TO BE A JOB WINNER, YOU MUST KNOW HOW TO:

Determine what kind of job is truly suited to your personality and abilities . . . ask for the right salary in the right way . . . adapt your resume to fit the special job situation and put your best foot forward . . . fill out a job application so that it becomes a key to opportunity . . . show up for an interview dressed like the person they want to see and with the answers they want to hear . . . follow up your first interview in a manner that will increase your chances . . . tune into the tremendous range of job possibilities that are available all around you at this very moment.

Now, this superb new guide will tell you exactly how to do it all—whether you are just entering the job market, are out of work, want to change careers, or are reentering the work force. We urge you to let it work for you.

HOW TO FIND WORK

MENTOR Titles of Interest

HOW TO FIND WORK

JONATHAN PRICE

A SIGNET BOOK

NEW AMERICAN LIBRARY

TIMES MIRROR

NAL BOOKS ARE AVAILABLE AT QUANTITY DISCOUNTS WHEN USED
TO PROMOTE PRODUCTS OR SERVICES. FOR INFORMATION PLEASE
WRITE TO PREMIUM MARKETING DIVISION, THE NEW AMERICAN
LIBRARY, INC., 1633 BROADWAY, NEW YORK, NEW YORK 10019.

SIGNET TRADEMARK REG. U.S. PAT. OFF. AND FOREIGN COUNTRIES
REGISTERED TRADEMARK—MARCA REGISTRADA
HECHO EN CHICAGO, U.S.A.

SIGNET, SIGNET CLASSICS, MENTOR, PLUME, MERIDIAN AND NAL BOOKS
are published by The New American Library, Inc.,
1633 Broadway, New York, New York 10019

First Printing, February, 1983

     3 4 5 6 7 8 9

PRINTED IN THE UNITED STATES OF AMERICA

Dedicated to Stuart Hunt

Contents

DECIDING WHAT YOU WANT TO DO

Chapter 1

Why Work?

Finding a job is often harder than doing the job. Why? Because there's no boss telling you what to do, no on-the-job training, no apparent technique. No one has organized it for you. And you may be rejected many times. In time, you could begin to doubt your own abilities.

What you need is a method. A simple, step-by-step procedure for getting a job. Nothing fancy—no $3,000 make-over-your-life courses. Just techniques that have been tested by thousands of successful job hunters—that's what this book provides.

You'll learn methods for figuring out what you want to do. Finding out where you can do it. Turning your weaknesses into strengths. Preparing letters and résumés that get you in the door. Conducting a persuasive interview. Following up on it, and then, when you're offered the job, negotiating a good salary. This method will help you get your next job—and the one after that. The payoff: knowing you *can* go out and secure a job you really want.

But *this* job—looking for work—will demand a lot from you. You'll discover that you may have to

- Reexamine your interests, your skills, your past.
- Rearrange your day, to make more time for your search.
- Rewrite and refine your résumé.
- Rehearse your answers to questions that bosses usually ask.
- Review your interviews, so you can follow up quickly and efficiently.

This book is organized to help you in each phase of your

search. In fact, each section addresses one of the main problems you face in finding a job:

- Deciding What You Want to Do
- Overcoming Barriers
- Getting in Touch
- Talking Your Way into a Job
- Discovering What Jobs Are Available

The first section will explore some basic questions:

- Why work at all?
- What kind of work interests you?
- How much money do you need?
- What kind of career will be best for you?

Then we talk about overcoming the barriers you may face if

- You're reentering the job force after years away.
- You're a member of minority.
- You need more training.
- You've gotten depressed looking for work.

To get in touch with employers who might offer the job you want, we look at

- How to locate openings
- What employers really want
- How personnel departments may work against you
- How to fill out an application
- What your skills really are
- How to start your résumé—and how to revise it for particular employers
- What letters to send along with your résumé
- How to use the phone to set up interviews

In "Talking Your Way Into a Job," we show you

- How to meet employers "for information only"
- When—and how—to prepare for an interview
- What the boss will probably ask you
- How to listen and respond in an interview
- How to follow up on a good interview
- What to do when you're offered a job

And then we describe more than three hundred jobs that are currently available in the United States.

With enough desire—and the method we outline here—you can find work that brings personal and financial rewards. Without that desire, you'll find that it is difficult to get started, that you're easily sidetracked, mired in problems. Just remember, you're working for what *you* want—and you can get it.

Do you really want a job, though? Let's run a quick analysis of the costs—and benefits—of unemployment and employment. The point: to gauge your real feelings, weigh the pluses and minuses, and answer the question; Why work?

By considering all your feelings, pro and con, you can sort them out and discover, perhaps, that although you may have brief sparks of enthusiasm for a job, you're basically cool to the idea. If so, this may not be the book for you. But if you find real desire for work, despite some twinges of reluctance, your conscious choice will help you press on to success. Desire—not an occasional pious thought—draws us on.

Think for a few minutes of the reasons you may have for disliking work. First of all, it's work. Does the thought make you tired? Did your parents insist you work, thus tainting the idea? Do you see work as humanity's punishment for original sin?

And then there's the schedule. Does it bother you waking up early every weekday? Going to the same place to do the same thing at the same time each day? Does routine make you feel hemmed in?

Perhaps you've had a job you disliked, or a boss who scared you. Were you bored, or ignored? Did you repress so much rage it hurt you physically? Was the building dirty and noisy? Did you feel left out of decisions? Was there too much, or too little, physical activity? Do you recall one job that made you mad enough to almost welcome unemployment?

Do you find your values conflict with those of most businesses? Do you worry that managers stress product over people? Do you dislike turning out a product that has little or no social value? Does the idea of "making it," scrambling for promotions, and succeeding on the job, seem hollow? Would you rather just ignore that, as long as you can somehow get by?

Such thoughts tend to undercut any job search, since they put reins on your desire. Let's look at the positive results of working, to reach a more balanced judgment.

First, working earns you money. With that extra cash, you get to decide what you want to do with your free time—not just what

5

you can afford to do. You can even set an exact date for future purchases, instead of daydreaming about "sometime." Does steady pay appeal to you?

Work keeps your talents sharp and teaches you to concentrate and to store your energy. Even though you may have taken the job for the salary, you do give of yourself, your skills, your concern; you practice generosity. One way or another, you create, you train, you constantly test your own understanding of yourself and of others. You see that your work makes some impact on the world. In all these ways, your particular work influences your soul. Are you willing to grow through your work?

Work offers you a steady community, too. As a crew, you and your coworkers form a group that is not as close as family, but may be friendlier.

So what do you think? Which do you value more, unemployment or work?

If you find your choice has hardened in favor of unemployment, good luck. You're opting out of a hard task—looking for a job.

And if you've chosen work, reflect on why. The more conscious the decision, the greater strength it can give you. So— Why do you want to work?

Chapter 2

What Kind of Work?

If you're not certain of what you want to do, you may want to look at different *types* of jobs that are available. To zero in on a particular job, ponder these questions:

- How much time do you want to put in during an average week?
- How easy, or hard, will it be to find—or start moving toward—a given job?
- Do you want a judgment job? An office job? A government job?
- Do you want to work under supervision, or on your own?

Here's a preliminary survey of some types of work. Put a checkmark next to whatever appeals to you—and try to understand why.

Entry-Level Jobs

Entry-level jobs—that is, the bottom steps on the great promotion staircase—come easier than the middle ones. Companies take in hordes to start as junior file clerks, management trainees, assistants, and administrative aides; then they promote a few to those middle-level slots. That way the middle managers will know the way their corporation works. Why bring in a stranger, when you can't tell what he or she is really like?

If you have a few years' experience, you'll have a tougher time getting into an entry-level position. Employers will call you

7

overqualified and, figuring you'll be bored, reject you. And if you send in a résumé in answer to an ad, most companies will turn you down. ("We promote from within.") So you'll have to go around the conventional want-ad-and-application route, talking your way into the "hidden" jobs that aren't advertised—the ones you hear about through a friend.

Blue-Collar Jobs

Physically, most blue-collar jobs demand that you think with your body, sense with your fingertips, keep your balance while carrying out the same task over and over. Starting salaries are lower than those of management trainees, but if you pick up complex skills over the years, you may eventually earn more than many vice-presidents. In fact, a lot of middle-level white-collar workers have dropped out of the office and gone into blue-collar jobs because of the pay. You might begin as a general laborer, hauling, cleaning, carrying, and digging, move up to helper, then apprentice; after three to six years of steady work, you could become a journeyman, a specialist entitled to top pay for the most ticklish jobs, then foreman or master. Community colleges, federal programs, and nonunion shops will give you the initial training you need.

You'll want to explore a blue-collar trade if you agree with most of these statements:

- I like to put my back—and hands—into my work.
- I would rather move the piano than compose a song.
- I like moving around a lot, and I don't mind getting dirty.
- I like union wages, protection, and benefits.
- I like immediate action more than long-range planning.

White-Collar Jobs

They're cleaner, all right. The worst smudges come from typewriter ribbons, or spilled toner dust on the copying machine. You probably won't have to lift anything heavier than a phone book. Mostly you sit and talk, or rearrange information on many pieces of paper. You often get tuition paid in evening classes.

You work with the same people for years, getting to know them, growing on the job.

If you start out as a secretary, cashier, file clerk, or teller, you can get promoted if you master the job quickly, and from then on turn your attention to the people around you, trying to figure out what work the company needs done that you can do. Many white-collar workers aim at professional or managerial roles, too: an administrative assistant might become assistant director, a secretary might head administrative services, a doctor might run her own institute.

You probably will veer toward some white-collar job if you agree with these statements:

- I like to organize.
- Thinking's an important part of any job for me.
- I like to weigh alternative theories, explanations, policies.
- Persuading people, helping them, teaching them, pleases me.
- I feel at ease in offices and on the phone.

Government Jobs

Uncle Sam employs more than 2½ million people. Every year 300,000 people apply for federal jobs; 10 percent get hired. State governments hire another 11 million. Any job you can do in private industry you'll probably find—under another title—in government service.

The salaries match or beat those in private business; the fringes are better; the pension plan's a plum. However, the multiplying rules, quadruplicate forms, and slow promotions may inhibit you from pursuing a government job. If these drawbacks don't seem that significant to you, call the Federal Job Information Center, listed in local phone books under U.S. Civil Service, or at 800-555-1212, to find out which qualifying tests come when. You'll find collections of old tests in most bookstores; buy one, and spend a few days practicing. If you score high enough, your name will go on a list of eligibles. Unfortunately, however, thousands make the list and wait for years to be hired.

You'll have to be active to land an interesting federal job. First, you have to locate the person who does the hiring, then talk your way into an interview. If that boss likes you, she asks the registry for the résumés of three people (one of whom is you), rejects the other two, and hires you.

If you've made personal contact first, you can get one of these "name requested" jobs, even if there's another freeze on hiring, or a budget cutback, or a well-publicized reduction in force. The bureaucracy goes on despite its leaders.

If you wait to be called from the list, you can expect to be offered a job in Guam, or a part-time slot, nights. Whether you want to be a spy, diplomat, FBI agent, or postman, you'll have to go through this same process, with the personnel departments of the Central Intelligence Agency, National Security Agency, State Department, Federal Bureau of Investigation, or Post Office.

Judgment Jobs

Richard K. Irish, a job counselor, recruiter, and headhunter, has placed hundreds of people in what he calls judgment jobs. Such jobs require you to weigh evidence, come to a decision, then use your social skills to get other people to carry it out. In problem solving, you learn about what makes other people work, relax, cooperate, and you yourself have a chance to become a leader, a decision-maker, even a mentor. As Irish says in his excellent book, *Go Hire Yourself an Employer* (Doubleday, 1978), judgment jobs "pay off with something more than a paycheck: [they] allow you to grow on the job, face challenges, feel relevant, and function effectively. On judgment jobs you are paid for the decisions you make." Examples: financial analyst, designer, marketing manager, program director, evaluation consultant. Most openings are hidden; plan to approach the boss personally, not through an application form.

Casual or On-Call Jobs

Many large corporations, especially hospitals, make you start their blue-collar jobs as a casual. That means you wait by the phone; if a regular gets sick, the supervisor calls you to come fill in. After a month or two, you'll probably be promoted to full-time status. Similarly, in some cities and counties, you can edge into teaching by being on call as a substitute; after a while, you may find a school and principal you like, then talk your way into a position there.

In-the-Meantime Jobs

If you're sure you want a career as a lawyer, then you may have to work nights as a security guard to put yourself through law school—or wait on tables, or do any number of short-term jobs that let you support yourself in the meantime. Not your first choice, these stand-by jobs may bore you, or wear you out. But if you keep your long-range aims in mind, you'll survive. Set yourself a deadline for quitting, and you'll know you're not stuck there for life.

The advantages: you can plan these jobs around your classes, even if that means taking the midnight shift—and they flesh out a thin budget.

Where to look? Consider any job you can already handle, no matter how menial: waiting on table, busing dishes, typing, guarding a warehouse, making telephone sales, sweeping out office buildings at night. Because of low pay and poor working conditions, lots of people quit these jobs, so there are often openings, even when not advertised.

Temporary Jobs

As a temporary, you put in a full eight-hour day, but the job itself may only last three days. You sign up at temporary employment agencies: they test your typing or bookkeeping skill; they ask about your warehouse or laborer experience. Then, if they're impressed, and if you really check in every day, they send you out on a job. You get paid a dollar or two more than the minimum wage by the agency, and the company pays them twice that for sending you. If a company likes your work, they may hire you full time.

Of course, you cannot count on continuous work unless you have very good skills and a friendly relationship with the counselor at the agency. Advantages: if you have classes two days a week, you can choose to work only the other three. Or if you do some work out of your home, you can call in whenever your own business slows down.

Tips: sign up with several agencies at once—and call all of them a day before you want to work. One place may not have any job for you, but the next will. Also, the counselors have so many people on their lists that they tend to send out anyone who's just telephoned. Don't wait for them to phone you.

•

Part-Time Jobs

Or you could become a part-timer—having steady work that averages fewer than thirty hours a week. Telephone salespeople, weekend replacements, survey takers, half-time secretaries—most work less than a full week. The pay's often low, but as with temporary positions, you can keep plenty of time free for fun.

Freelance Work

An architect in independent practice, an illustrator who works for a record company this week and an ad agency the next; an educational consultant; a writer who sells essays to different magazines—they all enjoy setting their own hours, meeting with clients only for an hour or two at a time, organizing and carrying out the job on their own. If you freelance, you are never entirely independent—you depend on the goodwill of your customers, you follow their general directions, you wait for their check-writing department to act. But you *feel* free—no boss looking over your shoulder.

How could you become a freelance? Put an ad in the classifieds—particularly the trade journals for your field. Talk to people who are already working as freelancers; ask them how they got started. And try to avoid a cash crunch at the start. Tony Hiss, a *New Yorker* writer, advises writers to put a year's living expenses in the bank before setting out to be a full-time freelancer. That way anxiety about the rent won't drive you to accept jobs you hate and do poorly. And your projects will have enough time to mature. You won't seem so frantic, so you will have an easier time selling yourself. A more common route: work nights and weekends to set your freelance business up while continuing a 9-to-5 job to pay your bills. This frustrating but practical method works, but it may take you as long as five years to establish your freelance business solidly enough so you can quit the other job.

Whatever path you follow, get in touch with people who are already doing anything at all like what you want—and ask how they got into the business. They can give more than advice; if

12

they see you are serious enough to follow their suggestions, they may even put you in touch with some of their clients.

Other Considerations

To pick *the* job for you, or to make sure the one you've chosen is right for you, you'll need to postpone the actual process of looking for work while you think over some fundamental questions.

About work:

- What are the actual tasks you enjoy?
- Where do you want to work—city, country, North, South, East, or West?
- What kind of working space do you like?
- How much or how little supervision do you want?
- How much do you know about the way the work is actually done?
- How long have you been interested in a given field?
- Do you enjoy risks and challenges, or do you yearn for security?

About values:

- Would you rather spend most time working with people, or ideas, or material objects?
- What accomplishments make you proud?
- Which values are you willing to pay for by refusing any job that might conflict with them?

We'll explore these questions in the next few chapters. For the moment, keep an open mind about possibilities.

Chapter 3

Clarifying Your Values

On any job, you deal with people, things, and data. Some people prefer a job that requires lots of physical dexterity and some judgment, but not much contact with other people. In proportion, the job's three components might look like this:

Data people THINGS

But perhaps you'd rather have a job where you don't have to do anything too complicated physically, but you do have to bring a lot of information to bear on a client's problems. That job might look like this:

DATA PEOPLE things

Before you settle on a job target, you may want to see if it gives the same importance you do to data, people, and things. The test that follows will help you decide how much weight you want to give each factor in a job—and how sophisticated you want to be when dealing with data, or people, or objects.

Put a check on the right if you would like a job *like* the one described. Not necessarily the same job—just one similar to it. If you feel negative, or neutral, leave it blank.

Data

You cannot touch data. Data are ideas or information that are expressed in numbers, words, or other symbols. When we ob-

14

serve, investigate, interpret, forecast, imagine, visualize, or plan, we gather data and manipulate it to help us on the job.

Level 6 Comparing
Check passport photo against person's face.   _____
Compare oscilloscope wave pattern with standard.   _____
See if charge customer has reached credit limit.   _____
Proofread contract word by word.   _____
Color-match cloth with paint chips.   _____
Spot passengers who fit a police description.   _____

Level 5 Copying
Take verbatim notes on a trial.   _____
Verify freight car numbers.   _____
Follow a blueprint.   _____
Write down cashier totals.   _____
Enter test results in tables.   _____
Record crew time and production volume.   _____

Level 4 Computing
Calculate locations for screws.   _____
Use formula to find object's center of gravity.   _____
Compute number of boxes needed.   _____
Determine what percentage of material gets wasted. _____
Estimate how much salable wood will come
out of this load.   _____
Add customer's bill and tax.   _____

Level 3 Compiling
Classify customers as credit risks.   _____
Organize and report sales figures.   _____
Collate different reports.   _____
Take inventory of available parts.   _____
Gather information from users.   _____
Collect and sort library references.   _____

Level 2 Analyzing
Analyze a patient's problems.   _____
Evaluate monthly performance by crew and
equipment.   _____
Determine current value of livestock.   _____
Analyze volume and type of telephone traffic.   _____
Examine and classify a job.   _____
Develop alternative solutions.   _____

Level 1 Coordinating
Organize the flow of work on a construction site. _____
Schedule each stage of a book's production. _____
Decide what repairs should be done first. _____
Coordinate different groups coming to a meeting. _____
Make sure that one operation does not conflict
with another. _____
Supervise inspections by different workers. _____

Level 0 Synthesizing
Figure out why sales have dropped. _____
Evaluate pollution levels and pinpoint causes. _____
Find a pattern in widespread illnesses in community. _____
Develop a new explanation for a common problem. _____
Diagnose reasons for production slowdown and
prescribe cure. _____
—Interpret political unrest and make recommendations. _____

People

Level 8 Taking instructions
Hand plumber the tools asked for. _____
Lower tube where you're told _____
Help without taking responsibility. _____
Follow prepared guides. _____
Cut strips to prescribed length. _____
Press button at assigned time. _____

Level 7 Serving
Wait on restaurant patrons. _____
Respond immediately to requests for candy. _____
Give a massage on demand. _____
Put through a collect call. _____
Drive client wherever she wants. _____
Deliver a rush order. _____

Level 6 Speaking
Dispatch taxis by radio. _____
Signal another ship. _____
Exchange information with client. _____
Give assignments to helpers. _____
Tell customers where to find departments. _____
Order crew to clean stairs. _____

Level 5 Persuading
Represent a community group. _____
Convince a homeowner to rewire. _____
Speak up for your point of view. _____
Lobby for a safety measure. _____
Promote certain foods. _____
Sell investment property. _____

Level 4 Directing
Amuse an audience. _____
Introduce records on radio. _____
Lead an exploration team. _____
Sing in a theater. _____
Put on a puppet show. _____
Give a lecture. _____

Level 3 Supervising
Decide on crew work schedule. _____
Assign workers their duties. _____
Solve conflicts on the job. _____
Improve the group's efficiency. _____
Motivate a team. _____
Demand a level of performance. _____

Level 2 Instructing
Plan and teach a whole course. _____
Train an animal. _____
Show a group how to communicate. _____
Demonstrate new procedures. _____
Explain department policy. _____
Make technical recommendations. _____

Level 1 Negotiating
Arrive at a joint decision. _____
Help a group reach a decision. _____
Bargain with seller. _____
Work out terms of a trade. _____
Share ideas for new program. _____
Discuss and agree on revised policy. _____

Level 0 Mentoring
Help individual look at self. _____
Advise people on their careers. _____
Give legal counsel. _____

Treat the whole person. ———
Guide people back to full lives. ———
Run vocational rehabilitation program. ———

Things
(Machines, tools, equipment, or products)

Level 7   Handling
Carry sheetrock to work site. ———
Move cement in wheelbarrow. ———
Clear dirt off highway with broom. ———
Load boxes until boss tells you to stop. ———
Haul sledge to marked spot. ———
Manhandle logs onto sluice. ———

Level 6   Feeding-offbearing
Dump flour into automatic mixers. ———
Remove each box from end of conveyor belt. ———
Insert sliced pineapple in each can. ———
Pick up loaves from bag-sealing machine. ———
Load crayons into hopper. ———
Lift raw material onto machine table. ———

Level 5   Tending
Adjust controls on welding equipment. ———
Look for malfunctioning in machine. ———
Turn valve to keep flow even. ———
Respond to warning light. ———
Change guide. ———
Flip switches in set order. ———

Level 4   Manipulating
Judge whether blade has been sharpened enough. ———
Choose proper material for job. ———
Use hands to guide objects into place. ———
Gauge accuracy of cuts. ———
Move pedals with feet and hands. ———
Select right tool for job. ———

Level 3   Driving-operating
Pull gear lifts or levers. ———
Start and stop a conveyor system. ———

Control hoist. _____
Run a crane. _____
Drive a tractor-trailer rig. _____
Operating a paring machine. _____

Level 2   Operating-controlling

Adjust machine in progress. _____
Turn valve to regulate pressure. _____
Decide when to slow the flow of liquids. _____
Monitor temperature to tell when to stop. _____
Watch gauges and dials to control pressure. _____
Judge when to start the machine. _____

Level 1   Precision working

Adjust alignment of moving parts. _____
Dismantle and repair devices. _____
Spot and correct imbalance. _____
Drill to very close tolerance. _____
Mesh gears in gearbox. _____
Fit together watch parts. _____

Level 0   Setting up

Supervise crew preparing plating tank. _____
Set up machine that cuts edges, flaps, and notches. _____
Put together printing equipment. _____
Assemble automatic pill machine. _____
Hook up harvester, tractor, and wagons. _____
Set up and adjust filter presses. _____

In each section (data, people, and things), the numbered sections progress from lowest skill (with the highest number) to the most sophisticated level (with a zero). The government uses these numbers to code jobs. If you look up any job in chapter 25, "Jobs Available," you will see a three-digit code assigned. This code indicates how complex a relationship a worker will have with data, people, and things. For instance, after "Critic" you will find the number 067: *0* refers to data, *6* to people, and *7* to things.

Each digit refers to the highest levels of skill needed—and includes all others before that. *Zero* means a critic has to synthesize lots of information—and, in addition, to coordinate, analyze, compile, compute, copy, and compare. *Six* in the second place means the critic only has to speak to other people, not really negotiate, instruct, or supervise. Seven in the third place means he has to handle a typewriter—but nothing more complicated than that (no feeding of machines, no precision working, no setting up).

Remember that a low number refers to a high level of skill—and includes all lesser skills as well. To define the levels of data, people, and thing skills you want on a job, turn back to the test section marked "Data." What is the lowest number (and therefore the highest level of skill) you have marked with at least three checks? Let's say that is your ideal data level. Put the number of that level here.   _____

Now turn to the "people" section. What is the lowest number (and therefore the highest level of skill) you have marked with at least three checks? That will be your ideal people level. Put the number of that level.   _____

Turn to the "things" section. What is the lowest number (and therefore the highest level of skill) you have marked with at least three checks? That will be your ideal thing level. Put the number of that level here.   _____

Put the three numbers together in order here:

DATA PEOPLE THINGS

Now you have a benchmark against which you can measure almost any job—your own prescription. Circle the levels you've chosen on this list.

DATA	PEOPLE	THINGS
0 Synthesizing	0 Mentoring	0 Setting up
1 Coordinating	1 Negotiating	1 Precision working
2 Analyzing	2 Instructing	2 Operating-controlling
3 Compiling	3 Supervising	3 Driving-operating
4 Computing	4 Directing	4 Manipulating
5 Copying	5 Persuading	5 Tending
6 Comparing	6 Speaking	6 Feeding-Offbearing
	7 Serving	7 Handling
	8 Taking instructions	

Now you can look up any job and see how it measures up.

Realize, too, that you get promoted from lower to higher skills. You might check to see what the lowest level of skill is that you will accept, to start. For instance, some people who want to be negotiators (People 1) would never start their career in a job where their only contact with people was taking orders (People 8). They might, however, wait on table (People 7) while studying techniques of persuasion at law school (People 5). You've figured out your ideal levels; now, what is your minimum?

The lowest Data skill I would accept in a job: #_____
Name: _____
The lowest People skill I would accept in a job: #_____
Name: _____
The lowest thing skill I would accept in a job: #_____
Name: _____

You now have a target level and a rock-bottom level—and your next job will lie somewhere in between. The ideal—at least for most of us—takes a few years to reach. But you'll get there faster for knowing what you're after.

Chapter 4

Deciding on
a Job Target

Without a real aim in life, we may wander. Knocked down by the first rejection, sent off in another direction by some new idea, slowed by surprises, meandering in circles, and we drift, chance takes over.

But a long-term goal can lead you past the temporary setbacks that push others out of their chosen course. Knowing what you want out of life, and what you're willing to pay for that, frees you to go after a job or anything else without hesitation. A real aim comes from your heart—not from ideas of what you ought to do, or what would be sensible. So examine what you *really* want. You may get it.

In the preceding chapter you may have come to a more precise idea of a career or a job you want, an area you want to explore. If you wonder whether that career corresponds to your own interests, pause a moment to answer these questions.

Career you have in mind _____

What unpaid activities have you done over the last five, ten, or fifteen years? Fill all the blanks.

1. For fun—sports, games, hobbies

_____
_____
_____

2. For social reasons

_____
_____
_____
_____

3. For religious reasons

_____
_____
_____
_____

4. For no apparent reason

_____
_____
_____
_____

As part of each activity, do you see *any* trace of that larger interest? If so, underline the activity. For instance, if your career aim is accounting, and you do the church books, underline *church books*.

If your career interest clearly dominates a given activity, circle the activity. For instance, if all you do for your square dance club is do-se-do and keep the books, circle that.

If your casual interests jibe with the career you have in mind, you're probably on target. If not, reconsider.

Only *wanting* will keep you going when problems arise. So what is it you want? Sketch out a picture of the life you'd like to be leading in five or ten years.

- What kind of home do you want?
- What kind of workspace?
- What kind of spouse?
- What kind of spare-time amusement?
- What kind of religious life?
- What kind of job?
- What exactly would you do on that job? (Name tasks.)
- What moments do you look forward to in that life?
- What parts of yourself will have grown?

Now that you've looked at the details of your dream, imagine actually living it. See yourself performing the tasks, living at home, playing. Envision receiving the money for your work. Count it.

Close your eyes and consciously daydream. The point: the more clearly you show your mind what you want, the easier it'll be for you to get it. (And if you don't relish visualizing that future, ask whether you really desire it.)

Now, what are you willing to give, in order to earn that? Are you ready to part with spare time, hours of sleep, money? Are you willing to put in the extra effort? Do you think your feelings will burn hot enough to help you keep your aim in mind for all those years?

Or do you somehow imagine you can get something extraordinary for nothing—no more effort than usual, no sacrifice, no risk? Do you secretly believe the world *owes* you a living? Many people think that. Result: they sometimes take away a small check, with the contempt of the person they've been begging from. And as their habit of dependence grows, their ability to act on their own behalf weakens.

So is your planning realistic? In the past have you put in that kind of labor? Have you overcome large obstacles? What inspired you? How did you learn the skills? How did you keep going?

And if you do feel you'll need to *earn* your good life, you have a chance of doing so. But are you offering people enough service for the returns you ask? Couldn't you do more?

Ask yourself about the work you envision doing in five or ten years. How could you make sure it benefited people more? In what ways is it something worth doing—not just for you, but for others? (If what you do helps people, you'll find you win supporters as you go, and you can talk enthusiastically about your work.)

Do you really believe you can offer these services, and earn that job, that house, that lifestyle? If you don't, or if you say, "Well, I think I can," you may find your actions strangely defeated by your own disbelief. (You get what you really think you will.)

Recall a time when you *believed* you could do something difficult—and you succeeded. Make a note here of that situation. Reflect on what you felt as you faced the hard times. Could those feelings help again?

You can convince your own mind by acting. Each step you take toward your aim persuades your own mind you intend to reach your goal. So act now. Not tomorrow.

Make up a plan for getting from now to then. Organize it in terms of the major hurdles you have to clear on the way—training, say; promotions; moves.

Hurdles I Have to Clear to Get to My Future Job
1. _____.
    How will I do this?   1.
                            2.
                            3.
    My own deadline for overcoming this hurdle_____.

2. _____.
    How will I do this? 1.
                                2.
                                3.
    My own deadline for overcoming this hurdle_____.
3. _____.
    How will I do this? 1.
                                2.
                                3.
    My own deadline for overcoming this hurdle_____.

What, then, is the first thing to do? Think about your immediate job target: how many hours will you put in to reach that, and what is your deadline?

To prepare, envision taking the first steps. In your mind, feel the objects, breathe on materials. See each step being done; check the results in your imagination.

Now make up your mind to do that. And ask your unconscious to send up some solutions to the "problems" (or hurdles, or obstacles). By morning, you should have some more ideas. Then act.

Remember: each act reenforces your will.

Chapter 5

Money

What's the lowest salary you can accept? What salary would let you keep up your current lifestyle? And how much more would you need to indulge in a few luxuries?

Knowing how much money you need can help you pick the right job, and rule out other jobs simply because the pay's too low.

Knowing, not guessing, can help you when the boss offers you a job, and asks, "What's the minimum you'd accept?" People often quote their past salary plus a few thousand, then get argued down. You need to know your own *real* minimum—the salary below which you will not work. Being sure of that, you will be able to make a better case for more.

Do you already *know*—or do you just ballpark a figure? For example, do you operate on a budget now? How precisely? Do you, for instance, record all expenses in a pocket-sized notebook? Do you check at the end of the month to see if you have stayed within bounds? If you have monitored yourself like that for five or six average months, then you already know how much you spend for what. If not, you can come to some rough conclusions using the following chart.

Fill it in for expenses *you* pay for, no matter how many people they benefit. We are talking about normal periods, not extraordinarily expensive ones. Compare your estimates with those of anyone else who can verify them, and with your checkbook.

Every Week
FOOD
How much do you spend on the average, each week for

food? Include meals at work, all visits to the supermarket, and dinners out—whatever you regularly buy. $_____

GAS
Include any gas you yourself pay for each week—no matter who drives the vehicle. $_____

ENTERTAINMENT
Take an average: if you take the kids to a drive-in every Saturday, how much do you spend? Include sports, dancing, anything you do for amusement. $_____

CHILDCARE
If you pay by the week, how much do you spend on babysitters, nursery, and day-care centers? (Don't bother to put school costs here; we'll get to those under yearly expenses). $_____

Total
weekly expenses $_____

There are 4.3 weeks in an average month, so to find out how much these four items come to in an average month, multiply the total by 4.3.   Result $_____

Every month
FOOD, GAS, ENTERTAINMENT, and CHILDCARE
Your total weekly expenses, above, multiplied by 4.3 to get the monthly total. $_____

HOUSING
How much do you pay each month for rent or mortgage?
$_____

CAR
Include your regular payment, plus the average monthly cost of repairs (no gas). $_____

CREDIT
Add up the time payments, and minimum charges from all credit. $_____

TELEPHONE
An average month—not the holiday long-distance charges.
$_____

ELECTRICITY AND GAS
Figure an average of summer and winter. $_____

WATER
Again, balance winter and summer usage to come up with a monthly average. $_____

INSURANCE
No matter who is covered, if you pay for it, how much is it per month? (Leave out benefits paid by employer.)

$_____

MEDICAL
Average these out: leave out whatever gets covered by insurance. $_____

CLOTHES AND CLEANING
How much do you spend each month on new clothes, and on cleaning the old ones? $_____

CABLE TV
Monthly rate. $_____

DUES
For clubs, union, professional associations. $_____

NEWSPAPERS $_____

SAVINGS
If you make a regular deposit in a savings account or credit union. $_____

DONATIONS
Contributions that you make each month to a charity or religious organization. $_____

OTHER MONTHLY EXPENSES
Write down what they are for. $_____
$_____
$_____
$_____

Total $_____

This total represents most of your expenses in an average month.

Multiply that by twelve to see how much you spend in a year, then add a few once-a-year expenses, too.

Monthly Total x 12 = $_____

VACATION
If you go every year, about how much do you spend?
$_____

BIG-TICKET ITEMS
Refrigerator, sofa, color TV—items beyond your regular expenses: how much, total, do you think you spent on them on average in each of the last three years? $_____

TAXES
Real estate taxes, sewer assessments, whatever *annual* tax is not withheld by your employer. This would include any income tax you owe beyond what gets deducted at work.
$_____

EDUCATION
Tuition, if your child goes to a private school; include books, lab fees, all expenses. $_____

OTHER ANNUAL EXPENSES $_____
Note here what they are for. $_____
    $_____

Total annual
expenses$_____

Now let's figure for an inflation rate of at least 15 percent to see how much money you'll need next year, just to buy the same goods and services next year.

Annual expenses $_____
        x   1.15
Expenses next year

That is how much you will need to take home, just to maintain your present standard of living. But your boss talks in terms of a gross salary—that is, before deductions have been taken out. If you know what your current gross income is this year, multiply

29

that by 1.15 to figure out how much you must make next year to break even.

Current gross income from all sources $_____
                    x   1.15
_____
Gross amount needed next year.

If you're not certain of this year's income, just start with the inflated expenses you anticipate next year and divide by three, to find one-third. Add that third to your expenses, and you'll come out on the low side of the gross income you need. (Deductions vary with your salary and number of dependents, but you can count on *at least* one-quarter of your salary going to Uncle Sam.)

Next year's expenses $_____
Divided by   _____ = _____
                          3   (A)

Add A to next year's expenses $_____
        A $_____
        _____
        Total $_____.

That's how much you have to ask for, as a minimum, just to keep living the way you are now. If you'd like to know how much that is per month, divide by twelve.

Gross annual salary $_____
Divided by   _____ = $_____
                         12   (gross monthly
                                  salary needed)

To find out what that means weekly, divide the gross monthly salary by 4.3.

Gross monthly salary $_____
Divided by   _____ = $_____
4.3   4.3   (Gross weekly
                                  salary needed)

And to turn that into an hourly rate, divide by forty, the number of hours in an average full week.

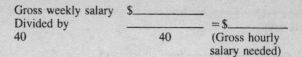

Gross weekly salary	$_____	
Divided by	_____	=$_____
40	40	(Gross hourly salary needed)

To see if a management job you want meets these standards, you'll have to call a few people in those slots and ask; want ads can give you an idea of the range. For most nonsupervisory positions, your librarian can give you a U.S. Department of Labor monthly publication called *Employment and Earnings*, which gives average salaries, nationwide. (As of 1980, the average nonsupervisor earned about $6 an hour, or just over $11,000 a year.)

Now, if you think you must take a pay cut—moving into a new field, or working fewer hours a week—then look back through your expenses, and think realistically. Which ones can I cut, or reduce? (Add up your cuts per month, and subtract the total from your monthly take-home pay. That would be your minimum. To find the gross, add a third of it.)

You now know approximately what you need next year, at a minimum, and at your current standard of living. More than that, and you're actually moving ahead of inflation.

So far I have left out benefits paid for by the company, because these are very hard to put a correct value on. But as you climb above the $30,000 level, these benefits help more and more, because *some* of them escape taxation. Count these as extras; but for the purpose of comparing two job offers, you might try to estimate how much each benefit package would cost if you were to buy it, including the "perks" as well. Also, ask if you *would buy* any of these things if they were not part of the benefits program. For instance, how much is the key to the executive washroom worth to you?

Overcoming
Barriers

Chapter 6

If You've Been Out
of the Work Force

If you've been out of the work force for a number of years, you may have to jump even more barriers than most people to reach the job you want. *Reentry* is what this track is called. And when you're going back into the job market after having been out of it for a while, your toughest obstacle can be your own attitude. It can keep you from

- Applying for a job you want
- Asking anyone for help
- Reading the want ads
- Following up on a job lead

The worst attitude is "I can't do anything." You're underestimating your real experience, putting down what you've actually done. Use chapter 10, "Taking an Inventory of Your Skills," to find out what salable skills you already have. Handling a home budget, organizing a school trip, running a volunteer bureau—these have honed your abilities. Even going to group therapy helps you perfect your ability to deal with people. Ignore *where* you learned a skill: realize what you *can* do.

Possibly the job search just seems "too hard." That's often true at first. You're not used to putting in these hours writing, calling, talking, calling again, thinking out a plan, following it, coping with rebuffs. You may have to go to sleep later than you're used to, and get up earlier. You'll have to make time to do work you never imagined was involved in finding a job. That means making yourself a schedule, creating a new routine, and defending that against your family and friends, who expect you to have the same time you've always had for them.

The best antidote is desire. Make a list of your reasons for getting a job. Meditate on it every day. Imagine what your life's going to be like when you're working full time. This way, when you change your lifestyle, you'll see that you are moving toward your goal. Each step you take makes the next one easier.

Start figuring out how you're going to manage to do household chores on days when you're out interviewing. Can anyone else help? Can you cut down on these? Can you endure a little mess now and then? And what about the kids? Perhaps they can stand being by themselves for a few hours after school. If you've got preschoolers, you're not going to feel comfortable until you've made day-care arrangements. Budget your time and money. Try to set a realistic schedule for job hunting—at least thirty hours a week. And figure that you're going to have to spend more than usual on new clothes, hair care, travel, lunches, childcare, research material, postage, typing, and copying your résumé. When you've anticipated problems, they don't seem so large.

And knowing that you're acting on a well-thought-out plan that leads toward something you really want will help you resist whining kids, resentful spouses, pouting friends. Sure they feel neglected. Count on hassles. And rehearse what you're going to say in your own defense. Explain why you're looking for work, but refuse to feel guilty about it.

You're worth it. And you're developing a businesslike attitude toward your job search. Create a mini-office for yourself. Make lists of leads, files of information, folders for your different résumés, and letters. Think of your search as a job—and do it as efficiently as you can. That will give you confidence in your own ability to get organized. And the orderliness will help you avoid panic when an employer calls you back and you have to look up what the job was.

Once you've begun, you'll find it fairly easy to overcome your unfamiliarity with the current job market. To find out where the jobs are, you can form a network, join a support group, call friends, use the library, and develop your own techniques to find out where the jobs are (chapter 17). You'll learn where there are and aren't openings, and how to repackage your skills so they look like what employers want.

But when you get in the door for an interview, you will find the employer's a bit suspicious. Most bosses worry that

- You're going to quit soon.
- You don't really have any useful experience.
- You'll need a lot of extra training.

And if you're a reentry woman, bosses may worry that you won't be able to handle the eight-hour day. Point out that mothers usually work eighteen hours, seven days a week. But what about the kids? Explain that you've made day-care arrangements. But won't you quit to have another kid? No, you've had enough. What the hell do you know about business? Talk skills—and mention key successes. You've got maturity and experience, so don't back down. They'll be lucky to get you. In case the employer doubts you, point out that nearly half the mothers in America now work at full-time jobs (compared to a quarter of them in the mid-fifties, and 9 percent in 1940). Three-fifths of all working mothers have children aged six to seventeen. Two-fifths have children under six. In most large cities, you'll find a support group dedicated to helping you break into the job market; it will provide more facts and figures—and better yet, leads.

If you were working for a while but have been out of work for more than six months, stress what you can do when you talk to an employer. Don't get backed into a corner, apologizing for being unemployed. Take the offensive. Say why you want steady work. Show your energy, vitality—the spirit you'll bring to work.

To many bosses, *unemployed* means lazy. Show that you're willing to put out a lot of energy to get the job—create an attractive résumé, brief yourself on the company, call and keep calling. Don't let depression keep you from trying. The more you work at getting a job, the more confidence you'll feel in your own abilities. Be businesslike in looking for work, and eventually work will come to you.

Chapter 7

If You're A Member
of a Minority

In looking for a job, you already know that you may be at a disadvantage if your skin is black, brown, yellow, or red; if your sex is female; if you're gay; if your body's disabled; or if you're over sixty. Of course, if we put together all nonwhite peoples, plus all whites who are female or gay or disabled or over sixty, we'd have a huge majority of the population. In America, unhandicapped heterosexual middle-aged white males are the real minority; but because a few of them control the budgets, and the thinking of most corporations, they've labeled everyone who's different a "minority."

And minorities have a tough time finding work. For example, for years the unemployment rate for blacks has been twice that of whites; 35 percent of black teenagers go without work, compared to fifteen percent of white teenagers; income levels for all nonwhites fall below that of 60 percent of all whites. As a result, more than 27 percent of black families hit the poverty level in 1975, compared to 8 percent of white families. And while women make up 40 percent of the work force, they have been able to win only 3 percent of the managerial or professional slots in "male-intensive" industries such as chemicals, coal, construction, food, glass, lumber, machine tools, metal, mining, paper, petroleum, plastic, rubber, transportation, utilities, and wholesale trade. "Women have more unemployment than men in every field, in every degree level, and within every age group," says Betty Vetter, the executive director of the Scientific Manpower Commission.

Few employers hire anyone older than themselves, and most still force retirement on anyone over sixty when budgets crunch. Few companies make their jobs accessible by wheelchair; and many bosses refuse to hire a programmer just because she can't walk.

How do you navigate past so much discrimination? You can't avoid it all. But you can become an overachiever, on the theory that you'll probably have to be twice as good to beat out "majority" competitors for the job. If you've got the talent, you can move into fields that can't afford to keep you down for long—music, sports, entertainment, poetry, publishing. In both these ways, you can have the pleasure of exercising your abilities to the limit. What might be shocking self-indulgence in a bank seems a crowd-pleasing expression in show business. What might be dangerous originality in a pedestrian job will, in a fast track, look like genius.

For a less dramatic route, you could look into companies where your "minority status" can help you, rather than hurt. You've seen lots of ads that end, "An equal opportunity employer." That doesn't mean much. They're claiming they don't discriminate. But it doesn't mean they've made any effort to change the traditional methods of selection. ("If you're white, you're right; if you're brown, stick around; if you're black, step back.")

What you want to look for are companies who've been forced (usually by lawsuits and government threats) to adopt an affirmative action program. That means they have to recruit minorities to meet quotas that they won't admit are quotas, monitored by a court, or a representative of the U.S. Department of Labor. In general, the bigger the company, and the more federal contracts it has, the more desperate it will be to hire you to meet its quota. Personnel managers from these firms joke about their dream applicant ("A black woman who's a paraplegic Vietnam vet") —but it they found one, they'd pay top bucks, since that person would put checkmarks in four columns (ethnic minority, female hire, handicapped, and Vietnam vet). This kind of tokenism may not end discrimination—but it could help you get a job.

In most urban areas, you'll find a community-based affirmative action program. (Ask any ethnic, age, or women's organization for the phone number). The staff knock on doors, trying to scare up jobs in businesses affected by government regulations. For example:

Carpentry	Longshore work
Cement work	Medical assistance
Construction	Pile driving
Cooking	Plumbing
Iron work	Retail clerks

Certain white-collar fields tend to offer more affirmative action opportunities than others:

Accounting	Law
Banking	Law enforcement
Clerical work	Management
Computers	Sales
Engineering	Sciences (life and physical)
Health Services	

Of course, most of these jobs require some training, and even if you pawn your TV set to take a course, there's no guarantee that just because you got an A, you'll get a job. Training for one of these fields just increases the odds in your favor. And you can bet that few of them promise advancement beyond the lowest fringes of middle management.

The best place to look for training with pay and promotion—pretty much on merit—is the U.S. government. Start with the military, where they need bodies badly and train you in particular skills you probably could never learn in civilian life. You can get a contract for the training you want *before* you join. Typical fields:

Electronics technician	Filmmaker
Aircraft repair	Legal aide
Radio technician	Nurse's aide
Pilot	Heavy-equipment operator
Musician	Air traffic controller

The federal government *does* have openings, but first you've got to take a test, then you may wait six months for a call. Some people have waited three years to get into the postal service. And remember that politics will direct money (and jobs) from one area to another. To get hired, you'll have to head for the departments whose budgets just got expanded. This year, that would be Defense. Next year it might be Agriculture. All you can count on is delay.

If you don't like uniforms, and don't want to deal with bureaucrats, look for help in grass-roots organizations. People in these groups have contacts throughout your community. They know many of the people who are hiring. But they also want to see if you're worth recommending. So volunteer to help. Show off your skills by furthering the aims of the group. You'll meet a lot of people, some of whom can give you job tips, and you may discover skills and interests you never knew you had. You'll get over the loneliness of looking for work by yourself, and you'll regain the confidence you need to impress an employer. Some grass-roots organizations:

ADVOCATES FOR WOMEN
256 Sutter Street
San Francisco, CA 94108
415-391-4870

ALL-CRAFT FOUNDATION
19–23 St. Marks Place
New York, NY 10003
212-260-3650

ALPHA KAPPA ALPHA
1751 New Hampshire Avenue,
N.W.
Washington, D.C. 20009
202-387-3103

AMERICAN ASSOCIATION
OF UNIVERSITY WOMEN
2401 Virginia Avenue, N.W.
Washington, D.C. 20037
202-785-7750

AMERICAN G.I. FORUM
P.O. Box 336
Beeville, Texas
512-358-2535

AMERICANS FOR INDIAN
OPPORTUNITY
1820 Jefferson Place, N.W.
Washington, D.C. 20036
202-463-8635

APPRENTICESHIP OPPOR-
TUNITIES FOUNDATION
400 Alabama Street
San Francisco, CA 94110
415-621-9712

BAY AREA CONSTRUCTION
OPPORTUNITY PROGRAM
367 Second Street
Oakland, CA 94607
415-342-3743

BETTER JOBS FOR WOMEN
1038 Bannock Street
Denver, CO 80204
303-224-4180

BOSTON WOW: WIDER
OPPORTUNITIES FOR
WOMEN
413 Commonwealth Avenue
Boston, MA 02215
617-261-2060

BUREAU OF INDIAN
AFFAIRS
Indian Federal Employment
Referral Program
Albuquerque, NM 87103
505-766-3043

CAREER PLANNING
CENTER, INC.
1623 LaCienaga Boulevard
Los Angeles, CA 90035
213-273-8123

CHICANA SERVICE
ACTION CENTER
Women's Pre-Apprenticeship
Program
2244 Beverly Boulevard
Los Angeles, CA 90057
213-381-7261

COALITION OF LABOR
UNION WOMEN
15 Union Square
New York, NY 10003
212-677-5764

COMMONWEALTH OF
PUERTO RICO
Department of Labor—
Migration Division
322 West 45th Street
New York, NY 10036
212-245-0700

COMMUNICATION WORKERS
OF AMERICA
Women's Activities Department
1925 K Street, N.W.
Washington, D.C. 20006
202-785-6700

COMPREHENSIVE VOCA-
TIONAL PROGRAM FOR
WOMEN
Brevard Community College
Clearlake Road
Cocoa, FL 32922
305-632-1111

CONCENTRATED EMPLOY-
MENT PROGRAM
730 Polk Street
San Francisco, CA 94109
415-771-7100

CREATIVE EMPLOYMENT
PROJECT—YWCA
608 South 3rd Street
Louisville, KY 40202
502-585-2168

DELTA SIGMA THETA
1814 M Street, N.W.
Washington, D.C. 20036
202-338-7727

GRAPHIC ARTS INTERNA-
TIONAL UNION
Project for Equal Progression
Program (PEP)
1900 L Street, N.W.
Washington, D.C. 20036
202-872-7994

HUMAN RESOURCES
DEVELOPMENT INSTITUTE
(AFL-CIO)
815 16th Street
Washington, D.C. 20006
202-638-3912

INTERNATIONAL UNION
OF ELECTRICAL, RADIO,
AND MACHINE WORKERS
(AFL-CIO)
Education and Women's
Activities
1126 16th Street
Washington, D.C. 20036
202-296-1200

JOB OPTIONS, INC.
Blackstone Building,
Room 704
112 Market Street
Harrisburg, PA 17101
717-233-4509

JOB SEARCH
Women's Resource Center,
YWCA
1111 S.W. 10th Street
Portland, OR 97205
503-223-6281

LEAGUE OF UNITED LATIN
AMERICAN CITIZENS
(LULAC)
10966 LeCont Avenue
Los Angeles, CA 90024
213-679-8225

NATIONAL ALLIANCE OF
BUSINESSMEN
1730 K Street, N.W.
Washington, D.C. 20006
202-254-7105

NATIONAL ASSOCIATION
FOR THE ADVANCEMENT
OF COLORED PEOPLE
(NAACP)
1790 Broadway
New York, NY 10019
212-751-0300

NATIONAL ASSOCIATION
OF HOME BUILDERS
15th and M Streets, N.W.
Washington, D.C. 20005
202-452-0200

NATIONAL ASSOCIATION
OF WOMEN IN CONSTRUC-
TION
2800 West Lancaster
Fort Worth, TX 76107
817-335-9711

NATIONAL FEDERATION
OF BUSINESS AND
PROFESSIONAL WOMEN'S
CLUBS
Talent Bank
2012 Massachusetts Avenue,
N.W.
Washington, D.C. 20036
202-293-1100

NATIONAL JOINT PAINT-
ING AND DECORATING
APPRENTICESHIP AND
TRAINING COMMITTEE
1750 New York Avenue,
N.W.
Washington, D.C. 20006
202-872-0083

NATIONAL ORGANI-
ZATION FOR
WOMEN (NOW)
1957 East 73rd Street
Chicago, Illinois 60649
312-324-3067

NATIONAL PUERTO RICAN
FORUM, INC.
214 Mercer Street
New York, NY 10012
212-533-0100

NATIONAL SPANISH-
SPEAKING MANAGEMENT
ASSOCIATION
1625 Eye Street, N.W.
Washington, D.C. 20006
202-785-3500

NATIONAL URBAN
LEAGUE, INC.
Equal Opportunity Building
500 East 62nd Street
New York, NY 10021
212-644-6500

OPPORTUNITIES INDUS-
TRIALIZATION CENTERS
(OIC)
Headquarters
100 West Coulter Street
Philadelphia, PA 19144
215-VI9-3010

PROFESSIONAL WOMEN'S
CAUCUS
P.O. Box 1057
Radio City Station
New York, NY 10019

PUERTO RICAN RESEARCH
AND RESOURCE CENTER
1519 Connecticut Avenue,
N.W.
Washington, D.C. 20036
202-677-7940

SERVICE EMPLOYMENT
REHABILITATION (SER)
9841 Airport Boulevard, Room
1020
Tishman Building
Los Angeles, CA 90045
213-649-1511

WOMEN'S EQUITY ACTION
LEAGUE (WEAL)
538 National Press Building
Washington, D.C. 20004
202-638-4560

ZETA PHI BETA
1734 New Hampshire Avenue,
N.W.
Washington, D.C. 20009
202-387-3103

And remember that the more training you have, the more you can parley your "minority status" into a reason the boss should hire you. With a college degree, you'll find many large corporations that have to deal with the public are shopping for spokespersons people can identify with. The companies want "tokens" in middle management. And if you get an advanced degree, you'll become such a hot commodity that companies may bid against each other to get you. Of course, their motives may not be pure—but at those salaries, you may be able to overlook such disingenuousness.

But what about outright discrimination? What can you do about it, if you feel you've been turned down just because you're black, or female, or handicapped? First off, know your rights under the law.

In order to prevent discrimination against minorities, federal and state laws spell out what your employment rights are, and what an employer may and may not do in a lot of tricky areas. Here are some of the details:

- An employment agency *must* refer you to any job you're qualified for, no matter what sex, race, or age *usually* does it.
- A company must let you fill out an application form when it allows other people to do so.
- A company *may* ask your marital status, sex, height and weight—but only if these are genuine requirements for the job. Very few jobs really demand a certain gender.
- A company *may* ask you to put down your race, sex, and age on a special form used to monitor its affirmative action program. But that information should not be on the main application form, where it could affect an interviewer or supervisor. And if you feel you've been discriminated against, the employer will have to *prove* that this data was *not* used against you.
- A company may not require high school graduation as a prerequisite for jobs in which that education is not really used. (In the past, these "education requirements" were used to reject innumerable minority applicants.)

- A company may not reject you just because you've been arrested. And it can only reject you for convictions if its business involves security (guards, police) or access to drugs and cash (pharmacies, hospitals, banks).
- A company may not ask about your charge accounts or home- and car ownership unless a car is needed on the job or you'll be dealing in large amounts of other people's cash (in which case they want to make sure you're not so desperate you'll pick up loose change).
- You may not be asked your birthdate or age before you are hired.
- You may not be rejected for hairstyle.
- Men and women, blacks and whites, must be offered the same salary for the same job.
- If you've been offered a job, the employer may not then withdraw the offer because you turn out to be a particular sex, race, religion, or age.

If you feel you've been discriminated against in your job search, you have a right to make a complaint, or sue. Call the Equal Employment Opportunity Commission's district office in your area (listed under U.S. Government, Department of Labor), and ask for the EEOC Form 5, Charge of Discrimination.

This form will ask you for the basic information:

- Cause of discrimination (race, religion, color, sex, national origin)
- Name of organization that discriminated against you (employer, labor organization, employment agency, apprenticeship committee, state or local government agency)
- Others who discriminated against you
- Their addresses
- Date of most recent or continuing discrimination
- Description of what was done to you and how others were treated differently
- Signature of a notary public (swearing you're who you say you are)

A number of people will help you prepare your case. Get in touch with groups such as

- Advocates for Women
- American Civil Liberties Union
- Asian Law Caucus

- Bar Association for your area (for a referral)
- Employment Law Center (San Francisco)
- Legal Aid Society
- Mexican-American Defense and Education Fund
- National Association for the Advancement of Colored People
- National Organization for Women
- Neighborhood Legal Assistance
- Urban League
- Women's Switchboard (Los Angeles)

You'll have to find some supporting evidence—someone else who heard the boss hire you, then fire you "because my boss says we can't have any women on that project." Tape recordings. The actual printed forms, with the illegal questions. When you go to a lawyer, you can expect to be asked for more and more proof. In some cases, you may join a class action, teaming up with hundreds of other people who've been rejected by the same company; these suits have the best chance of winning, since they outline a *pattern* of planned discrimination.

What good does it do to complain? You might get a job offer, to keep you from pursuing your complaint. (This is common—but do you really want to work for someone who discriminates? You'd hardly be starting off on a basis of mutual trust.) You might eventually get a cash payment to cover salary you *might* have earned. But your lawyer will probably pocket most of that. In a class action, you might make a few hundred dollars ten years later.

So when you bring a complaint, you mainly help others who come after you. You add your small voice to the growing indictment, forcing employers to edge closer to obeying the law. You also earn the long-standing hatred of the boss, and in certain businesses with close ties between personnel departments, you'll be universally blackballed. (No one will tell you that, since this practice is illegal; but your name will be mentioned on the phone, or marked on the computer file. You'll be known as a troublemaker.)

Still confused? To find a job—rather than to correct a social injustice—go to the grass-roots organizations that speak for your particular "minority." Talk with the National Organization for Women, the Center for Independent Living, the Mexican-American Legal Defense Fund, the Gray Panthers, the Asian Caucus, the Urban League. Go to their meetings, chat with counselors. You'll want to ask

- Where are there some affirmative action programs for my type of job?

- Which companies still discriminate?
- Where can I get into an affirmative action training program for a new job?

Most important, be methodical in your search. You know your résumé's going to have to be twice as attractive as that of a "majority" applicant's. So put in the time to create a snappy sheet. Create cover letters that stand out from the crowd. Keep calling, and talking, and checking out leads. Eventually, method—and a little luck—can outwit even the most pervasive prejudices.

Chapter 8

If You Want
More Training

If you want to learn a new trade, or refresh skills you haven't used for a few years, you may want to take some training. The benefits:

- You perfect some salable skills.
- You establish a track record, showing you can put in regular effort over a long time, moving toward your goal.
- You pick up useful information about jobs and trends in the field.
- You develop friendships with other people in the field—the basis for an information network later.

The drawbacks:

- You may have to postpone getting the job you want.
- To support yourself while taking the training, you may have to take a low-paying job at hours that fit around your class schedule.
- You may end up paying thousands of dollars to learn a job and find that there aren't many openings.
- It's hard to become a student again, if you've been out of school for a while.

So before you choose a particular training program, you'll need to consider some questions like this:

- Are there really going to be jobs available in this field when I graduate?
- Can I stand learning this trade? (Or am I just doing it because I think there may be a job in the field?)

- Am I excited by this trade?
- Would I learn it even if it didn't lead to a job?
- Can I afford the courses, and the loss of income for the months I'll be devoting my time to training?
- Is the training I want approved by the Better Business Bureau, state department of education, the union, workers in the field, and employers?

If most of your answers are yes, then check out the possibilities in detail:

- Trade schools
- Home study
- Community college and adult education
- On-the-job training
- Military training
- Federal Programs

Trade Schools

There are more than seven thousand privately owned, profit-making trade schools in the U.S. Most charge between $1,000 and $3,000 a year for courses that take up to three years to teach you a high-paying trade—word processing, electronics repair, computer programing. Few require a high school diploma for admission, but to start certain courses, you must prove you can read and write English and do elementary math. Basically, if you've got the cash, you're admitted.

The best schools will offer you:

- Student-teacher ratios of less than fifteen to one.
- Teachers who are currently active in the profession.
- A real placement service. (Most claim to help with placing you in a job afterward. But you should demand at least one full-time placement person for every hundred students about to graduate.)
- Help in securing federal, state, and other scholarships.
- Accreditation of the school by the state department of education, the Veterans' Administration, and the professional associations in your field.
- A detailed description of the courses you will get for your money. (They contract to provide this material, and you can sue if you don't get it.)

Beware of fast talk and special deals. Ask some employers what they think of this training. Go to the school and see what the students say. Consult your employment counselors, and union leaders. What good is a school if every boss laughs at it?

If you want a list of accredited trade schools, write for the *Directory of Accredited Private Trade and Technical Schools,* from the National Association of Trade and Technical Schools, 2021 L Street, N.W., Washington, D.C. 20036.

Home Study

You may want to sign up for study-at-home courses if you live way out in the country, if you work the same hours as trade schools are open, or if you have a few more years to serve in the armed forces. Five million people now take correspondence courses offered by some twelve hundred high schools, the federal government, labor unions, religious groups, and universities, as well as purely "correspondence" schools.

You'll miss out on the chance to learn through class discussion and you won't be able to ask the teacher for help. Plus, not having a class to go to, with regular assignments, you may find it hard to complete the home course.

But for fees ranging from $5 to $2,000 (most average $500) you'll be able to learn at your own pace, and you'll pile up credits you can boast about in your résumé. Before you spend the time and money, you might check your local library to see if you could borrow the same information for free. Ask employers whether they'd be impressed by your having completed the course. To find some accredited schools, write for the *Directory of Accredited Home Study Schools,* from the National Home Study Council, 1601 18th Street, N.W., Washington, D.C. 20009.

Community College and Adult Education

At many community colleges, you'll find first-rate almost-free classes in trades such as programing, and mechanical drawing. As long as you're a local resident, you qualify for admission to most such classes. When there are laboratory fees, supply costs, or tuition, the school will help you find scholarship money.

To fit into a working person's schedule, most classes take

place in the evening. But some, like basic typing, English as a second language, and office skills, go all day, since the school figures you'll need these *before* you get a job. Sign up early—there are a lot of people pressing to take advantage of these bargains. And state employment offices nudge applicants this way, too.

For copies of the courses available through junior colleges, community colleges, and adult education divisions of local universities, go to the library—or call the schools.

On-the-Job Training

On-the-job training usually isn't. Ads talk about on-the-job training (or OJT) but when you get on the job, they just show you how to do this particular task, and you get paid a low rate, as a "trainee." But you rarely get the carefully thought-out training you thought you would.

You will learn quickly—if not thoroughly—from a person who works right there with you. And you'll learn the way *this* company wants the job done—not just those general techniques you'd get in a class.

Of course, some big corporations do develop first-rate training programs for new employees—particularly if you're going to become a middle-level professional. Usually, you'll go to school for a few weeks, then work in one department for a month, take some more classes, then go to another department, making the rounds and learning as you go. This is expensive, so most companies will only do this for you if they're convinced that you're going to make a fine bank manager one day, or head auditor, or vice-president.

But the best training you can get will be if you can wangle a job as the extra person in a fairly small but very active business—you'll have to do a little of everything right off. You'll get to make mistakes, decide important questions, and write up contracts. Within a year, you'll know more about the business than the management trainee being carefully led through the different departments over at the huge corporation. Harder work, yes—but probably better training.

Military Training

If you can get into the armed forces, you can write your own "career" before you join up, so the service will train you in the field you want to learn. There are at least two hundred courses available—some of which apply to civilian jobs (such as electronics, data transmission, driving, flying, cooking, repair).

Basic training takes one and a half to three months; then you go to the formal training you contracted for—usually a few more months, sometimes as long as a year. Your salary will be low ($6,300 to $7,500), but you get food and housing, plus lots of fringe benefits. You'll usually work an eight-hour day, five days a week. But you are in the service. You must obey orders; if the captain tells you to work overtime, you do. You're around dangerous machines—and you could even get shot at.

To find out what's available, talk to recruiters from every service. Insist on finding out what you'll learn, and make sure there's really a *current* opening in the service for that specialty. Then talk to civilian employers: would they respect this training? Hire you afterward?

For general information, write to

- Army Opportunities, P.O. Box 1776, Mount Vernon, NY 10550.
- Commandant (G-PMR), U.S. Coast Guard, Washington, D.C. 20580
- Director, Personnel Procurement Division, HQ, U.S. Marine Corps, Washington, D.C. 20380
- U.S. Air Force Recruiting Service, Director of Recruiting Operations, Randolph Air Force Base, TX 78148.
- Navy Recruiting Command (Code 40), 4015 Wilson Boulevard, Arlington, VA 22203

Federal Programs

They come and go. Some last a few weeks, some a year. You can earn the minimum wage while learning a job; some programs even help you find a job afterward. Contact your local state employment office or the U.S. Department of Labor.

Chapter 9

Coping with
Turndowns and Burnout

So you sent out ten letters, and only got two replies—both rejecting you? Or you've been looking for work for the last four weeks, and the only interview you've gotten was with your bank, about your overdrawn account? You say you thought you had a job all set, and it fell through? You're worn out from filling out application forms, and you groan when you open the want ads.

Sure, you're going to have moments when you feel frightened, hopeless, helpless, dejected, ejected, downcast and furious. That's normal. Unfortunately, many people let these feelings stop them from pursuing their job search.

But you can turn your mood around. First of all, get out and talk to your friends. If you've teamed up with others who are looking for work, meet with them. Talk about what's really making you depressed. But talk with people who can ask a few realistic questions, like these:

- Are you running out of money? Have you really checked your bank statements, your budget? Do you have a budget? Have you figured out some in-the-meantime job, to take care of current expenses? At the current rate of outflow, when are you going to run out of money—and out of credit? Exactly how long can you postpone getting a hand-to-mouth job?
- Have you really been looking? If you're unemployed, you have at least forty hours a week you can devote to this job of finding a job. How many hours did you put in? Do you keep an exact count? How many ads did you reply to? How many employers did you call? How many people did

you get in touch with, asking about work they may have heard of? (Keeping careful records, with statistics like these, can help prove to your own mind that you are doing something; you are working.) And if you haven't done much, how come?

- What do you really want to do? Do you prefer unemployment? What kinds of jobs do you really like? Are you going after those? Or are you forcing yourself to go after ones you think you can get, but you hate? That's enough to make anyone depressed. If you're not going for what you want, you'd better ask yourself, When am I going to?
- Have you given yourself credit for what you have done, so far? It's hard to learn to boast about your progress when you don't have a job offer in hand. But you should. Realize when you've put in a good day's work looking for work. Congratulate yourself. Give yourself a treat. You might even let yourself feel rich, by indulging in a luxury— when you feel rich, it's easier to think like someone who doesn't need a job. And of course, jobs come to people who don't need them.
- Are you taking care of yourself? Look in the mirror. Are you developing sags under your eyes? Pimples, and headaches, and ulcers, and aching feet? Remember, the anxiety and the uncertainty will exhaust you, if you're not careful, just as all that walking around will. So eat well; exercise a lot; take extra vitamins. And watch some comedies. You need to laugh more.

A real friend will ask you all these questions. Answer them, out loud. The more you talk about what's going on—truthfully— the easier it will be to endure. Hiding the facts from others lets you go on feeling guilty about what you haven't done. Covering up your terror lets you go on attacking yourself with thoughts like:

If only I'd done X . . .
I'm too lazy.
I'm just not worth hiring.
I'll never get a job. I don't deserve one.
I should go back to school, because I can't do anything.

Talking about these feelings lessens their sharpness, lets you see that they're a bit exaggerated. And talking about the facts— what you have or have not done—lets your mind sort out your situation objectively. At least you'll know where you stand. (When you don't talk about these facts, you can go on worrying, without knowing for sure.)

Alone, or with friends, ask yourself how you really feel about the employers who've ignored your letters, or refused to call you back, or just plain rejected you. Depressed, sure. But don't you feel some anger, too?

Try this exercise. Write down on a piece of paper the names of some employers who've snubbed you or turned you down. Now crush it. Think about crushing those bosses. Now set the paper on fire. Call those employers any name you think of. Sounds a little silly, but you'll be surprised how much better you feel. How come? You've gotten the anger out—instead of keeping it inside and turning it on yourself. Blame the people you're angry at—not yourself. Expressing your legitimate anger can help you start moving again, too.

When you're angry, you see that the employers are keeping you from something you want. So think some more about what it is you want. Review the reasons you really want work. Not just the hysterical ones ("I've got to get some cash"). Recall the other ones—your need for accomplishment, for challenge, for companionship.

Here's another exercise to try. When you notice yourself saying "I've got to," rephrase that to "I want to." See how that feels. And if you think "I really need," rephrase that to "I really want." Realize that you have made a *choice* to get a job.

Visualize success, too. Imagine how it will feel, what you'll tell your friends, what you'll do to celebrate, what your first day on the job will be like. See it in your mind's eye, touch it, smell it. Spend half an hour just daydreaming—but consciously daydreaming. Do it on purpose. You're stimulating yourself, reminding yourself of your real desires. Those desires will show your unconscious what direction to think in. And then surprising ideas, sudden hunches, and enlightened impulses will start popping up—pointing you on unexpected paths toward the job you want, setting you in motion.

And desire will give energy to your activity, too. Recognize that there is a method to finding work, and that if you just start following it again, you'll be sure of a job, eventually. So focus on activity. Mark the want ads. Revise your résumé. Write cover letters. Do something! Make a list of people to call. As you get back into action, your mind will relax, because you will then be doing something to take care of yourself rather than waiting for some employer to break in your door with a job offer. You won't be a passive victim anymore.

It's not unusual to feel burned out when you're looking for work. But you can stand out from the crowd by concentrating on what you want—and using your aim to lift yourself out of the common despair.

Getting in
Touch

Chapter 10

Taking an Inventory of Your Skills

You probably have at least a hundred skills you can transfer to your next job—even if you've never actually done that job before. From earlier jobs, from volunteer days, from hobbies, from work around the house, you've acquired general abilities that will help you do most of whatever needs to be done on the job you're applying for—the rest you can learn there.

But to get the job, you have to convince the boss that you can do it—that you have the necessary skills. You must mention these talents prominently in your cover letters, applications, résumés, and interviews. That's why you'll find it helpful to put together a list of your transferable skills. For example, if you'd never been a stockbroker and began today, you could draw on skills you acquired shepherding kids on school trips to the Stock Exchange, making speeches to local civic clubs, reading the financial pages, planning your family investments. On your résumés, these skills might show up like this:

- Instructed groups in basics of stock market.
- Made public speeches, persuading local dignitaries to contribute over $100,000 to charities.
- Monitored daily trends, as research for investment plans.

That's why we call many skills "transferable."

Once you acquire a skill, you own it. It goes with you, and you can "transfer" it to a new job. So you can probably do more than you usually give yourself credit for. As a homemaker, for instance, you've learned to budget, shop, clean, organize time, make repairs, communicate, and teach. As a student, you learned techniques of learning, writing, reporting, and communicating.

Even if you've been unemployed for five years, you've been doing *something*—and if you look at that carefully, you'll spot some practical skills.

Here is a list of actions you may have performed, a checklist of skills. Imagine you're a supermarket full of abilities, and we're taking an inventory of your skills. Check off anything you can do. Don't be modest.

And don't rule out a skill, just because you're not perfect at it. Also don't leave out a skill, just because you never acquired it on a paying job. If it's a skill, it's a skill—and you should check it.

Fill in the blanks, too, when you can give more details. For instance, if you check "Repaired," you might write in what you fixed. All these details will be very valuable when you actually get around to writing up your résumé.

In parentheses you'll find examples of each skill—these are just examples to give you an idea what I mean by each word. Your own experience will be wider, so don't rule out a skill like building just because you built something other than a house, garage, or table. It's still building, so check it off, and write in whatever you made.

Ignore the right-hand column until you've gone through all the items. (I'll explain what to do there at the end.)

Did this:	To what or whom	Examples	Type of skill
Classified		Sorted out addresses by zip code; separated hot from cold wash	
Organized		Set up group trips, parties, political campaigns	
Did troubleshooting		Located leaks, engine problems, spotted foul-ups in an organization	
Analyzed		Figured out a pattern in purchases, production, voting	
Set up systems		Systematized office procedures, factory lines, mailing program	
Established priorities		Figured out what to do first, second, third, or what is most and least important	

Did this:	To what or whom	Examples	Type of skill
Researched		Collected statistics, quotes, studies, information	
Interviewed		Talked with applicants, asked questions of customers or clients	
Administered tests		Gave knot-tying exams, handed out instructions for mass tests	
Evaluated		Judged a program to see if it met its goals, suggested new standards	
Created		Began a new program, system, way of doing things	
Changed		Altered existing arrangements, machines	
Initiated		Started a new procedure	
Persuaded		Talked others into collective action, a fund drive, say	
Led		Took leadership role in union, club	
Administered		Organized work for others, gave orders, checked up on performance	
Sold		Sold products door to door, or from behind gas pump or counter	
Negotiated		Talked with numerous people, moved them toward mutual agreement	
Recorded		Wrote sales up on slip, filled out invoices	
Computed		Figured out the cost of cookies, sales tax, production totals	
Used languages		Programmed languages, foreign languages	
Filed		Put letters in alphabetical, chronological, or numerical folders	
Dealt with public		Talked on the telephone, greeted visitors, hosted parties	

Did this:	To what or whom	Examples	Type of skill
Handled phones		Answered, forwarded calls, took messages	
Taught		Lectured, led discussions, set up curriculum	
Addressed groups		Spoke to assembled strangers, town meeting, fellow employees	
Composed letters		To friends, businesses, newspapers	
Wrote reports		From one page to a hundred, reporting on accidents, problems, successes	
Edited		Improved grammar, clarity in others' writing	
Produced brochures		Turned out writing and pictures for public	
Issued policy		Made formal announcements of rules, procedures	
Received complaints		Took notes on citizen complaints, dealt with unhappy customers	
Counseled		Listened to and talked with upset students, street people, referred them to hospitals, therapists	
Advised		Told others how to work, play, dance	
Planned		Drew up blueprints, or outlines	
Gave support		Gave ideas, warmth, and comfort to a group	
Took inventory		Of products, supplies	
Kept the books		Entered figures in accounts-receivable, accounts-payable, general ledgers	
Set up budget		Figured out income and outflow, item by item	
Inspected		Examined cloth, cars, gardens, looking for defects	
Assembled		Put together parts of machine, process	

Did this:	To what or whom	Examples	Type of skill
Built		House, garage, tables	
Repaired		Appliances, bridges, trails	
Performed		Songs, theatrical roles, mime, magic	
Shaped		Clay, bronze, ice sculpture	
Designed		Posters, ads, dances	
Drew		Sketched landscapes, faces, abstracts	
Danced		Modern, jazz, classical	
Coached		Baseball, swimming, mountain climbing	
Made art		Created conceptual pieces, performances, video art, oils, drawings	
Advertised		Garage sales, beer, restaurants	
Assessed needs		Figured out what people or companies need	
Assigned work		To campers, kitchen help, factory workers	
Communicated		Via letters, radio, TV, or just word of mouth	
Guided		Foreigners on tour, visitors at tourist site	
Coordinated		Volunteers, various efforts	
Packaged		Shoes, food, programs	
Installed		Locks, electrical wiring, office equipment	
Marketed		Planned sales strategy, made high-level contacts, presented sales pitch	
Trained		Taught new staff how to do jobs, instructed Girl Scouts in knot tying	
Cleaned		Washed, swept, dusted, mopped, waxed, scraped	
Operated		Ran machines such as forklift, drill press, ten-key adding machine	
Drove		Ten-ton trucks, school bus, car	
Piloted		Plane, boat	
Secured grants		Got funding from private foundation	

Did this:	To what or whom	Examples	Type of skill
Serviced		Maintained, did light repairs on machines	
Cultivated		Prepared soil, raised flowers and vegetables	
Lifted		Boxes, bodies, dirt	
Painted		With brush, roller, or spray, indoors or outdoors	
Selected		Chose proper tool or material	
Compiled		Filled out forms or charts, reporting data	
Requisitioned		Sent in orders for supplies	
Patrolled		Guarded neighborhood, building, or camp	
Distributed		Handed out leaflets, mail, posters	
Decorated		Store windows, stage sets, platforms	
Provided		Gave services such as haircuts, meals, information	
Demonstrated		Showed others how to use equipment or perform activities	

As you've built up your list, you may have noticed that your skills tend to cluster into certain areas of interest. Perhaps you've checked off four or five skills, all of which have to do with speaking and writing. In that case, you'll want to pull those skills together under a larger label, "Communication skills."

By bunching together your related skills, you show an employer that you have depth and experience in that general area. You may end up with three to five major areas. Go back through the inventory and tie together groups of skills, using your own labels (preferably) or some from this list:

Supervisory skills	Public contact
Communication	Sales
Teaching	Research
Financial	Clerical
Leadership	Performance
Helping	Art
Mechanical	Service
Maintenance	

Now extract the information from the inventory, so you can use it on your letters and résumé. For each area of ability, put the general label (such as "Communication skills"), then copy out the details (which might be "wrote articles for company newspaper, performed in holiday pageants, interviewed dissatisfied customers, received complaints, recorded them, wrote reports, and made suggestions").

_____
(Category)
        _____
        (Skills, with details)

_____
        _____

_____
        _____

_____
        _____

_____
        _____

If you memorize these lists, you will be able to persuade an employer that although you may not have done the job before, you have the skills—and more.

To make sure you have not overlooked any skills, make a list of each job you've done, and under each write down what you did there—not just the main tasks, but everything. (Something that was not important there may turn out to be just the extra that gets you your next job.) Borrow ideas freely from our list of jobs available (Chapter 25), but mainly examine your memories. Use lots of active verbs in the *past* tense—"Did this, acted on that, performed *x* or *y*."

_____

(Job)

_____
(What you did)

_____   _____

_____   _____

_____   _____

_____   _____

In some circumstances you will want to be able to talk about your clusters of skills without being too specific where you acquired them. In other circumstances, you'll want to be able to discourse at length about each job and what you really did there. Both approaches help you recognize and remember all that you have to offer.

You'll be itemizing these skills in your letters, résumés, and interviews. Having them clearly in mind will help you respond without hesitation when an employer asks, ''But what can you do for us?''

Chapter 11

Starting Your Résumé

A résumé offers an employer a brief summary of your work history, and education—in your terms. Unlike an application, a résumé is your form; you decide what goes into it, what gets left out, what you want to emphasize. In this sense, a résumé can help you

- Show that you understand what skills are needed for the job you want.
- Stress that you have several important skills to offer this particular employer.
- Point out the abilities you developed on jobs that at first glance seem far removed from the one you're applying for.
- Interest an employer in interviewing you.
- Provide a "talking paper" from which you can discuss your qualifications during an interview.
- Offer the employer *your own* digest of your experience, in a form that can be easily copied, handed around, and saved.
- Remind the employer how to get in touch with you by phone or mail.
- Show the employer that you can prepare a neat, understandable document.

Employers expect you to send them a résumé for any professional or managerial positions and for most clerical and sales jobs. Without a résumé, you go to the back of the line.

Basically, a résumé acts as an introduction. If you're answering a newspaper ad for a job you've already done, you may want to send a résumé with your letter. If you're filling out an application at a bank or a hospital, where the personnel department will be deciding whether to interview you, you might clip your résumé on top, to say more than the application allows. If you've lined up an interview through a friend, you'll want to take your résumé in; start talking without it, but when the discussion turns specific, pull it out to show you've already prepared for these questions.

Don't send a résumé off at first when you're switching careers. It's too easy for employers to reject you when they see you've *never* done *anything* like their job. Instead, start out with a letter that highlights a few of your relevant successes and leaves out just where you scored these triumphs. This will pique interest without revealing any damaging information. That way you can get an interview. Once you've established personal contact and sold the employer on your abilities—*then* you can pull out the résumé, if you need to.

Since a résumé describes your previous experience in terms that apply to your new job, you may have to create a new, or partly new, résumé for each type of job you consider. For instance, a woman who had been a volunteer publicist for three years might want to get into public relations or advertising (she's had a few courses in that). She could come up with two different résumés, describing her volunteer work as publicity in one, advertising in another. That's why I recommend typing your résumé—in a new way for each job—rather than typesetting it. You should have a unique résumé for *each* job you want.

And that's why you have to make up your mind what job you want *before* you write the résumé. You name the job you're after at the top, to tell a confused personnel department exactly which job you're after, and to reassure the boss that you're not just looking for *any* job. You know what you want. Then you figure out what skills are important in that job, and describe your previous jobs or rephrase that job description to resemble those skills. Make the skills you used on your previous jobs *translatable* to the job you want.

How long should the résumé be? One page is best. No more than two. A résumé sums up; it does not tell your whole life story.

What kind of résumé is best for you? That depends on what you have to hide and what you want to emphasize.

IF

• You are changing careers

- You have not worked for a year or more
- You have done a lot of short-term jobs, with different companies
- You have gaps at least six months long in your work history
- You got your job training in prison or in a government program
- You know one of your former employers is giving you a bad reference

then you will want to use a *skill résumé*. A skill résumé gives no company names, no exact dates. It clumps together those five painting jobs you did in three states into one skill: "Painter." And it totals the time you put into painting, no matter where, to give the time as "one year." After all, you have that much experience, all told. By avoiding specific dates, you can stress the depth of your skill, and you can escape the embarassing questions, "How come you skipped around so much? Why are you changing careers?"

IF

- You have an unbroken work history since you left school, except for maybe a few months' vacation between jobs
- You have a good explanation for any gaps (you went into the army, went back to school)
- You have worked for long periods at one or another company (three or more years)
- You are applying for a job just like what you have now (and you have no gaps in work history),

then you may want to use a *chronological résumé*, in which you list every job you've had, from the present back into time, giving the dates and names of employers. You list skills only under job titles, not separated out. Thus, the jobs themselves, and the sheer length of your employment, will speak well enough for you so that you don't need to emphasize the particular skills involved.

IF

- You're changing careers, but you've had a fairly steady employment history (no big gaps, no mysterious or un-mentionable employers)
- You're reentering the job market and you want to mention volunteer jobs you've done, or long-ago jobs you think relate to the job you're applying for

- You've moved from another country, where you did similar jobs
- You want to emphasize skills, but you also want to show you have nothing to hide in your work history,

then you will want to draw up a *mixed résumé*, starting with your major skills, under a heading like "Experience," then putting in a section called "Work history," a very concise list of jobs, dates, and companies. In this way you show that you have the ability to do the new job, and that you've been a consistent worker before, but you avoid having an employer exclaim right off, "But that's not the same job! It's not the same career!" Often such résumés fall into two pages: the first outlines your major skills, the second gives the details of previous jobs and education.

So before you go any further, you need to make two decisions.

A. What job or jobs are you going to be applying for?
   1.
   2.
   3.
B. Which type of résumé is best for you, when you apply for each job? (Check one type for each job.)

(JOB)	Skill	Chronological	Mixed
1.			
2.			
3.			

No matter what kind of résumé you make up, it will include certain information.

1. Your name, mailing address, and phone number, so the employer can get in touch with you. If there's no one to answer your phone during the day, include some number at which messages can be left. Perhaps a friend or relative—someone who stays home all day. Or sign up with an answering service for a month or two. Remember, an employer may only try to reach you once.

2. Your education. Put down the last high school you attended, the most recent college or graduate school. If you graduated, say so, and include the exact degree—but only put dates if you're using a chronological format. (If you did not graduate, you at least show you attended, and many employers will assume you graduated; few check, unless you've had no work experience.)

If you have just left school, state your major, list relevant courses, and mention any awards or honors you received. If you paid your own way, or won a scholarship, say so. Mention extracurricular activities only if they have some relevance to the job.

If you earned an equivalency diploma (the G.E.D.), say so, and give the date.

Also mention any training you've had—military courses, summer seminars, evening classes, government programs. Put down the title of the course, the host organization, city, state, and length of time the course lasted. For instance, an accounting course might appear this way:

> Inventory Accounting Procedures course, Surefinah Foods, Fargo, North Dakota (one month).

Don't worry if some courses seem irrelevant. Studying shows you're conscientious. Only leave out the downright embarrassing.

And if you have foreign education, describe it as "equivalent" to whatever our similar level would be. Be sure to give an exact English version of the name of your school, and include the address, and dates. Consult with an American to be sure you can translate the terms, and then describe the contents of your major courses, so other Americans can figure out exactly what you studied. For instance, a woman who studied "pedagogy" in Switzerland described her work this way:

> Equivalent to Master's in Education, at University of Lausanne, Lausanne, Switzerland (1978–1980). Courses on Pavlov, Skinner, Piaget, IQ Testing, Statistical Evaluations, Infancy, and Early Childhood Learning.

3. Some personal data. Put in information that has real relevance to the job; otherwise omit. For most jobs a list of hobbies is all right but unnecessary. Some people like to put down their special interests, hoping the boss will share one. But be sure you really know flower arranging, if you put it down, in case the boss says he just won first prize and asks about intricate details of Japanese arrangements. Also, only include pastimes if they are unusual. For instance, "TV watching" will not help you much. "Cooking" doesn't sound like a special interest, but "Gourmet cooking" does. Some other tips for the personal data section:

• If you speak foreign languages, say so.

- If you've moved from another country and have been authorized to work here, say so.
- If you've had writing published, make up a short bibliography, headed "Publications." Include the title (underlined if it was a book; in quotation marks if it was something shorter, like a chapter, a poem, an essay), then a period. Then the title of the magazine or book the shorter piece appeared in, underlined, followed by a comma, and the name of the publisher, comma, place of publication, comma, year of publication, comma, and relevant pages, period. (Omit pages for a full-length book.) Thus:

  "Grinding Tools." *Parade*, Iowa City, Iowa, 1981, pp. 3–4.
  Scraping and Scratching Technology. Grinder Press, Des Moines, Iowa, 1980.
- If you've been on radio or TV, list the shows in capital letters, the call letters of the station, and the dates. You could head this "TV and Radio Appearances."
- If you've given more than three or four speeches recently, you might list them, putting the title in quotation marks, then giving the name of the sponsoring organization or event, address, and date as:

  "The Republic and You," Lincoln Day Dinner, Torreyville, Indiana, February 16, 1981.
- Don't put down your height, weight, race, religious background, or political party.
- Avoid mentioning controversial items, such as the fact that you organized a union at your last job.

4. References. You need some people to vouch for your character; best are friends who've known you for years. Tell them what to say about you when a boss calls. Prepare them for these calls. (Relatives won't do. And congressmen are not a good idea—unless they really know you. Better an unknown who can talk about you in detail than a famous politician who says, "Wonderful person, whoever they are.") Don't put the names on the résumé. Say "References available on request." That way your friends won't be bothered unless the employer calls you first.

If your school maintains a placement service with a file of reference letters ready to be sent out, put its address down.

These sections form the beginning and end of any résumé, no matter what kind. Fill in the details here, to start your up-to-date résumé:

Name   Home Phone:
Address   Messages:
Job Objective (the job you are applying for):
Experience *or* Work history (you will complete this section
in the next chapters)
Education
        Date (if using a chronological résumé, include date;
             omit on a skill résumé, or if you did not graduate)
        Graduated (if you did)
        Name and address of high school
        Date
        Graduated
        Name and address of college

Personal Data

References available on request

The heart of the résumé, though, lies in your experience and
work history. That is where you get to advertise your skills. And
that is what we turn to next, describing your abilities one way for
a skill résumé, another way for a chronological résumé, and a
third for a mixed résumé.

Chapter 12

Making Up
a Skill Résumé

A skill résumé puts the spotlight on your ability to do the job you're applying for. It stresses your skills—not job titles, dates, company names. But which skills should you emphasize?

The ones needed on this job. So the first thing you need to do is figure out what skills the job requires. Does it take math sense? Administrative ability? Negotiating savvy? And once you figure out the various skills involved, which is the most important?

Job you want _____

Types of skills required _____*Most important

_____

_____

_____

_____

Take these types as major headings for your résumé. You're going to show, in detail, that you have each of these skills. How? Well, for starters, look back at your Skills Inventory. You can probably sort some of those inventoried abilities into the "types." For instance, if you checked "computed" and filled in "macro-economic forecasts for East European countries," then you might put that under the general heading "Forecasting Skills," needed for a job as an economist at a major international bank. Your cluster of skills might come out like this:

Forecasting Skills: Computed macro-economic forecasts for East European countries; administered five-person study group focusing on East German balance of payments and likelihood of repayment of outstanding loans; wrote monthly reports, with recommendations in areas of currency exchange and loan policy, for major bank dealing with East Germany, Poland, and Rumania.

If you sense that the job you are applying for invovles telling other people what to do, you might expect the boss to want to know about your supervisory skills. And, borrowing from your inventory, you might create this paragraph on your résumé:

Supervisory Skills: Created and administered $500,000 budget for five-person department; planned and monitored the work of five researchers; set up standard procedures, measurement criteria, general policy; hired and fired.

And if you want to emphasize the length of time you've worked in the field—even if it was in four states and three companies, with long gaps between jobs—you could put a time total in parentheses. Not dates. Just a total amount of time you've devoted to this activity. Like this:

Forecasting Experience   **(5 years)**
Computed macro-economic forecasts for East European countries; administered five-person study group focusing on East German balance of payments and likelihood of repayment of outstanding loans; wrote monthly reports, with recommendations in areas of currency exchange and loan policy, for major bank dealing with East Germany, Poland, and Rumania.

This looks as though you spent five years at one job doing forecasting. It lets you avoid embarrassing gaps that show up in a chronological résumé when you have to do something like this:

1975–1976	Assistant Economist, Toronto National Bank
1979	Research Director, Hibernia National Bank
1981–1982	Economic Writer, Bank of America

Those gaps may show up eventually. But at least you'll have shown the employer that you can do the work, that you have the skill—no matter where you learned and practiced.

You'll need to boast about at least three skills. Perhaps another part of this job will involve giving presentations to bank officers. "Presentation Skills" might then be another type. And scanning your inventory for any evidence of this skill, you might come up with a paragraph like this, covering a month here, a month there:

Presentation Experience (3 years)

Presented audio-visual reports to groups of loan officers; briefed State Department management on economic policy; gave university lectures on the prospects for the Rumanian economy; represented major bank in meetings with mass media and local groups.

In this way you total up all those isolated months and show all such experience in one lump—much more impressive than if you list it in a series of short jobs here and there.

Because you are not giving dates to your work experience (just total time devoted to a particular skill), avoid putting in dates when you list your education. The degree is important, the date is not.

If you are combining skills acquired on half a dozen different jobs, leave out the company names in your descriptions, unless they are very impressive. Reason: if you mention half a dozen names, the employer can tell that you've jumped around a lot—spoiling the very effect you're after. Remember, you're trying to show that no matter where you worked, you've piled up a lot of valuable experience. Turn attention away from job titles and dates; make employers look at what you can do.

What would a completed skills résumé look like? Here's one:

ANTHONY HIGGINS

2535 La Costa Lane
Suite 213   Home: 415-555-1212
San Francisco, CA 94107   Service: 415-525-4119

JOB OBJECTIVE: Economist

EXPERIENCE

FORECASTING   (3 years)
- Computed macro-economic forecasts for East European countries.

- Administered five-person study group focusing on East German balance of payments and likelihood of repayment of outstanding loans.

- Wrote monthly reports, with recommendations in areas of currency exchange and loan policy, for major bank dealing with East Germany, Poland, and Rumania.

SUPERVISING   (2 years)
- Created and administered $500,000 budget for five-person department.

- Planned and monitored the work of five researchers.

- Set up standard procedures, measurement criteria, general policy.

- Hired and fired.

PRESENTING   (1 year)
- Presented audio-visual reports to groups of loan officers.

- Briefed State Department management on economic policy.

- Gave university lectures on the prospects for the Rumanian economy.

- Represented bank in meetings with mass media, and local groups.

EDUCATION
M.B.A., University of California, Berkeley.
B.A., University of California, Berkeley.

You'll notice that in the final form, individual achievements are bulleted, so they stand out more. In general, the more white space you leave around an item, the easier it will be to read. Notice, too, that you don't have to bother saying this is a résumé. Obviously it's a résumé. And for a job like this, your hobbies won't make a lot of difference, so leave them out.

Eventually you're going to have to be specific about where you worked, and when. But you'll make your first impression with a résumé like this. When the boss sees you've got the skills, she won't be so tough on your erratic work history.

Use a skill résumé when you are changing fields, too. That way you can't be rejected right off by a boss who looks down your list of job titles, sees that you weren't doing exactly what he's looking for—and assumes you can't do it. A minister who wanted to go into youth counseling took an inventory of his skills, then sorted them out in the main areas he felt would be needed on his new job. Some of his original entries looked like this:

Addressed Groups Gave weekly presentations to groups of two hundred or more; delivered informal addresses to high school students; prepared instructional materials for teen after-school group.

Counseled Counseled disturbed teenagers on drugs, family problems, sex, and love; led recovery group in drug rehabilitation center for juvenile delinquents; made weekly visits to people suffering from blindness, handicaps, bereavement, alcoholism, addiction, and marriage problems.

Planned Planned recreational programs, choir singing, and study groups; scheduled visits from other ministers; organized each class.

Administered Administered $100,000 annual budget, with staff of four and large physical plant; hired and fired; recruited forty volunteers to carry out the rest of the work. Set general policies; encouraged workers to develop own objectives and to carry those out.

You can see that occasionally the minister let slip that he was a minister. So as he revised these notes, he changed "visits from other ministers" to "visits from outside counselors." And he figured that someone hiring counselors doesn't want to hire a lecturer, so he revised "Addressed Groups" to read "Public Contact." In each category, he also selected the most impressive item and put that first. Since counseling was the job, he put that category first. And when he came to education, he decided not to put the initials of his degree (B.D.) or to spell it out (Bachelor of Divinity). Instead, he just wrote "Bachelor's degree," and the college. In all these ways he emphasized his abilities and down-played his role as a minister, so that the director of a youth center wouldn't take a quick glance at the résumé, and say, "Oh God, not another minister!" This way the minister appeared to be a counselor—a job he could do, and had done.

The final résumé:

TOM WRIOTHESLEY

51 Nartine Place   414-567-8899
Detroit, MI 48228

JOB OBJECTIVE: Youth counselor

EXPERIENCE

    COUNSELING   (5 years)
- Counseled more than seventy-five disturbed teenagers on drugs, family problems, sex, and love.

- Led recovery group in drug rehabilitation center for juvenile delinquents.

- Made weekly visits to people suffering from blindness, handicaps, bereavement, alcoholism, addiction, and marriage problems.

    PUBLIC CONTACT   (6 years)
- Made weekly presentations to groups of two hundred or more.

- Delivered informal addresses to high school students.

- Prepared and delivered instruction for teen after-school group.

    ADMINISTRATION
- Administered $100,000 budget, with staff of four and large physical plant.

- Recruited forty volunteers to carry out the rest of the work.

- Set general policies, encouraged workers to develop own objectives and to carry those out.

EDUCATION
    Bachelor's degree, University of Michigan, Ann Arbor.

Miles Trumbull has just graduated from a prominent state university in the Midwest, majoring in nutrition with a minor in African studies. His job objective: to work for some branch of the United Nations, or the World Bank, on agricultural policy in developing nations. He has never had a full-time job, but he did help several professors on their summer research projects in Africa. And he figures that he didn't just learn facts in school—he learned how to "do," so he presents what he learned as skills—not courses.

MILES TRUMBULL

1114 Main Street   219-933-8776
Hammond, Indiana 46327

JOB OBJECTIVE: Consultant in agricultural development

EXPERIENCE

ANALYSIS

- Traced effects of hedging in international commodities market in chocolate, 1976–1982.

- Diagnosed causes of protein-calorie malnutrition in three West African nations.

- Prepared plan for offsetting nutritional anemia in Africa. This proposal was adapted by Professor W. B. Low, and presented at the Pan African Congress, 1981.

PUBLIC CONTACT

- Met with one hundred African students in the U.S., interviewed them on attitudes toward traditional law, and the after effects of colonialism in Tropical Africa. (Study presented at UNESCO Conference, New York, October 1981.)

- Worked in Benin with local and federal government programs introducing farmers to new crops and fertilizers.

- Created four major conferences on what American black college students can do for their peers in Africa. (More than three hundred participants.)

LANGUAGE

- Speak reasonably good Hausa—can read newspapers, write Ajami script.

- Speak some Yoruba.
- Read and write French.

EDUCATION:
    B.A.   Indiana University, 1982, Major in Nutrition, Minor in African Studies.

    Yoruba   One-month course in Yoruba language and civilization, in Benin.

Here's another skill résumé. It's from a woman who has been working as a secretary. She is applying for a position in sales, so she has made her secretarial experience sound like sales work. She once sold raffle tickets to her child's school, and worked for the PTA, so she put that in. She has chosen a skill résumé for two reasons: she hasn't actually done the job she is applying for, and she wants to cover up the fact that she has been out of the work force for six years, raising her daughter, so she wants to avoid dates.

ANNE KORVATH

1898 San Clemente Road   Home: 415-535-1244
Roisterville, CA 94706   Messages: 415-545-6464

JOB OBJECTIVE: A challenging position in computer sales.

EXPERIENCE   (5 years)

  SALES

- Sold door-to-door and on the phone, with record averages.
- Persuaded members of community to work in fund drive that netted $500,000 in three months.
- Won passage of five important bills in town council.

  PUBLIC CONTACT

- Interviewed candidates for jobs, evaluated their potential, made recommendations.
- Greeted visitors, handed out brochures, helped them fill out order forms.
- Did heavy phone work, with general public.

  SUPERVISION

- Trained new workers in our office.

- Supervised two assistants.
- Improved overall productivity of our department by 22 percent, and won merit award for my supervision.

EDUCATION:
Roisterville High School.
Extension Courses in COBOL, BASIC, and PASCAL, University of California, Berkeley.

Training in use of IBM Personal Computer, for office records, Accounts Receivable, Accounts Payable, and General Ledger.

References available on request.

So if you have some reason for avoiding dates, or job titles, or if you just want to emphasize your skills, turn back to your inventory, and pull out details that will prove you can do the job you're after. Remember that your main headings should be the major skills needed by the job—not just things you've done a lot of. And remember to rephrase whatever you've done so it sounds as though you've already—in a way—done the job you're after. Here's a rough outline for you to fill in:

(Name)
(Address)   (Phones)

_____   _____

_____   _____

Job Objective _____

Experience
_____ (General skill needed for this job) _____ (years)
  • _____ (Most impressive achievement)

  • _____

_____ (Next most important general skill needed for job) ____(Years)

• _____ (Most impressive achievement)
_____

• _____

_____

_____

• _____

• _____

• _____

EDUCATION

_____
_____
_____

Chapter 13

Making Up a
Chronological Résumé

A chronological résumé isolates each job you've had and emphasizes the dates: excellent if you've had an unbroken work history, with long stays at each job and good explanations for any gaps (military service, return to school). Not so hot if you've had many short jobs, or if the jobs bear no easily visible relationship to the job you want, or if you have huge unexplained stretches when you were out of work. (The dates will give you away, so use a skill résumé instead.)

In preparing your chronological résumé, start your "Experience" section with your most recent job, giving the date, your job title, the company, then a description of what you did there. Repeat for each job you've done, back to schooldays.

The unbroken sequence of dates will suggest you are a steady, reliable worker. But exactly what did you do? Under each job title, you get a chance to advertise your skills. Put the most important first. Mention money, and statistics when possible—how many strokes per minute can you keypunch? How many people did you welcome to the model home? Look back at the descriptions you made of each job (in chapter 10, "Taking an Inventory of Your Skills"), and add skills from the clusters you formed there. Check again to see if that particular job—or one like it—is described in chapter 25, "Jobs Available." Remember, use the past tense to describe what you did, and start each phrase with a verb.

And since you give dates for the jobs, make sure you include them for school, training, and military service as well. Don't leave out awards, prizes, promotions.

Here are five examples of chronological résumés. Hermione had gone as far as she could in the Federal First Bank. She'd been assistant head teller for a few years, then head teller, but the branch manager showed no signs of quitting or dying. So to move up, Hermione had to move out. She prepared her résumé chronologically to show she was a steady reliable worker who had been promoted before—someone ready to become branch manager.

Hermione Fontana

333 Hartman Street	Home: 203-345-9999
Pittsburgh, PA 15206	Work: 203-555-1212

JOB OBJECTIVE: Position as branch manager.

WORK HISTORY

1978–present	Head Teller, Federal First Bank, Pittsburgh, Pa. Supervised staff of twenty tellers, assisted auditors, trained new tellers, handled difficult questions. Developed new procedures, cutting teller-time per transaction by 25%, made hiring and firing decisions.
1975–1978	Teller, Pittsburgh Savings and Loan, Pittsburgh, PA. Received deposits, paid out moneys, sold travelers checks, prepared daily totals. Won three merit awards. Promoted to Assistant Head Teller after first year.
1973–1975	Accounting Clerk, U.S. Army. Entered accounts payable and accounts receivable; promoted to take charge of making entries in general ledger for base.

EDUCATION

1974	Accounting Course, U.S. Army (1 month).
1969–1973	Jefferson High School, Pittsburgh, Pa. Took business course, including classes in ten-key, typing, and accounting procedures. Voted social secretary for my class.

References available on request.

Tom Brand started graduate school thinking he wanted to build bridges, but shifted to petroleum production halfway through. Once he got his Ph.D., he didn't feel like working too hard, so he took a part-time position with Pollo Oil, earning about half what he could have. In 1976, though, he got married to Erma, and they bought a house. He went to work full time, but Pollo just didn't need engineers badly enough to promote him, or give him a raise. He signed up with Wildcat in 1979, and now he wants to get a management job with a major oil company. He leaves out the "part-time" stuff, and describes his current job as if he were *already* the chief petroleum engineer at Wildcat.

Tom Brand

| 315 Derrick Road | Home: 214-389-1512 |
| Dallas, TX 75228 | Work: 214-555-1212 |

JOB OBJECTIVE: Chief petroleum engineer

WORK HISTORY

1979—Present Production Engineer, Wildcat Oil
Company, Dallas, TX.
- Increased oil and gas production in 15 operations.
- Recommended placement of 23 new wells, to maximize use of resources.
- Stimulated flow by heating subsurface.
- Solved problems such as invasion of subsurface water, slow drilling rate.
- Trained 3 assistants.
- Established standards and procedures for all engineers in company.
- Formulated company-wide plans for exploration, drilling schedules, and construction of crude-oil treating units.

1975—1979 Assistant Petroleum Engineer, Pollo Oil
Company, Dallas, TX.
- Developed well-drilling plans.
- Analyzed costs for new operations.
- Supervised mud compounds and tool bits.
- Monitored production rate of established wells.

EDUCATION

1970—1975 Earned Ph.D. in engineering, University of Texas, Austin, TX. Dissertation on installation of casings and tubings.

1966—1970 Earned B.S., majoring in engineering, University of Texas, Austin, TX.

1962—1964 Sam Houston High School, Austin TX.

PERSONAL DATA

Speak Spanish.
Am willing to travel or relocate.

References available through placement service, Graduate
Division, University of Texas, Austin, TX.

Yvonne Marchetti started work during college, helping the
public relations office with articles on prizes won by faculty
members, money given by alumni, buildings going up, tuition
going up, and government financing coming down. She made
enough to pay for her books and entertainment. But she also
learned the trade. She switched her major to journalism, spent a
summer working full time in the public relations office, and got
tips from the boss on places to go for a job after graduation. She
followed up on one, and got an assistant slot at a local hospital.
After a few years there, she switched to a much larger hospital in
New York City. After five years there, she moved over to the
Red Cross. After four more years there, she decided she wanted
to run her own office, in a somewhat smaller organization. So
she said that her job objective was to become head of public
relations. And since the fact that she had an unbroken work
record of steady progress would help get her in the door to
interviews, she chose to use a chronological résumé. Here's what
it looked like:

YVONNE MARCHETTI

352 Bleecker Street   Home: 212-924-1583
New York, NY 10014   Work: 212-679-4493

JOB OBJECTIVE: Head of public relations

WORK EXPERIENCE

1978–1982   Assistant Vice-President for Public
                 Relations, Red Cross Headquarters, New
                 York, New York.

                 • Supervised staff of ten, developing pub-
                   licity campaigns, assigning and mon-
                   itoring staff work.

                 • Devised Save Blood Campaign that netted
                   more than $35 million in three months.

                 • Supervised time buying and ad placement.
                   Saved $1 million over previous
                   scheduling, reaching much larger
                   audiences.

1973–1978	Lead Writer in Public Relations, Bellevue Hospital, New York, New York.

- Developed TV commercials and newspaper ads for five annual campaigns. Won Cleo for two spots aired locally.

- Supervised the work of three other writers.

- Developed contacts with local TV, radio, and newspaper personnel. Arranged over five hundred interviews with our staff.

1971–1972	Assistant in Public Relations, Bridgeport Hospital, Bridgeport, Connecticut.

- Wrote two hundred press releases used in local newspapers and on local radio and TV.

- Arranged interviews for doctors and executives.

1968–1971	Trainee in Public Relations, University of Bridgeport, Bridgeport, Connecticut.

- Wrote press releases on grants, awards, new buildings, personnel promotions, and appointments.

- Promoted to Writer.

EDUCATION

1967–1971	B.A. in journalism, University of Bridgeport.

Henry Sauerbaum wants to join an ad agency doing statistical studies of consumer attitudes. He has had no relevant jobs—he mowed grass one summer, waited on table during the year, and just graduated. And he doesn't really feel qualified to do a complete study without guidance, so he doesn't want to claim he has the skill. But he's taken a lot of courses, and he wants to make it clear that he's a top student. So he divided up his undergraduate career into four years, and highlighted the most relevant courses.

HENRY SAUERBAUM

15, Place St. Laurent
Montreal, Canada   514-276-0098
H42 4Z9

JOB OBJECTIVE: Statistical analyst, in market research

EXPERIENCE	Courses at University of Texas, Austin, as statistics major, 1978–1982. Graduated with honors.
1978–1979	Statistical Inference: Explored probability theory, Neyman Pearson theory, large sample theory. (A)
	Statistics One: Testing hypotheses, organizing data, chi-square tests, basic design of sampling surveys. (A)
	Calculus: Iterated integrals, convergence tests, Taylor's theorem. (A)
1979–1980	Advanced Calculus: Higher order linear differential equations, Laplace Transform, vector analysis, ideas of Gauss and Stokes. (A–)
	Analysis: Point set topology, Riemann-Stieltjes theory. (A)
	Marketing Research: Introduction to basic techniques, practice using computer packages. (A)
	Philosophy of Mathematics: Russell, Godel, Bernays. (B)
1980–1981	Analysis of Variance: Interpreting observations, factorial experiments, orthogonal contrasts. (A)
	Population Sampling: Random, stratified, cluster, nonresponse. (B)
	Multivariate Analysis: Practical experiments in psychology and consumer behavior: factor analysis and correlations. (A)
1981–1982	Random Numbers: Methods of generation. (B)
	Computers in Statistics: Least squares, robust regression, Eigenvector-eigenvalue computations, Monte Carlo methods. (A)
	Seminar in Simulation: Discrete events, languages, design. (A)
	Senior Paper on IBM Statistical Computer Programs: Advantages and drawbacks. (Honors)

Alan Oberon learned computer programing in college. He had a hard time finding a first job. "All they ever said was 'Come back when you have some experience.'" Finally he got a job mounting tapes, and once he was in the company, he talked his way into doing some patches on programs that were already running—just barely. He worked on large distributed systems for a few years, and became an expert on telecommunications. He got promoted to project leader, but he could go no farther. He wanted to become a systems analyst, but he felt his boss hated him, so he decided to look elsewhere. Here's his résumé. It's chronological because he wanted to show that he had made steady progress, without jumping from job to job the way many programmers do.

ALAN OBERON

1800 Lincoln Avenue   Phone: 404-315-7653
Atlanta, Georgia 30338

JOB OBJECTIVE: Systems analyst

WORK HISTORY

1980–present	Project Leader, Pay 'N Park Drug Stores, Atlanta.

- Did feasibility study, analysis, and design for large distributed system, involving thirty-four stores in three states, recording each sale, reporting back to an inventory system.

- Supervised team of four programmers, developing, implementing, and testing a system involving more than seventy-five individual programs.

- Had the system up and running smoothly after only eighteen months.

1978–1980	Programmer, Pay 'N Park Drug Stores, Atlanta.

- Maintained online system, updated and enhanced ten programs. Became specialist in telecommunications problems.

- Used IMST, VSAM, IBM 3033's. Wrote in COBOL, and FORTRAN.

1977–1978	Operations Technician, Pay 'N Park Drug Stores, Atlanta.

- Ran programs, did troubleshooting on Modems, disk drives, air conditioning.

- Offered advice to programming teams on scheduling, file management, and volume of jobs.

EDUCATION
1973–1977   B.S. University of Georgia. Majored in Computer Sciences. Studied COBOL, FORTRAN.

By presenting his résumé this way, Alan showed an unbroken work history at the same company since graduation. But he also emphasized the steady progression he had made up the ranks. The dates, and the company name, show the steadiness; the rising titles, his achievement.

A final résumé. George Hicks is a package designer. He has never been out of work, even though he's moved around. The companies he's designed for? Little ones at first, then giants. So he wants the names on the résumé. Also, he knows that each boss he's had will give him a great recommendation. So he made up his résumé this way:

GEORGE HICKS
15 Sutton Place   Work Phone: 212-PL5-4350
New York, New York 10022

JOB OBJECTIVE: Head of product design

WORK HISTORY

1980–Present   Chief Designer, Disk Boxes, Manuals, Keyboard, and Console, Personal Computers Inc.

- Created design for the equipment, and the documentation that accompanies it.

- Won prizes at three computer fairs. Design placed in Museum of Modern Art permanent design collection.

1978–1980   Package Designer, Soilex Corporation, New York.

- Redesigned entire line of packages, including six product lines, in at least three sizes each.

- Created new logo for product, stationery, and all corporate communications.

91

1976–1978	Assistant Package Designer, Re-Entry Envelope and Box, New York

- Created new line of gift boxes, sold through greeting card shops. Line realized $3.5 million in profits during the first three years.

- Supervised ordering of papers, cardboards, and printing.

EDUCATION

1972–1976	B.F.A., Parsons School of Design.

Here is a blank form to use in making up your own chronological résumé.

Name

Address   Phones

Job objective

Work history

    Dates   Title, company, address
                    What you did

    (Repeat)

Education

    Dates   Graduated (If you did), School, Address

Personal data

References available on request.

Chapter 14

Making Up a
Mixed Résumé

Sometimes you'll want to combine the two kinds of résumé, starting out by advertising your skills, then following up with a detailed list of your jobs. Why do this?

If you're changing careers, you may want to point out that you can do the job, that you have the skills and the experience—before you reveal that none of your previous jobs fits into the expected career path leading to the job you're applying for. You'll mention them at the end, to show you've worked steadily.

If you're coming back into the job market after years away, you'll want to point out that you can do the job before you mention that you have not worked steadily since school. Your volunteer jobs are worth mentioning, but if you start out with those you may be dismissed as "just a volunteer."

Some people like to start with skills, then throw in the actual jobs at the end, to prove they are not afraid to list the companies they worked for, with job titles, and dates—so a boss can check.

Serena Munro's two kids were twelve and thirteen when she decided to go back to work. She'd worked for her husband while the kids were growing up. Serena balanced his books and consulted with minor clients. The business: locating loan money. So she came to know the backrooms of banks, picked up a lot of financial jargon, and learned to sell herself. She decided to look for a job selling bank services, including loans, to medium-sized businesses. So she started by listing the skills she thought necessary and concluded with a history of the part-time and volunteer jobs she'd had.

12 El Placadero
Dallas, Texas 73208   214-667-8890

JOB OBJECTIVE: A position in bank services sales

EXPERIENCE

    SALES   (10 years)

- Sold businesses to loan officers, convinced businesses to go with particular banks.

- Represented firm before local groups, making weekly speeches and arranging head-to-head discussions.

- Prepared all bills and pursued all late payments.

    FINANCIAL   (10 years)

- Handled General Ledger, Accounts Receivable, Accounts Payable, Quarterly and Annual Tax Returns.

- Had constant contact with all departments of major national banks, with particular emphasis on Real Estate and Capital Development.

WORK HISTORY

Office Manager, Munro Financial Services, Dallas, Texas (1971–1981).
Chief of Volunteers, El Paso Hospital, Texas (1971–1974).

EDUCATION

B.A., University of Texas, Austin (1970).

Bill Fulton taught high school chemistry for seven years, and then the school board closed down the school and laid him off. He worked for a while selling vacuum cleaners but couldn't make enough money that way; tried working in a bookstore but got fired after a fight with a customer; used up his unemployment benefits; decided to look for work as a trainer in the chemical industry. He asked friends about this, and they told him that business is afraid of teachers. So he wanted to show that he could do everything a trainer does (just about what a teacher does, anyway), before admitting that he'd been a teacher, salesman, and bookstore clerk. Here's how he did a mixed résumé:

BILL FULTON

71-713 Washington Street   Phone (216) 213 2233
Cleveland, Ohio 44110

JOB OBJECTIVE: Training coordinator

EXPERIENCE

CURRICULUM DEVELOPMENT

- Created courses introducing newcomers
  to chemistry, developed and
  administered pre- and postevaluations.

TRAINING

- Trained over 300 people in basic
  concepts of organic and inorganic
  chemistry, 140 in physics, 300 in
  biology.

- Won merit awards for excellence of
  training.

ADMINISTRATION

- Coordinated the activities of other
  trainers in the science area. Set general
  guidelines.

- Evaluated, recorded, and ran statistical
  surveys on pre-and posttraining results.

- Set up schedules for twenty other staff
  members, and assisted on scheduling of
  approximately one hundred students
  every three months.

JOB HISTORY
1973–1980   Teacher of Science (Chemistry, Biology,
                   Physics) in Regis Philbin High School,
                   Cleveland, Ohio

1980–1981   Sales Coordinator, Hoover Vacuum
                   Cleaner Company, Cleveland, Ohio

EDUCATION

1969–1973   B.A. University of Akron, Akron, Ohio

So if you're changing jobs, and you've got a fairly solid work
history behind you—at least for most of your time since school—
you might want to try the mixed résumé.

Don't bother with the mixed résumé if you have a regular
series of jobs in the very field you're applying for. A chronological résumé will do fine.

And if you really have something to hide—a big gap in your work history, or wildly different jobs in different states, none for very long—you won't want to list them at the end, anyway. Stay with the skill résumé.

You may find you want to use a skill résumé for one job, a mixed résumé for another, depending on what you want to emphasize— or leave to the last. Basically, you'll have to make up a new résumé for every job you go after, because you must customize every description, every boast, every detail so that it shows you're perfect for this very job. That's why I say you'll find you're never finished with your résumé. Every want ad tells you it's time to revise it.

Chapter 15
Revising
Your Résumé

Of the writing of résumés there is no end—until you get a job you like. Say you've created a rough draft of one résumé. Now you'll need new and different versions of your résumé whenever

- You apply for another *type* of job, which demands a different ordering of skills.
- You respond to the particular demands of a newspaper want ad, tailoring your résumé to its wants.
- You come home from an interview, having promised to send in a résumé—made up just for that job.

You don't have to rewrite the whole résumé each time—usually just the "Job Objective" and "Experience" sections. Sometimes you'll want to organize chronologically, sometimes functionally. You already have modules ready to plug in: your clusters of skills, your detailed descriptions of the jobs you've done. When you read what an employer wants, you may want to put one skill first, play down another, omit a third—or, to conform to that employer's terms, retitle each skill.

If the employer advertises for an administrative assistant and your résumé says "secretary," cross that out and put in "administrative assistant" as your job objective. Then revise the experience section to emphasize supervisory skills, ability to carry out projects on your own, management potential. Don't leave out clerical skills—that's what the job will probably consist of—but because the employer believes this position demands more responsibility than most secretaries can handle, rearrange your clusters to show how responsible you've been. You might even leave out job titles, or alter them slightly, to keep from being pigeonholed as "just a clerk."

Face it: you may need a new résumé for every job you apply for. The more interesting the jobs, the more you have to rewrite to fit unique requirements. After a half-dozen tries, you can develop what I call the "All-Purpose Interchangeable Résumé System." Let's say you've created résumés for three types of jobs—office manager, executive secretary, and administrative assistant. You've used similar material for each, but emphasized different clusters of skills. Think of what you've been rearranging as modules—roughly interchangeable units that you can cut and paste wherever you need them. That, plus a little tinkering with key phrases, plus a lot of typing, can help you turn out one or two new résumés an hour.

Revising your résumé, then, is an on-going process. It will keep your typing speed up. And you will gradually memorize your key selling points—very useful for those moments in an interview when the employer falls silent.

As you revise your résumé, for the first or fortieth time, consider the people reading it. They may have hundreds of résumés on their desks, with an hour to winnow out half a dozen candidates to invite for interviews. You cannot expect your résumé will get more than thirty seconds' attention, at first. If you show you know the job, have even a few qualifications, you may get a thorough reading.

What can get you rejected without a reading?

- Sloppy typing: lines uneven; strikeovers: spelling mistakes
- Too much text packed too close together, too hard to read
- No job objective—or one so vague it doesn't seem to apply
- Too little white space
- Poor duplication: gray and blurry copy; purple ditto; smudged original
- Bad paper: original typed on onion skin (it smudges); original typed on erasable bond (it smudges); lightweight, flimsy; garish colors (use white or cream)
- Vague descriptions of skills or jobs: no "feel" for what you did; no excitement; drab, colorless, boring

So while you're revising, and isolating key achievements, you can improve the force of what you say if you

- Insert numbers, percentages, dollar figures.

—Which sounds more impressive: "Improved sales," or "Improved sales by 23 percent in 2 years?"
- Start each item with a verb.
  —Don't say "I was in charge of pickling." Say "Pickled."
  —Don't say "I was responsible for wiring." Say "Wired."
- Make sure your job objective is specific.
  —Don't say "Seek meaningful position." Say "Seek position as office manager."
  —Use the employer's terms each time.
- Use some jargon to prove you know the business (but not too much).
  —Read ads, trade journals, talk with people in the business to find out the essential buzz words, if you don't know them.
  —Use only the most important.
- Emphasize successes and results—not just routine duties.
  —Don't say "Worked with elderly and infirm." Say "Helped thirty two senior citizens regain flexibility through daily yoga class."
  —Don't say, 'Talked with town officials." Say "Persuaded town council to install four new playgrounds in working-class neighborhoods.

Then type your résumé perfectly. If you can, use a film ribbon, not a cloth one, to get precise images; then the slight blurring that occurs on some copying machines won't matter. Make sure you leave plenty of white space—use wide margins, indent key material, isolate and underline headings. Revise this:

Marketing: Increased sales 23 percent in two years, hired fifteen new sales representatives, fired six, trained entire sales force in new techniques, daily plan system, faster close, coordinated strategy with repair crews, bi-weekly call-baks.

And it might come out like this:

Marketing:
- Increased sales 23 percent in two years.
- Hired fifteen new sales representatives, fired six.
- Trained entire sales force in new techniques.

  —Daily plan system.
  —Faster close.
  —Coordinated strategy with repair crews.
  —Bi-weekly call-backs.

Get your résumé offset or copied on 20-pound paper—that's solid, but not too heavy. Insist on super-crisp copies.

Save your originals. (A copy from a copy will go gray and blur.)

In fact, make up a folder for yourself. Clip the ad you answered to the résumé you sent. That way, if the employer calls, you'll know what you said you could do. And with that file, once you've made up half a dozen versions of your résumé, you'll be able to cut and paste, add and subtract, highlight or hide, without the agony that often goes into your first.

Here's an example of multiple revisions—one person's life redone so he can apply for three different jobs. The man: Charlie Roussillon. His mother is French-Canadian, his father American. A history major in college, Charlie joined the State Department, planning to become a Foreign Service officer; instead, he ended up doing research on France during the day, then taking a master's in economics at Georgetown University at night. He couldn't stand the bureaucracy though, so after three years he quit to work for Morgan Guaranty Bank as a junior economist, focusing again on France. He became friends with several editors on the business pages of *The New York Times*, and when banking began to pall, he coaxed one editor into letting him report on the French economy from Paris. While there, he met Nicole and married her. She worked for the government, developing telecommunications. After a few years in Paris, Charlie got a call from one of his contacts from Morgan Guaranty—a businessman about to launch a new division in France. Would Charlie like to become a vice-president—at five times what the *Times* was paying? Sure. But when Mitterand's socialist government took over, Nicole lost her job, and Charlie's business got nationalized. They decided to go back to New York. Charlie looked over his work record—covering ten years, now—and decided that he would look into jobs as an economist at banks and brokerage houses, as a reporter at magazines and newspapers, and as a businessman specializing in developing the French market. Here are the three basic résumés he came up with, describing what he had done in terms appropriate to the jobs he aimed to get.

CHARLES ROUSSILLON

16 rue de Gaulle
Paris, 14eme, France   Telephone: 45-67889

JOB OBJECTIVE: Position in international finance

WORK EXPERIENCE

International Financing   (4 years)

- As Vice-President for International Operations, set up $15 million corporation in France, using local credit.

- Prepared fifteen major studies for four Fortune 500 corporations seeking financing in French market, carried out plans involving $3 billion in loans and credits.

Economic Analysis and Forecasting   (10 years)

- Drew up macro- and micro-economic forecasts for industries and national economy of France.

- Synthesized market research and monitored trends in government, private sector, and international marketplace, developing quarterly, annual, and five-year projections.

Presentation   (10 years)

- Wrote weekly executive summaries for officials of Morgan Guaranty Bank (economy of France).

- Contributed weekly article to international and domestic editions of *New York Times*, for three years.

- Articles in technical journals. (See list attached.)

- Have addressed industry and government groups in France and U.S. (Over four hundred lectures in ten years.)

EDUCATION

B.A., history, University of Pennsylvania, 1972
M.A., economics, Georgetown University, 1975

CHARLES ROUSSILLON

16 rue de Gaulle
Paris, 14 eme, France   Telephone: 45-67889

JOB OBJECTIVE: Position in economic reporting

WORK EXPERIENCE

JOURNALISM   (5 years)

- Wrote weekly articles for international
  and domestic editions of *New York
  Times*, focusing on French and
  European economic issues.

- Prepared thirty one articles for
  magazines such as *Fortune, Insider's
  Report, Essais sur Finances Internationales*, and technical journals.

RESEARCH   (10 years)

- Prepared fifteen major studies for four
  Fortune 500 companies seeking
  financing in French market.

- Drew up macro- and micro-economic
  forecasts for individual industries, and
  national economy of France.

- Synthesized intelligence data,
  insider information, and press
  comments to project trends in the
  government, private sector, and
  international marketplace, developing
  quarterly, annual, and five-year
  projections.

JOB HISTORY

1972–1975	Junior Foreign Service Officer, in intelligence, State Department, Washington, D.C.
1975–1978	Economist, Morgan Guaranty Trust, International Department.
1978–1981	Reporter, *New York Times*, based in Paris, France.
1981–1982	Vice-President, Contel, Paris, France.

EDUCATION

1972	B.A., history, University of Pennsylvania
1975	M.A., economics, Georgetown University, Washington, D.C.

CHARLES ROUSSILLON

16 rue de Gaulle
Paris, 14eme, France   Telephone: 45-67889

JOB OBJECTIVE: Economist

WORK EXPERIENCE

ANALYSIS AND FORECASTING   (10 years)

- Developed quarterly, annual, and five-
  year projections of national economy
  of France, and individual industries
  within that.

- Refined computer projection techniques
  for macro- and micro-economic analysis.

- Contributed thirty-one articles to
  magazines such as *Fortune, Insider's
  Report*, and *Essais sur Finances
  Internationales*, and technical journals.
  (See attached bibliography.)

INTERNATIONAL FINANCING   (4 years)

- As Vice-President for International
  Operations, set up $15 million
  corporation in France, using local credit

- Advised four Fortune 500 corporations,
  helped them secure $3 billion in loans
  and credits in the French market.

- Specialized in European Common
  Market.

JOB HISTORY

1981–1982	Vice-President, Contel, Paris, France
1978–1981	Economic Reporter, *New York Times*, based in Europe.
1975–1978	Economist, Morgan Guaranty Trust, International Department
1972–1975	Economic Analyst, Junior Foreign Service Officer, United States State Department, Washington, D.C.

EDUCATION

1972	B.A., history, University of Pennsylvania
1975	M.A., economics, Georgetown University

103

Chapter 16

Cover Letters

Why send a letter with your résumé?

To snare the reader's attention—fast
To distinguish yours from the other two hundred résumés
lying on the employer's desk
To avoid being turned down just because of some minor
detail in your résumé

When should you use a cover letter, then? Almost always—
particularly when

- *Answering an ad.* If you have even half the qualifications
  asked for, answer the ad. More than 75 percent of the
  people who get hired don't have *all* the "required" experience. But they found a way to show the employer they
  understand what he wants, and they've taken the time to
  rethink their experience so it seems to match his needs.
  (Don't rush. Most mail comes in during the first four or
  five days after an ad appears, so wait a week before you
  reply, and take the time to write a unique letter—one
  especially designed for this employer. Then he'll have
  time to read it, and it will demonstrate you've made an
  effort to think in *his* terms. That's considerate.)
- *Leafleting.* If you're sending out your résumé to three
  hundred companies, make sure you show you have already handled the main tasks involved in a *particular*
  job—not just "any work available." Don't make employers figure out where to put you—they'll put you out the
  door. Decide exactly what job you want; put down the

major requirements; and demonstrate that you have already achieved successes in those areas. With this shotgun approach, you can expect to get about half a dozen interviews from every hundred letters.

- *Teasing.* If you're changing fields, your résumé may work against you, since you haven't put in two to five years in a certain job title. You want to point out that you can *do* the job before the boss finds out you haven't actually held the position, so you write a teaser letter, outlining your skills, but not enclosing a résumé. Point: to interest the boss enough so you get invited to a personal interview. (That's when you bring your résumé.)

The best cover letter shows that you understand the boss's problems—and that you can solve them. But most people write terrible letters:

They assume they'll get ten minutes' reading time, so they put off selling themselves until the fourth paragraph—and get dumped in the wastebasket.
They answer ads for jobs they can't possibly qualify for.
They do not respond to the boss's needs and the "requirements" stated in the ad.
They use a full page to say, "Attached you will find my résumé."
They send in hand-written or poorly typed letters on odd-shaped personal stationary.

If you don't want your letter crumpled up in the first five seconds, start by getting the employer's name right. Don't write to "Gentlemen." There aren't any left—and anyway, the boss may not be male. Scratch "Dear Sirs," too. Find out who you're talking to, if you can. Phone the company. Ask how the name is spelled. And if you're answering a "blind" ad (where you can't see the person who placed it—just a box number), skip the salutation altogether, or try one like these:

- Dear Want Ad Box #137
- Dear Employer
- Hello

Type like a pro. That's the last thing you do, but the second thing an employer notices—right after spotting that you've misspelled the company name. More than half of all cover letters show that the writer

Has not changed the ribbon in six months
Figures any old piece of paper will do
Does not have any business stationery
Cannot afford an office-quality typewriter
Does not care what picture the reader forms of the writer

Consider the employer's split-second impression of you. Bosses ask themselves

Does this person respect my company—and me?
Is this person businesslike?
Can this person help me do my job?

That's what you need to address in your first sentence—and in your overall organization. So get to the point. Say you're interested in the job, and say why. Maybe you see it as a challenge. Maybe you're an expert in this area. Maybe you're ready to move up to this kind of responsibility. Whatever your main reason, state it in your first sentence.

Then organize your letter around the needs your reader has already expressed in the ad. And if you're not answering an ad, determine what you consider the demands of the particular job you want. Write down each need, then in a sentence or short paragraph sketch out how you've met that need in the past.

- If the ad says "Ability to supervise," then put down "Supervised staff of thirty-five in Accounting Department at Genstar."
- If the ad says "Experience in training required," recall the time when you "Trained more than one hundred U.S. Steel foremen in new work procedures, resulting in 23 percent increase in productivity."
- If the ad says "Clinical dietitian only," you could say, "Planned diets and supervised meal service for over three thousand patients in Haddock Hospital, 1973–1974."

These bulleted sentences, floating in white space, highlight those achievements and show you can handle similar jobs for the employer. Instead of forcing a boss to read your whole résumé, you're putting your finger on the sections that are relevant to his requirements. You make it easier for him to imagine you working for him.

Notice, too, that these capsulized success stories start with active verbs ("Supervised . . . Trained . . . Planned"). You sound more energetic when you lead with an action—rather than a series of qualifying phrases like, "As Vice-President for Marketing at U.S. Steel, in Bethlehem, Pa., for more than three years . . ."

Use figures, dollar amounts, company names, exact titles—unless you think one of these might clash with a requirement. It's too coy to leave out convincing information like this. But only use jargon where the ad does—otherwise, write ordinary American.

Don't keep referring to your résumé. (You could say you're enclosing it, but say that at the end.) But do look it over. If what you're saying here differs markedly, reshape the résumé.

Yes, this means writing a new cover letter (and possibly a new résumé) for each application. That's the point: to sound unique. You've taken the time to answer the reader's questions. Most people don't—and their badly photocopied form letters flop onto the trash pile.

At the end, request an interview, and suggest a time when you'll be available to come in to talk. You could even say you'll call to set an exact time. In this way, you've got an excuse to call and sell yourself again—and you're making it easy for the boss to grant an interview.

Here's an example. The ad said, "Translator, Spanish-English. Must be fluent in English and Spanish, acquainted with promotion. Ability to supervise helpful. Box 157, this paper."

Trini Rodriquez wrote:

> I'm intrigued by your ad for a translator, because your requirements match my history so closely. Here are some highlights from my six years as a full-time Spanish-English translator for Olivetti Business Systems.
> - Translated ten operations manuals for Olivetti Business Systems (English to Spanish).
> - Wrote twenty-four English and Spanish promotion brochures for typewriters.
> - Supervised staff of eight, writing and translating correspondence from and to Olivetti sales personnel in nine Central and South American countries.
> I'd like to talk with you about ways my experience could be useful to you. Please call me at 699-2731, days, or 577-3213, evenings. (Spanish translation attached.)

She got the job. And the boss said, "We got lots of responses to our ad. But you were the only person who *answered* it."

Gertrude Gillespie felt she had nothing much to offer an employer, because she'd just graduated from college and she'd only held down jobs as a waitress at a hotel near the Grand Canyon during the summers. But she'd done a lot of volunteer work as part of her studies in speech and hearing. So, although she'd been "just a student," she was able to present her homework as real work, in a cover letter. And, to avoid revealing her lack of work experience in paying jobs, she omitted her résumé. Here's the letter she sent; it got her the interview.

> I'd like to be an intern in your speech therapy program. I've just graduated from the University of New Mexico with a major in hearing and speech sciences. Highlights of my training:
> - Ran laboratory for instrumental phonetics. Served twenty regular students. Prepared detailed analysis of each client.
> - Tested laryngeal control in thirty-five speech-impaired students. Prepared courses of treatment, for physician approval.
> - Measured auditory function in one hundred clients, wrote up reports, consulted with physicians on courses of treatment.
> I like working with people who have hearing and speech difficulties. I expect to continue my studies in this area, working on my master's in the evenings. Let's get together and talk.

Here are some other cover letters. When Charlie Rousillon answered an ad that read, "Sr Economist, Mjr Ntl Bnk, Midtown, Reply with salary requirements to Box 33, this paper," he pulled out his "Economist" résumé and chose a few highlights, to pique the reader's interest. He didn't have much to go on in the ad, so he just stated his background boldly.

> I'm an economist with ten years' experience in analysis, forecasting, and international financing. Some highlights from my experience:
> - Developed quarterly, annual, and five-year projections of macro and micro economics in France and Europe.
> - Helped four Fortune 500 Corporations secure more than $3 billion in loans and credits in the Frech market.
> - Prepared weekly executive summaries for Morgan Guaranty officials, in International Division.
> - Contributed thirty one articles to magazines such as *For-

tune, Insider's Report, and *Essais sur Finances Internationales.*

My expertise focuses on international finance and national forecasting, particularly in Europe. I'm looking for a salary in the $40,000 to $50,000 range. If you need someone with my qualifications, please give me a call in Paris, at 45-67889. I can arrange to come to the U.S. for an interview at any time. I enclose my résumé.

And when Tom Brand started looking for a management job in a major oil company, he decided to leaflet—sending his résumé out to fifty major companies. He found out whom to write to, then typed individual letters to each one, saying:

I'm looking for a job as your chief petroleum engineer. Here are some highlights from my seven years' experience:
- Increased oil and gas production in fifteen operations for Wildcat Oil, over two-year period.
- Established standards and procedures for all engineers in company, trained new staff.
- Formulated company-wide plans for exploration, drilling schedules, and construction of crude-oil treating units.

I'd like to talk with you in person about what I could do for your company. Just give me a call at 214-389-1512.

Tom Wriothesley, the minister who wanted to go into youth counseling, didn't want anyone to know he'd been a minister, because he thought that would get him rejected right off. So he wrote a cover letter that was basically a tease—it aimed to arouse interest, to make the boss call him, and to avoid any direct admission of his past job history.

TO THE BOSS:
Yes, I want to be a youth counselor at your center. I have five years' experience in counseling:
- Counseled more than seventy-five disturbed teenagers about drugs and related problems.
- Led recovery group in drug rehabilitation center for juvenile delinquents.
- Made weekly visits to outpatients suffering from alcoholism and addiction.

I'd like to talk with you in person about ways I can contribute to your program. Please call me at 414-567-8899.

Chapter 17

Where Are the Jobs?

Only one opening in four gets advertised. Less than one applicant in twenty gets a job through an employment agency. So how are you going to locate the right openings for you?

Start with the ads:

- Your local paper. The Sunday edition has the most ads; many of those are repeated on Monday and Tuesday. Wednesday often brings a new crop, and those peter off through Friday. If you find a column of ads for your specialty, you can figure there are lots more jobs waiting. If your job's not even mentioned—or the only one like yours turns out to be three states away—don't get discouraged.
- Go through the library's collection, looking at the last two months' worth of Sunday classifieds.
- *The Wall Street Journal*, for management slots (Tuesday's Mart). The Eastern edition has the most ads; but local ads show up in the Pacific, Southwest, and Midwest editions.
- *The New York Times* Sunday edition. If you're not in New York, make a deal with your local distributor to get the classifieds. The Finance section carries dozens of pages of executive help wanted ads.

And follow local business news:

- Companies moving in or expanding need new blood.
- If someone's been promoted, congratulate them, and pitch your ideas on reorganizing a department.
- Keep up with trade magazines, and the personnel notes. Add those names to your list of people to call.

Compile a complete list of companies you think might need your expertise:

- Start with your local yellow pages. Look up your job, then any category of company that might need you. Later we'll discuss ways you can call in and get some names.
- Go to the business library, and look up companies in fields you're familiar with. The *Standard Directory of Advertisers* sorts companies out by product, or locale— and gives you the names of officers. Ask the librarian for reference volumes (often published annually) for your field. Look at *Moody's Manuals*, Dun and Bradstreet's *Directories*, Thomas's *Register of American Manufacturers*, and Standard and Poor's *Register of Corporations*.
- Check with trade associations. They usually have a list of the companies in the field.
- Call your Chamber of Commerce. They publish lists of local firms, often annotated to indicate gross sales, number of employees, and products.

Be businesslike when you make these lists. Get the exact address, the right spelling of the boss's name, the phone extension. When you send a letter, or make a call, note that—because three weeks from now you'll have forgotten, and it's not going to look too good if you send the same letter twice.

Advertise. Tell your friends exactly what kind of job you want (not "just something to tide me over.") And point out your qualifications, so they can talk you up if they hear of an opening in their company.

> More people find openings this way than through agencies or ads.
> You come recommended.
> Your friend can tell you what to say on the interview.

So don't be shy. Don't snub some friends because you think they won't know any openings. Call everyone. Be systematic at this, precisely because we're never methodical about calling our friends. How many weeks has it been since you talked to *everyone* who'd be glad to help you?

And create a network. As you meet bosses, and other job seekers, ask for more names. Call those people. Give *them* names and information. And a month or so later, call everybody back. You keep a network alive by *communicating*. (And don't

111

stop calling when you get a job. The people you've linked up with in the network can help you do your job better, or find another one—and you can enjoy helping *them*.)

Set up a support group. A dozen people, all looking for work, meeting with you once a month to trade hot tips and evaluate new résumés, can help you in a lot of ways. They

> Keep you from feeling depressed, and isolated.
> Reassure you that you are making sense—or tell you you're fouling up.
> Offer neutral advice on letters, résumés, interviews, and new lines of approach.
> Rehearse you for an important interview.
> Keep you on schedule when you get lazy.
> Brainstorm for new job possibilities when your old ones seem stale.

Keep looking. Study the local labor market to see if your old job's likely to survive. Where are the future jobs? Is another industry on the rise, and could you fit into that? Maybe the economy's exhausted in your area, and you'll need to head Southwest. You can track the trends in a number of places:

- Department of Labor publications, such as *The Occupational Outlook Handbook*, and monthly updates. The department also puts out a pulp newspaper, *Occupations in Demand*, saying which states need which workers
- Bureau of Labor Statistics publications
- Popular articles in *Business Week, Fortune, The Wall Street Journal*, and the local paper
- State departments of employment—these often issue local forecasts, saying which jobs should increase in your area.

Remember that every year at least two million new jobs are created, and four million old jobs are left vacant when people retire. And another twenty million people successfully change jobs every year. So there *will* be some jobs out there.

Occupations the government expects will offer at least 50 percent more jobs by 1990 include

Bank clerks	Computer service technicians
Boilermakers	Dental assistants
Business machine repairers	Dental hygienists
City managers	Engineers (all kinds)

Flight attendants
Health service administrators
Homemaker aides
Industrial machinery repairers
Licensed practical nurses
Lithographers
Marketing researchers
Mining engineers
Nursing aides
Occupational therapists
Occupational therapist assistants

Physical therapists
Physicians
Respiratory therapy workers
Sewage plant operators
Shoe repairers
Speech pathologists
Systems analysts
Teachers' aides
Travel agents
Typists
Word processors

Can you fit into one of these areas? If you're interested but ignorant, start reading. Ask people what the job is like. Do some information-only interviews, and ask someone who does the work what it's like and what you'll have to do to adapt.

All you need is one job. You may have to read a hundred ads, look up five hundred companies, call two dozen friends and relations, establish a network of forty or fifty people, explore two or three possible new careers—just to land that one job. Think about the numbers—the more companies you've tried, the closer you're getting to the opening that's waiting for you.

To keep the numbers working for you, make sure you maintain businesslike records. Keep

- A copy of every ad—and the reply you send.
- File folders with three or four extra copies of *each* résumé, so you have one ready if you get a call for an interview right away.
- A list of all jobs applied for (with company name, phone number and address, date you sent your letter, and whatever responses you've gotten. This way you'll know when to call up—or give up hoping. (Usually a month without answer means forget it.)
- Folders with information about new fields you might go into.
- An annotated list of people in your field—your own network—complete with phone numbers and the date you last called or wrote them.

Being methodical about this paperwork will help prevent panic (where *is* my résumé?), and it will show you that you really *have* been working at finding a job. (Without evidence, the mind can turn on you, calling you lazy and undeserving.)

Congratulate yourself on the number of letters you've sent, calls you've made, each day. Volume counts. Some people hesitate to send out a hundred letters because they've heard you'll only get five or six favorable responses. But you only need one job.

And until you get it, think of your job as one part mail clerk, one part phone sales, one part hustle, and one part daydream. The more systematic you are, the likelier you are to find a position you like—fast.

Where are the jobs? Just a phone call—and an interview—away.

Chapter 18

Using the Phone

The best machine you can use to find a job is your phone. Walking the streets, knocking on doors, getting sore feet, filling out applications, you'll probably hit half a dozen companies before knocking off for the day. But with the phone you can reach forty or fifty companies in the same time. Use the phone

- To reach people without forcing your way in the door
- To talk with other workers who can give you tips and advice from their desk (networking)
- To discover openings before they're advertised
- To create openings for yourself, by angling for an interview
- To find out if the company really has an opening before you take the time to go in and fill out forms for a job that may not exist
- To discard some companies before you bother making up a new résumé for them

Most of us feel at ease with the phone—on personal calls. But the idea of calling a total stranger and asking for a job frightens us. We don't want to be laughed at, snubbed, belittled. We would rather not call than get turned down.

And if we do manage to dial, most of us do not sound very businesslike. If you haven't worked in phone sales before, ask someone to watch as you make some calls.

- Do you slur your name?
- Does your tone sound arrogant? Naive? Desperate?
- When saying why you've called, do you hem and haw?
- Do you fail to push your own skills?
- Do you accept the first "No!" and hang up?
- Or do you give up after making only two calls?

To sound as if you know what you're doing, prepare a pitch. Condense the highlights from your cover letter. What's the gist of what you want to tell the employer? Think of this outline as a rough script. You don't have to follow it—but it'll be there in case you lose track of what you're saying.

That should help you develop a confident and friendly tone. Confident because you're qualified. And you can reel off dates, facts, names, and dollar amounts to prove to anyone that you're capable of doing the job. You've rehearsed your pitch. You know exactly what job you're after, and you figure the company'll be lucky to hire you.

Be friendly, too. You don't have any reason to hate—or fear—the person who answers. Think about this. Your tone reveals your attitude. If you're abusive, or tentative, you show that you imagine that any boss is a bully, or worse. How's this one going to feel? Why not be considerate, then? Consider the call from the boss's point of view. Realize that you're interrupting—but you could help boost department productivity, if hired. So your tone *could* demonstrate:

- You realize this may not be a good time to talk—and you'll be glad to call back.
- You respect the boss's work.
- You understand some of the problems the boss faces—and you think you could *help* solve them.
- You can condense a lot of information into a short time.
- You are polite, but you keep pushing for an interview. ("Perhaps we could meet at your office next Tuesday. I'll be in the area that morning. Would that be convenient?")
- You're a go-getter, but you listen.

Don't snub the receptionist, either. If you put a secretary down, you'll never reach the boss. Here your tone can make the difference between contact and freeze-out. If you sense the secretary's bored, chat. If rushed, get to the point. (Don't recite your life's tragedies.) If the boss is out, make an appointment to call again. Find out when the boss might be free; give your name, and say you'll call at that time. When you do, you prove that you do what you say you will—unlike most callers. And if the secretary likes you and remembers you, you'll eventually get through to the boss.

And don't be put off. If the receptionist doesn't know who's in charge of your kind of job, suggest different names for the

116

department, outline the job, volunteer to speak to anyone in the area. If the boss doesn't sound too eager (''Budget cutbacks''), go ahead with your pitch anyway. If you can't reach someone, call again and again until your name's on so many slips of paper that the boss calls *you*. You do get points for push—it's a quality most employers want.

And since you're playing the numbers, set yourself a daily schedule. Establish a quota: you'll make x calls by lunch, y by supper. Check off each phone number when you've reached the boss. To avoid calling the same place twice, and to keep track of who's asked you to call back on Tuesday afternoon, you may want to summarize your calls this way:

Company	Boss's name	Phone number	Call back?	Results?

Congratulate yourself for each call you make. Don't worry about rejections and stalls. When you're calling, your job is to call. The more calls you make, the likelier you are to stumble on an opening you like.

Begin each call with a name. Even if you have to make a few calls to find it, get the exact name of the person who's in charge of your area. In large companies, the receptionist may refer you to personnel, where a voice will say very quickly, ''Is this in reference to employment?'' If you answer, ''Yes,'' you're stuck. The voice will say, ''Come in and fill out an application. Thank you, goodbye.'' So some people pretend to be reporters, representatives of trade associations, vendors, a fellow manager, or a convention publicist. If your story sounds plausible, and you're willing to leave your number, you can probably trick the name and number out of the personnel people. But it's long hard work. So look the name up (in the books mentioned in chapter 17, ''Where Are the Jobs?'') or get it from a friend. The personnel department should be your last—not your first—call.

And when you finally reach the boss's secretary, be ready with your pitch. Don't lie here, or you'll get caught. (Secretaries talk to their bosses.) They make key decisions: do you sound like some crazy job applicant, or a responsible person with some real business with the boss? The best way to slip past a guard-dog executive secretary: sound like another boss. Expect to get through. Sound as if you're familiar with the boss. (Don't say so; just sound at ease.)

If the secretary asks why you're calling, you have some choices:

- You could claim, "It's a personal matter." But the boss may say, "I don't know this person. Hang up."
- You could say, "I'd prefer to discuss this with the boss." But you may sound like a snob. And most secretaries will just take your name and number.
- You could sketch your experience, and say you'd like to talk with the boss about "future openings."

I recommend the last. Don't ramble on. But give the gist of your qualifications. Don't ask about *current* openings, since there may not be any—and you'll be talking to a dial tone in another second. You want to get through to the boss—so ask about something the secretary can't know about. And enlist the secretary's support. Take time to explain at length, if the secretary sounds sympathetic. A recommendation from the secretary can put you ahead of twenty other candidates.

When you do talk to the boss, focus on scheduling a personal interview. A busy employer may ask you some tough questions, to prove that you won't fit in. Don't cave in. Keep coming back to your reason for calling: you'd like to come in to outline *in detail* how your experience might help solve particular problems. Ask how they handle a certain function. Use questions to show you know the field (only a fellow expert could pose that question) —and to get the boss talking. Outline your experience, but turn aside probing questions with your repeated offer to come in and talk. If you get agreement, suggest a time when you're free. Don't let your eagerness blot out common sense; if you have an eleven o'clock interview on one side of town, you can't be sure of making a noon interview on the other. Keep coming up with times you could visit until one clicks. Then confirm the following, by saying them out loud:

- The exact time and date

- The address (and directions, if you need them)
- The accurate spelling of the boss's first and last name (for your follow-up letters)
- The boss's phone (in case you have to change the time later)
- Exactly what the boss wants you to bring along (samples, portfolios)

Take the time to go over these details. It shows you mean business, and it will help you avoid panic. (If you get to the reception desk and the guard doesn't recognize the employer's name, you've got a number you can call.)

If you're calling someone else who does your job, start off by saying you do that too, and you'd like some help. Explain you're looking for work. Then ask questions you've prepared, such as:

- Is their company hiring?
- If not, who is?
- What do they think are the trends in the business?
- Where do they want to go next?
- Where can I meet more people who do this work?

In the course of the conversation you can easily mention the highlights of your own experience. These may give the person ideas for you to pursue.

Respect the phone, then. It can get you through closed doors:

To find out where the openings are
To set up interviews
To sell yourself

And remember what the Bell System tells its operators. You can hear a smile.

TALKING YOUR
WAY INTO A JOB

Chapter 19

Meeting Employers
"For Information Only"

If you're changing careers, you'll need to do some "information only" interviews:

- To learn about your new field
- To meet with a boss when your work record *alone* wouldn't get you in the door
- To talk yourself up a job that did not exist before

Most bosses dread interviewing job applicants—particularly ones they suspect they'll have to turn down. And if you come from some other field, and ask directly for a job interview, you'll probably just get a polite turndown.

But if you show you're interested in the boss's work, you can come in as an outsider, ask intelligent questions, establish a friendly rapport—without putting anyone on the spot. You flatter the boss by seeking advice, philosophy, tips. You don't press for a job. In fact, you don't even know *if* you want to go into the field. That's why you've come—for information.

What can you learn from an information interview?

- What an expert sees as the coming trend in the field—the dangers, the opportunities, the areas you might step into
- What day-to-day problems a boss has to face in this area
- How the boss got the job
- Who else you ought to talk to
- What qualifications the boss looks for in applicants

Sure, you're going to hear some pompous nonsense, and some obscure jargon. But take notes.

And while you're talking, you can show the boss—informally, of course, almost incidentally—

- You have a good grasp of the field—what the work is, what some problems are, what's needed in an employee.
- You're eager to learn—and you actually listen.
- You can probe for a *real* answer, rather than accepting the "formal" or "party-line" response. (So you wouldn't be bamboozled by some other department.)
- You're polite, but determined.
- You've done well in your previous work, but you have valid reasons for wanting to change.
- Your experience may give you a unique perspective on the boss's biggest problem. You *might* be able to help.
- You have a general idea of what you want, but you're coming to an expert (the boss) for advice on particular steps.
- You're energetic and businesslike in carrying out a task even the boss recognizes as difficult—changing careers.
- You can act on advice (very rare trait). If the boss suggests you call someone, call—the boss will hear about it and figure you can follow up on suggestions.

Why not ask for a job, then? Wait. You said this interview was for information. If you surprise the boss with an appeal for a job, you'll look tricky. You've lied. You've just wasted the good will you've built up.

So wait a while. Think over what the boss has said. Talk to the people she suggested. Let them call her back, with good reports. Write a thank you letter saying you've decided to go into the field, enclosing your new résumé, and asking her to keep you in mind if she hears of any openings. A few weeks later, she may call you with a tip.

In this way, you're tapping into the informal network of professionals, experts, people "in the trade." They'll send the word around. Execs you've never heard of will hear your name. So instead of being "another damn applicant," you're an interesting person, someone who might have some good ideas. Pretty soon, someone'll call and ask *you* to come in "to see if you can help us with our problem."

So you're developing word-of-mouth recommendations, sending out signals on the gossip line, setting yourself up as a fascinating possibility, rather than a depressing reject. You're also increasing your potential salary. (After all, you may have to be *persuaded* to take the job.) And with each interview, you know more about the business, so you're actually becoming more valuable.

Who's best to talk to? Anyone whose work you admire. That's someone you could—and would like to—learn from. Next, anyone who really knows the job—a supervisor, experienced worker, even a trainee. As you go on, you'll pile up a long list of names—use these, and keep asking for more.

To set up an interview, call and say who sent you, or where you've heard of them. Go to restaurants and bars where these people lunch; mix and meet. If you spot someone—anywhere, in the park, at a party, on a boat—talk to them right away. Or ask for a half hour of their time later. Point out what you're now working as, explain you're thinking of going into their field, and ask for their help. Most will be flattered, and intrigued.

Think out what you are going to ask. Here are some questions you might use to home in on the boss's biggest problems:

- How do you keep costs down?
- How do you get work out fast?
- How do you hype sales?
- Are you expanding? How?
- How do you speed up turnaround?
- What are you doing about inventory?
- What do you enjoy most about this work? Least? ·
- Who else could give me useful information about this work?
- How do you motivate workers?
- What's the hardest problem you face?
- What hassles have you had with employees?
- Where do you want your department to go in the next few years?

Obviously you can show—by comment and question—that you sympathize with the boss's problems and could help in their solution. For instance, if the boss feels that her team needs some training in closing sales, then you could nod, and talk about the time you taught that skill to thirty traveling reps for a cosmetics company. If she's got to expand into a new territory, you could ask what kind of market studies they've done, and you could recall times when you've helped companies move into unfamiliar turf.

And find out what the boss thinks is good background for a job candidate:

- What courses should I take?
- What skills should I acquire?
- How did *you* get your first job in this field?
- What's the most important thing you look for in an employee?
- Which of my experiences will be most useful to me in this field?
- What drawbacks will I have to overcome?

Do at least a half a day of homework for any interview with someone you want to impress. By showing you already know key facts about the boss's business, you can demonstrate that you might fit into their organization. So use the business library and make some calls, to discover

- Total sales for the company last year.
- Rank in industry.
- Major products. (What's next?)
- Subsidiaries or divisions.
- Trends in the industry—and what this company is doing about them.
- What's threatening the company, if anything?
- How do workers like the place? (Ask them.)
- Why am I interested in their company?
- What do other companies think about this one?

Study the products. Learn some of the shop talk. Read the trade journals. Soak yourself in that environment. Figure out what you *could* offer.

In fact, sketch out a few ideas you can unleash in an interview. Prepare a brief speech. You probably won't use it, but that will help you get ready to pitch your ideas. Think through your own experience: which parts will be most relevant?

Remember that you don't have to ask all these questions. You probably won't uncork more than half. But thorough preparation will make you at ease with terms the boss takes for granted. You'll seem quick, understanding, and well informed.

But don't let your prepared questions freeze your conversation. Let the interview go. If the boss wants to talk about pensions, encourage this. You can still get your questions answered. But whatever the boss thinks is important *is*—at least, if you want to know what the boss values.

Listening and asking are probably twice as important as reciting your qualifications. So show you care about this person. Ask questions that show you're following what the boss says. Pursue the boss's evolving ideas. Yes, suggest how you've solved similar problems. But don't insist that the boss do what you did. Relax. Heck, you might even tell a joke. After all, you are not the one being interviewed—the boss is.

Chapter 20
Getting Past Personnel

Whenever possible, avoid personnel departments. Why?

- They have no power to hire, except occasionally at the rock bottom. They just refer you on to the foreman.
- They screen out an average of at least a hundred—often several hundred—applicants for every one interview they grant.
- They rarely know about middle-level vacancies until the boss has almost made a hiring decision.
- They match people to artificial requirements and flunk you if you don't match exactly.
- They protect the busy boss from your intrusion.
- They spend at least half their time handling in-house matters such as workman's compensation claims, raises, disciplinary proceedings, union friction, salary statistics. You are not a high-priority item.

But for the moment imagine you haven't been able to get around the personnel department. Maybe you're answering a newspaper ad that just gives a post office box number (no company to call, no way to trace the supervisor). Or the person you sent your résumé to rerouted it to personnel, and it sent you the standard application form. Or you just walked in off the street. What to do?

Realize that although the personnel department claims it was set up to find a qualified candidate for every job, it's usually snowed under with applicants. So most personnel departments develop standards and systems that help reject more than 95 percent of all applicants—leaving a manageable few to interview and send upstairs to the actual supervisor.

The screening process begins with the receptionist. She gets to see you when you may not be on your "interview" behavior—and as soon as you go, you can bet the recruiter will ask her what she thinks. If she approves, that will sway a decision your way; if not, forget it. So bring your own pen—don't borrow hers. Don't blame her for the wait. Don't complain to her about filling out the application. (Most companies see the application as a test of your willingness to "go along." If you refuse, they figure you'll balk at harder work.) If she points out some question you haven't answered, thank her and fill it in—don't say, "Aw, what difference does that make?" Don't waste her time—she's got three dozen rejection letters to get out by noon, and the phone keeps ringing.

In many companies the receptionist has been ordered to make notes on your application as soon as you leave. BV means "bad vibes"—she thought you were hostile, or weird. D means she suspected you were drunk or drugged. P means you wore too much perfume, and she's been told that's a sign you're covering up marijuana smoke. Other codes may indicate inappropriate dress, poor English skills, stupidity, or whininess.

Treat the receptionist in a businesslike way. Don't assume that because she's the same ethnic or racial background as you that she will help—she'll feel you're using her. Don't flirt, figuring your charm will get you by; how would you feel if someone pretended they liked you, when you knew they just wanted a job? Do tell her you're interested in the job. If she shows she wants to talk, you might say you hope you'll get a speedy response, because you're considering other offers. You can figure she'll repeat everything you say to the recruiter.

The next person who screens your application checks to see:

- Does your current or last salary fall within the range established for their job—not too far below, or above?
- Are you asking a ballpark figure—not too much or too little?
- Does your job history meet the minimum requirements established by the supervisor?
- Have you held most jobs for at least a year, some for three or four years?
- Have you filled out every blank, not just most of them?

If any answer comes up no, your application gets rejected.

(Imagine this checker is prissy, devoid of imagination, intent on getting rid of you. Misspellings drive him crazy; if you leave out a phone number, rage makes his lips go white.)

If the answers are all yes, the checker may hand your application over to the reference checker. That person calls former employers to confirm dates, salary, job title. Any real discrepancy (more than a month or so, more than $1,000 a year) and you may get the heave-ho.

If you survive these scrutinies, you may eventually be asked for an interview. At that point, you can feel pleased with yourself—you've made it through where hundreds of others fell. Yes, the process is as bloody and foolish as the charge of the Light Brigade. And you must think defensively to make it through the ruinous cross fire.

The first thing you need to defend yourself against are those apparently innocent questions on the application form. Let's turn to those now.

Chapter 21

How to Fill Out
an Application

An application, the first job of work you do for many companies, offers you a series of tricky decisions, hard-to-recall memories, and ambushes. Who can remember the zip code at that company five years ago? And what was the supervisor's name? And what can you say about your conviction for car theft when you were sixteen?

Often you have to ponder such questions while you sit in a green plastic chair, writing on your knee. On the spot, you may make mistakes, or forget. So I recommend you prepare beforehand, by filling out this sample application at home. You'll have time to look up old addresses, salaries, dates. You can make some calls, see if a company is still in business, prime a former supervisor to give you a good reference.

Remember, every blank counts. Be sure to put in every zip code, phone number, yes and no. And if something does not apply to you, put "N/A," which stands for "Not Applicable." For instance, if you've never been convicted of a felony, you would check "No." But then comes a question: "If yes, explain." Well, you might think that it's not yes, so you don't have to explain. Right, but the checker worries that you haven't filled out the slot. So be reassuring: write in "N/A." Go over the completed application one more time, looking for inadvertent blanks; a badly designed form can fool you into leaving something out. Don't.

Here, then, is a sample application, with typical questions, followed by notes on how to answer the hard ones.

A. INSTRUCTIONS

Print. Use pen.
Furnish all requested information. If you fail
to answer all questions fully and accurately,
you may delay consideration of your application, and lose employment opportunities.

Position you are applying for:

Date of application:

Date available for work:

Are you available to work: _____ Full Time _____ Part Time
_____ On Call _____ Swing Shift
_____ Casual _____ Night Shift

B. PERSONAL

NAME:
STREET ADDRESS:
CITY: STATE: ZIP:
PHONE:
HOW LONG HAVE YOU LIVED THERE?
PREVIOUS ADDRESS: STREET _____ (DATES:___)
CITY STATE: ZIP:
SOCIAL SECURITY NUMBER:
CHECK ONE: ___SINGLE ___MARRIED ___DIVORCED
___WIDOWED ___SEPARATED
SPOUSE'S NAME:
SPOUSE'S OCCUPATION:
SPOUSE'S WORK ADDRESS: ORGANIZATION:
STREET:
CITY: STATE: ZIP:

WORK PHONE:
DATE OF MARRIAGE:
CHILDREN: NAMES: AGES:

HOW WILL YOU GET TO WORK? _____ PUBLIC TRANSPORTATION
_____ OWN CAR
_____ WALK
_____ OTHER: _____

ARE YOU WILLING TO RELOCATE? ___ YES ___ NO
DO YOU OWN YOUR OWN HOME? ___ YES ___ NO
DO YOU RENT? ___ YES ___ NO
DO YOU HAVE ANY FAMILY RESPONSIBILITIES THAT COULD
PREVENT YOU FROM:
WORKING FULL TIME ___ YES ___ NO
TRAVELING ___ YES ___ NO
IF YES, EXPLAIN:

132

ARE YOU BETWEEN THE AGES OF 18 and 65: ___YES ___NO
DO ANY OF YOUR FRIENDS OR RELATIVES WORK AT OUR
COMPANY?

___ YES ___ NO   IF YES, GIVE NAMES:
HAVE YOU WORKED HERE BEFORE? ___ YES ___ NO
IF YES, GIVE DATES AND JOB TITLES:

WHAT CIVIC, PROFESSIONAL, TRADE, OR BUSINESS ORGAN-
IZATIONS DO YOU BELONG TO?

WHAT ACTIVITIES DO YOU DO IN YOUR SPARE TIME? (Hobbies, social activities)

C. HEALTH
WHEN DID YOU HAVE YOUR LAST PHYSICAL EXAMINATION?
GENERAL HEALTH: ___ POOR ___ FAIR ___ GOOD
___ EXCELLENT
DO YOU HAVE ANY MEDICAL OR MENTAL DISABILITIES?
___ YES ___ NO IF YES, EXPLAIN:

HAVE YOU HAD A MAJOR ILLNESS IN THE LAST FIVE YEARS?
___ YES ___ NO IF YES, EXPLAIN.

HAVE YOU RECEIVED COMPENSATION FOR INJURIES?
___ YES ___ NO IF YES, EXPLAIN.

CAN YOU EASILY LIFT 10 POUNDS? ___ YES ___ NO
25 POUNDS? ___ YES ___ NO
50 POUNDS? ___ YES ___ NO
DO YOU HAVE ANY CHRONIC ILLNESS THAT COULD REQUIRE
ABSENCE FROM WORK? ___ YES ___ NO
IF YES, EXPLAIN:

HOW MANY DAYS WORK DID YOU MISS DUE TO ILLNESS
LAST YEAR? (EXPLAIN):

NOTE: A PHYSICAL EXAMINATION IS REQUIRED OF ALL
NEW EMPLOYEES: IF THE RESULTS DO NOT CORRESPOND
TO YOUR ANSWERS, YOU WILL BE FIRED.

D. LEGAL STATUS
ARE YOU A CITIZEN OF THE UNITED STATES?
___ YES ___ NO IF NO, WHAT NATIONALITY?

IF YES, CAN YOU PROVIDE A BIRTH CERTIFICATE, IF
REQUIRED?

133

IF YOU ARE NOT A CITIZEN OF THE UNITED STATES, ARE
YOU LEGALLY ALLOWED TO WORK IN THE U.S.?
___ YES ___ NO   IF YES, EXPLAIN:

DO YOU HAVE THE LEGAL RIGHT TO PERMANENT RES-
IDENCE IN THE U.S.? ___ YES ___ NO
HAVE YOU EVER BEEN CONVICTED OF:

ROBBERY	___ YES	___ NO
ASSAULT	___ YES	___ NO
EMBEZZLEMENT	___ YES	___ NO
THEFT	___ YES	___ NO
PERJURY	___ YES	___ NO
MURDER	___ YES	___ NO
ANY OTHER FELONY	___ YES	___ NO

IF YES, EXPLAIN:

ARE YOU CURRENTLY ON PROBATION OR PAROLE?
___ YES ___ NO   IF YES, EXPLAIN:

HAVE YOU EVER BEEN REFUSED BONDING? ___ YES ___ NO
NOTE: You may omit 1) traffic fines for which you paid a fine
of $50.00 or less; 2) any offense committed before your eigh-
teenth birthday which was finally adjudicated by a juvenile
court or under a youth offender law; 3) any conviction the
record of which has been expunged under federal or state
law, and 4) any conviction set aside under the Federal Youth
Corrections Act or similiar state authority.
HAVE YOU SERVED IN THE U.S. MILITARY SERVICES?
___ YES ___ NO
    IF YES, WHAT BRANCH?   SERIAL #:
        DATES OF SERVICE:
        TYPE OF DISCHARGE:
        RANK AT TIME OF DISCHARGE:
DO YOU CLAIM VETERAN PREFERENCE? ___ YES ___ NO
    IF YES, CHECK TYPE: ___ ACTIVE DUTY
                        ___ 30% OR MORE DISABILITY
                        ___ LESS THAN 30% DISABILITY
                        ___ NONCOMPENSABLE DISABILITY
                        ___ PURPLE HEART RECIPIENT
                        ___ SPOUSE
                        ___ WIDOW(ER)
                        ___ MOTHER
WHILE IN THE MILITARY SERVICE, WERE YOU EVER
CONVICTED BY A GENERAL COURT MARTIAL?
    ___ YES ___ NO
    IF YES, GIVE DATE, CHARGE, PLACE, COURT, SENTENCE:

DO YOU HAVE A VALID DRIVER'S LICENSE?

WHAT OTHER FEDERAL OR STATE LICENSES DO YOU HAVE?

E. SKILLS
    CHECK EQUIPMENT YOU OPERATE:
    ____ DICTAPHONE   ____ CRT ENTRY
    ____ WORD PROCESSING (TYPE:_____)
    ____ COPYING MACHINE   ____ AUDIO TAPE RECORDER
    ____ SLIDE PROJECTOR   ____ FILM PROJECTOR
    ____ VIDEO TAPE RECORDER
    OTHER MACHINES YOU OPERATE:

    CAN YOU OPERATE A TEN-KEY ADDING MACHINE?
    ____ YES ____ NO ____ BY TOUCH ____ BY SIGHT
    DO YOU KEY PUNCH? ____ YES ____ NO   STROKES:
    DO YOU TAKE SHORTHAND? ____ YES ____ NO WPM:
    HOW FAST DO YOU TYPE?
    LIST OTHER SKILLS THAT RELATE TO THE JOB YOU ARE
    APPLYING FOR:

    WHAT LANGUAGES DO YOU KNOW?
                      SPEAK   READ   WRITE
    FLUENTLY
    WELL
    PASSABLY

F. EDUCATION

LEVEL	NAME OF SCHOOL AND ADDRESS	DID YOU GRADUATE YES/NO	CIRCLE HIGHEST GRADE COMPLETED	DATES
GRAMMAR			4 5 6 7	
HIGH			9 10 11 12	
COLLEGE			1 2 3 4	
GRADUATE			1 2 3 4 5 6	
OTHER			1 2 3 4 5 6	

    HAVE YOU RECEIVED A G.E.D. HIGH SCHOOL EQUIVALENCY
    CERTIFICATE?
    LIST COURSES YOU HAVE TAKEN THAT MAY RELATE TO
    THE JOB YOU ARE APPLYING FOR:
    LEVEL   COURSES   # OF CREDITS
                                  SEM. HRS/QTR. HOURS

    LIST OTHER TRAINING, LOCATION, LENGTH OF COURSE,
    NUMBER OF HOURS:

    LIST HONORS, PRIZES, AWARDS, FELLOWSHIPS RECEIVED:

G. EMPLOYMENT HISTORY
   ACCOUNT FOR PERIODS OF UNEMPLOYMENT EXCEEDING
   THREE MONTHS. BEGIN WITH MOST RECENT POSITION.

NAME OF COMPANY	DATES EMPLOYED	
ADDRESS	FROM	TO
	(MONTH/YEAR)	MONTH/YEAR)

AVERAGE NUMBER OF HOURS PER WEEK:

SALARY: BEGINNING $ PER
        ENDING $ PER
PLACE YOU WORKED:
EXACT TITLE OF YOUR POSITION:
NAME OF YOUR IMMEDIATE SUPERVISOR:
   PHONE NUMBER (AREA CODE)
WHAT KIND OF BUSINESS OR ORGANIZATION?
YOUR REASON FOR LEAVING:

DESCRIBE YOUR SPECIFIC DUTIES, RESPONSIBILITIES, AND
ACCOMPLISHMENTS IN THIS JOB:

YOUR NAME AT THE TIME:

(Repeat G four times.)

H. PERSONAL REFERENCES
   DO NOT LIST RELATIVES, OR FORMER EMPLOYERS.
   NAME
   ADDRESS
   PHONE
   OCCUPATION
   YEARS KNOWN

   NAME
   ADDRESS
   PHONE
   OCCUPATION
   YEARS KNOWN

   NAME
   ADDRESS
   PHONE
   OCCUPATION
   YEARS KNOWN

I. AFFIRMATIVE ACTION AND EQUAL OPPORTUNITY REPORT
   HOW WERE YOU REFERRED TO OUR COMPANY?
          _____ BY AD
          _____ BY CURRENT EMPLOYEE
          _____ BY FORMER EMPLOYEE
          _____ BY PRIVATE AGENCY

_____ BY STATE AGENCY
_____ BY NONPROFIT REFERRAL
_____ BY TEMPORARY AGENCY
_____ BY SELF
_____ OTHER:_____

RACE/ETHNIC ORIGIN
PLEASE CHECK YOUR ORIGIN OR ANCESTRY, REGARDLESS OF
BIRTHPLACE OR NATIONALITY.
_____ WHITE (NOT OF HISPANIC ORIGIN)
_____ BLACK
_____ HISPANIC
_____ ASIAN
_____   —CHINESE
_____   —JAPANESE
_____   —FILIPINO
_____   —ALL OTHER
_____ AMERICAN INDIAN OR ALASKAN NATIVE
SEX: _____ MALE _____ FEMALE
ARE YOU HANDICAPPED? _____ YES _____ NO
ARE YOU A VIETNAM-ERA VETERAN _____ YES _____ NO
ARE YOU A DISABLED VETERAN?
_____ YES _____ NO
_____ RATED AT 30% OR MORE DISABILITY.
_____ RELEASED OR DISCHARGED FOR A DISABILITY
INCURRED IN THE LINE OF DUTY.

J. OATH
   I CERTIFY THAT ALL OF THE STATEMENTS MADE BY ME ARE
TRUE, COMPLETE, AND CORRECT TO THE BEST OF MY KNOWL-
EDGE AND BELIEF, AND ARE MADE IN GOOD FAITH.
   I UNDERSTAND THAT ANY DISCREPANCIES, FALSEHOODS, OR
OMISSIONS MAY BE CAUSE FOR DISMISSAL.
   I AUTHORIZE THE COMPANY TO UNDERTAKE PERSONAL,
CREDIT, AND EMPLOYMENT INVESTIGATIONS TO VERIFY THESE
STATEMENTS, AND I CONSENT TO THE RELEASE OF INFORMA-
TION CONCERNING MY PREVIOUS WORK HISTORY, CAPACITY,
AND FITNESS BY EMPLOYERS, EDUCATIONAL INSTITUTIONS, LAW
ENFORCEMENT AGENCIES, AND OTHER INDIVIDUALS AND AGEN-
CIES TO AUTHORIZED INVESTIGATORS FROM THIS COMPANY.
   I UNDERSTAND THAT THE COMPANY MAY REQUIRE A MEDI-
CAL EXAMINATION, FINGERPRINTING, PROOF OF AGE, PROOF
OF U.S. CITIZENSHIP OR LEGAL RIGHT TO RESIDE PERMANENTLY
IN THIS COUNTRY, AND A FIDELITY BOND AS A CONDITION OF
EMPLOYMENT.
DATE: SIGNATURE:

Instructions

Position? Put down the company's name for the job; use the exact title, or else personnel will get confused.

Date available? If you're applying for entry-level, blue-collar work at a hospital, you'll have to start as a casual, or on-call; you replace sick-outs; then if they like you, you can go permanent. On some jobs, you'll get ahead of the competition if you're willing to work nights, swing shift, or part time. Check as many boxes as you can.

Salary you require: write down "Open," or "Negotiable." If you put an exact figure, be sure it's what they already intend to pay. If you put down a figure that's too high, you lose the job; too low, and you may be the lowest-paid worker in your department.

Personal

Several questions here are illegal—about your marital status, spouse, kids, for instance. "Separated" sounds the most dangerous to employers, since they figure you're in the middle of a drawn-out divorce. Best advice: tell the truth, here, since even a casual credit check can turn up this information.

You don't have any family responsibilities that could prevent you from working full time, do you? If you do, take care of these matters before you apply for the job.

Do list anyone you know who works there, and tell them to talk you up. An inside reference will help.

Organizations? Put down only noncontroversial ones. If nothing's left, put "none."

Social activities? Again, put clean-cut hobbies, or sports. Baseball, chess, swimming. Nothing too dangerous.

Health

Your general health is excellent. The only illnesses or disabilities you should mention are those that would show up in an interview or on the job. And even then, just check "Yes," and put "Will discuss on interview." That way you can avoid getting turned down cold—and you get to tell your own story. The rule of thumb: will this affect my job performance? If yes, put it down.

You do not have to put down a nervous breakdown or minor ailments. If you've had a major workman's compensation case, where you were out of work for more than a month, confess. Less than that, forget it.

Legal Status

If you have been convicted of a felony—not just arrested—since your eighteenth birthday, check yes, and write, "Will discuss on interview." Do the same with questions about probation, parole, and military courts martial. You don't want to shock them on paper; wait until you get a chance to explain in person. Skip traffic tickets.

A felony is any crime punishable by a term of more than one year in jail, but not state misdemeanors (which sometimes allow longer sentences). Any "major" crime counts as a felony: murder, assault, burglary, grand theft, embezzlement, perjury, tax evasion, jumping bail, violating parole, transportation of stolen goods, illegal possession of high explosives. Do not mention crimes you were conviced of before your eighteenth birthday; omit any conviction which has been legally expunged from the record, or set aside.

Skills

Figure you will be tested on typing, keypunch, and shorthand, if you claim these skills. So give exact words per minute. On other machines, claim anything you think you could operate, given a few minutes' instruction on this particular model. Copier, slide projector, shredder, headset, transcription, or Dictaphone—almost anyone can operate one of these after about two minutes' instruction, so go ahead and claim them. When the employer leaves you a wide-open blank like "Other skills," pour in every applicable skill from your résumé. Fill it up.

But aim your skills at the level of the job you want. If you're applying for an editorial position, put in your skill at proofreading and copy-editing, but leave out typing, since that's more appropriate at a lower level. It's assumed you can type—or that you'll give stuff to your secretary to do. Look back at your inventory of skills, and if you haven't put them elsewhere on your application, slip them in here.

Education

Circle highest grade completed in *each* category. (If you went to school abroad, circle the U.S. equivalent, and write "equivalent" next to the numbers.) Put down the last school attended at each level. Do not leave out any schooling, unless it's downright embarrassing. Under "other training" include any short courses in the military, or in other organizations. Be sure to put length of the course, or total number of hours.

Employment History

Reasons for leaving? You were never "fired" or "terminated"; you never just "quit." You "sought advancement." You "sought more responsibility," if your next job *did* offer more responsibility. You "immigrated to the U.S." You "sought better work conditions." You "had to help in family emergency." Or you "retired to have children."

If you were fired, call that employer and try to persuade the boss to give you a better recommendation—or at least a neutral one. If they balk, point out that it is illegal to pass on negative comments on your work, and it is illegal for a boss to say you were fired.

If you've been unemployed for longer than three months, you'll need some explanation other than "kicked back on unemployment insurance." Maybe you were self-employed at some job like construction, painting, tutoring, typing at home. Perhaps you went back to school (employers rarely make a distinction between evening and full-time school). Perhaps you went on a round-the-world trip.

References

The longer you've known someone, the more impressive they'll be as a reference. Put in any friend who's willing to make you sound terrific—and tell them what to say.

Affirmative Action and Equal Opportunity Report

To preserve federal contracts, these reports go to the government, when the company must prove it is complying with Titles VI and VII of the Civil Rights Act of 1964, Title IX of the Education Amendments of 1972 (45CFR 86), Sections 503 and 504 of the Rehabilitation Act of 1973, the Age Discrimination in Employment Act of 1967, and Sections 402 and 407 of the Vietnam Era Veterans Readjustment Act of 1974. This means the company has to *prove* that it does not discriminate on the basis of race, color, age, national origin, religion, sex, handicap, veteran status, or disablement. If the company says it is an Equal Opportunity Employer, that means it promises not to discriminate. If it says it is an Affirmative Action Employer, that means it is making an extra effort to hire minorities, so the odds will be stacked against white males, and to a lesser extent, against white females, unless the job you are applying for is extremely specialized. Such companies often have quotas or percentages to meet, and minority status can help you overcome lack of skills, since they may hire you to make their numbers look good.

In such a company, bring up your status as a handicapped person, disabled veteran, or Vietnam-era veteran and point out what you do and do not need to help you function on the job. (Do you need ramps, special equipment, changes in layout or responsibilities?)

The Vietnam-era veteran is anyone who served more than 180 days, any part of which fell between August 5, 1964 and May 7, 1975.

Oath

Mostly threat, but these certifyings and swearings give the company a legal way to get rid of you later, if facts turn up to prove you lied on your application. So tell the truth, as best you can; never claim you worked for a company when you didn't. Don't cheat on salaries, or dates.

Chapter 22

Preparing for the Interview

There are three times when you need to prepare for an interview—a few days before, that day, and at the end of the interview itself, as you set up another. Half a dozen details you've failed to polish can give the boss a wrinkled first impression of you. But when you've taken care of those small items (do you have new heels on your shoes?), you'll find you feel more confident, and you can turn your attention to the main point of the interview—getting a job. And even though few employers would say that they turned you down because of a smudged shirt, each preparation—even dry-cleaning your tie, or photocopying another sample of your work—helps sway their opinion in your favor. You make the odds swing to your side.

Take dress, for instance. A few days before you're scheduled to go for the interview, put on the outfit you'll wear:

- Is it slightly better than what other employees wear to work on a dull day? (You'll want to seem dressed up, but not too much.)
- Do you look as if you could get right to work, if asked?
- Is everything fresh, clean, and pressed?
- Is your purse new and attractive?
- Is your make-up understated?
- Do you need a haircut? (The shorter a man's hair, the better recruiters like him, according to a study by Stanford University researchers.)
- Should you have a manicure? (Even for a warehouse job, dirty fingernails will lose you points.)
- Are your shoes well-heeled and polished?
- Do you feel mildly embarrassed about something in your

appearance? (If so, fix it, so you don't spend the whole interview wondering if the employer noticed the cigarette burn on the back of your sleeve.)

Sure, fixing yourself up costs money. But you're investing in a job. Once you've gotten a few paychecks, these costs will seem trivial.

And, sure, you need time to go to the cleaners, and the hair salon. That's why I recommend doing this self-examination a few business days before the interview. If you're just starting a job campaign, you'll want to clear up some longer-lasting problems, too:

- Get your teeth cleaned, particularly if they're stained with coffee or smoke. And if you have a broken tooth, have it repaired. (This will also drive away bad breath.)
- Buy yourself a job-hunting outfit. You're likely to have moments of depression when you're out looking, so you might as well feel good.
- Reduce. Yes, fat people have a harder time getting jobs than thinnies do.
- Get new glasses. You may be used to those tippy, off-angle, scratched lenses, but an employer may not be able to see you behind that dangerous mess you call glasses.
- Spend enough money to get an excellent purse, belt, and shoes. When the accessories shine, you can get away with a much less expensive suit. You'll seem attractive, but practical; rich, but not extravagant.
- Definitely get a hairdo designed to snare the job you want. You should be able to find out exactly what bosses like in your field. For a month or two you can stand to look like that. After you get the job, you can go frizzy again.
- If you're bringing samples of your work, make sure your briefcase or portfolio looks fairly new. Yes, a rumpled sack shows you've worked hard. But it also suggests you didn't care enough—or couldn't afford—to put on an appealing show.

First impressions will make you money, or lose you the job. When you dress as if you don't need the salary, you'll be offered more. But if you feel it's a chore to overhaul your appearance, or a threat to your creative spirit, or an encroachment on your independence, then you're going to be expressing your resentment by not obeying the conventions, by not dressing up, by looking like a slob. Who wants to hire a bum? And even if you're just walking around in old clothes, thinking you should be judged by what you do, not what you look like, you're ignoring the fact that for *most* bosses, what you put on *is* a large part of what you do, for the interview. After the interview, they may not care what you wear to work. But they expect you to show your respect by picking the lint off your image. If you don't, they'll feel subtly insulted.

More hard work. Find out about the company beforehand. Ask anyone in the business what they think of the place. Use the library. Read the annual report. Look it up in the Yellow Pages. Visit an outlet. You'll be one step ahead of the interviewer if you already know their

- Main products
- Competition
- Plans for the future
- Territory
- Way of doing business
- Total sales
- Particular problems in your area

Most people don't find out anything about a company before they walk in the door. So they can't tailor their presentation to the boss's particular needs. They're surprised. They're often nonplused when they find out the company's not doing at all what they expected. They have to ask what the boss means by local shop talk.

When you come in aware of the company's uniqueness, its strengths and weaknesses, its plans as reported in the trade press or rumor mills, you can show that you have a real reason to prefer working for it rather than for its competitor. In effect, you're selecting it. That's flattering to the boss. And it puts you in the position of a chooser—not someone waiting to be chosen.

With a friend or your support group you can rehearse the tough questions you expect, focusing on this particular job. If there's an ad, use that. Show why you're right for the job. And have your partner critique your pitch. In this way, you can refine your story, and make sure you're really matching your skills to what you know about their needs.

And read over your résumé and cover letter, so you know what the interviewer's idea of you may be. (Do this carefully when you've sent out a number of quite different résumés.) And make sure you have some extra copies of the résumé, and samples of your work—even if you sent some. What you mailed in has probably been penciled up, stained, and smudged as it was passed from one person to another. When you bring fresh material, you make sure that the boss's boss will be looking at something impressive—not a blurry copy of a badly mauled copy of a written-over copy.

The day of the interview, leave yourself plenty of time to dress, collect your materials, and get to the interview site early. Rushing makes you sweat, and forget.

So before you get ready, give yourself an hour or so to relax and read the paper. Breathe deep and clear your mind. If you notice you're walking too fast, slow down. Tell yourself: it's not *that* important. Browse through the business columns. Your eye may focus on an item you can bring up as chitchat—the "latest." Eat a real meal.

And when you do dress, consciously slow down, so you can pay attention. Actually read your résumé to make sure you're picking up the right one. Before you do, look yourself over in the mirror—and wave good luck.

Leaving your house early will give you a chance to plan the interview on the way, rather than worrying about getting there on time. You can check out your clothes, your résumé, the address, thoroughly. You'll know you've really gotten ready.

Showing up a half-hour ahead of time helps in a number of ways. It may take you twenty minutes to get from the receptionist to the supervisor's office out back. Or the address may be wrong, and you have to find a phone book to get the right one, and then it's five blocks away. Or the minute you arrive, you're handed an eight-page form that *has* to be filled in before your interview.

As you enter the company's space, be inquisitive. Get the "feel" of the place. Try to figure out what attitudes are dominant here, what problems you intuit. Yes, your impressions may be based on very slender evidence. But keep looking. Why? The activity keeps you from feeling as if you have to please the boss; you're asking whether the company pleases you. Also, you may learn something—how rich the company is, or how cheap, whether people seem friendly to each other, or half-dead.

Of course, you're going to feel tension when you face a job interview. So don't deny the nervousness. Use it. Turn it into enthusiasm. Review in your mind what *interests* you about the job—other than the pay. You're about to talk about something that matters a lot—show that in your energy and vivacity. Get ready to get up. (Don't sit there with a pile of books and an ashtray keeping you from getting up when the boss appears.)

But when the boss does greet you, take your time. Give a real handshake. Say you're glad to meet, but wait to be shown where to sit. You might offer a compliment on the space, or on something you've learned from your research. If the boss seems open to it, chat about neutral subjects, while you feel each other out. Figure out what kind of a person you're dealing with.

Watch, then—don't rush into a spiel, or a joke. But don't just wait there humbly for the boss to ask awful questions. You'll just look sullen and unhappy.

Once you feel some rapport, you might start by asking the boss to say what he or she thinks are the most important qualities for this job—"in your own words." This lets you know what you've got to show you can do. (Otherwise you're just guessing. And you may be earnestly proving you can do X when the boss wants someone who can handle C, D, and E.)

That kind of question launches you into the core of the interview. And from then on, when in doubt, ask a question. Some of these you can prepare. Asking about the boss's operation is not impolite. It shows you are interested. You might wonder about:

- How many employees work here?
- What's your best-selling item this week?
- How do you handle complaints?
- What are the biggest problems facing this department right now?
- What changes is the boss about to make?
- What are the boss's plans?
- What direction is the company headed?
- What kind of equipment do they use?

Each of these offers you a chance to expatiate on your last job, after the boss replies. You're setting up a topic you want to talk about.

All this preparation! It seems such a bother—almost as hard as working. It is. But when you take the time to prepare each detail, you feel more comfortable, and in a hundred minor ways, you show you are a person who can *do* whatever is necessary to get what you want, even if some of the tasks cost money, challenge your usual ways of behaving, or make you look like a serious business person.

Only Marines are *semper paratus*, always prepared. But you can probably stand following the Boy Scout motto for a few weeks. So be prepared—at least until you get the job.

What Bosses Ask

Remember this: employers want you to do well on an interview. Then they can hire you, cancel their appointments with other applicants, and get back to business.

Unlike an application, which we've seen is designed to filter you out, an interview is set up so you can *prove* you're right for the job.

You should realize that the boss wants to be able to hire you. Why waste the time, if you don't already look hirable?

Go in friendly. After all, you've probably been chosen out of dozens, maybe hundreds of other applicants. Feel pleased with yourself and the interviewer.

Many people see the interview as a necessary but unimportant torture on the way to a job—somewhat like getting your hair cut before going into the army. These people do not prepare; they merely bend their head, grit their teeth, and walk in, ready only to endure. Enduring, though, does not get you a job.

The employer wants to know what's *not* on your résumé and application: what you are like as a person, how you think, what you do when you are caught off guard. Will you make a pleasant coworker? Do you seem to know where you're going? Are you really reliable?

But some employers feel embarrassed, or nervous, asking you about personal information. So they rely on certain key questions. Some are tricky. Others open the door for you to step in with your sales pitch.

By thinking out your answers to some of the most often asked questions, you can prepare for the surprises. You will never be able to guess all the topics that may come up. But you can anticipate the ones that might give you trouble. For instance, what would be the most flustering subject the boss could bring up?

Think of the most positive way you can discuss that. Going over this beforehand lessens the shock when it comes up.

When an employer gives you carte blanche to talk ("Tell me a little about yourself"), you may be thrown into confusion, not knowing where to begin, or what to focus on. So I recommend rehearsing a mini-lecture on what you have to offer. Look over your list of skills, and pick the five that would best help this employer.

1.
2.
3.
4.
5.

Next to each skill, make a note of some story you could tell to show that you really have used that ability. For instance, where was it? When? Who else did you work with there? What was a particular time when you used the skill? You do not need to write down what happened—just put down a word or two that will remind you of the incident.

Now memorize the five skills (and stories) so that you can recite them out loud without looking. Do not count on being able to improvise. In the pressure of an interview you may draw a blank unless you spend the time now to plant these ideas firmly in your memory.

Then, when you spot an opportunity to talk freely, unreel your list, and talk in detail about each skill. The interviewer will be glad you *volunteer* information. (Most people answer with only yes or no, or one fact—and most people are not hired). Talk up.

You only have a few minutes to persuade the employer to hire you. Seize any chance you get to launch into a discussion of what you have to offer.

And when the employer asks a question you expected, pause to breathe and think. Preparation helps, but when you're on the spot, don't answer by rote. Listen to what you're saying; watch how the interviewer responds; change as you go. The interviewer wants to see your spontaneous reactions even more than your résumé—so rehearse before; then when you sit down, ad lib.

As you go through these questions, figuring out your best answers, don't feel locked in. These are just exercises. When you are actually talking to an employer, you'll be ready so you can relax, and adapt the basic idea to the circumstances.

Some typical questions:

What Is Your Greatest Strength? Your Greatest Weakness?

Your strengths are your skills. Focus on the ones you think

most important on the new job. An opportunity for you to deliver your little lecture.

Weaknesses? This is a pit covered with straw.

The best "weaknesses" are real habits you have—ones that please employers, but not lazy coworkers. For instance:

- "My greatest weakness? I guess I'm compulsive. I really want to finish my job on time, and I know that can upset some of my coworkers."
- "I'm a perfectionist. I maybe spend too much time making sure everything comes out just right."

Depending on the job, figure out a "weakness" that is just what the boss wants to hear.

And remember, he may ask you for examples. He may probe for proof. So be sure that you do pick a tendency that you really have. If you're going to "confess" some supposed flaw in your character, make sure you can boast at length.

QUESTION: What is your greatest strength? Your greatest weakness?

MY ANSWER: _____

_____

_____

_____

_____

Are You Planning to Have Children?

An illegal question. But if it's asked, you need to respond, if you want the job.

What's behind it? The suspicion that if you are a woman you will get pregnant and leave. (The employer wants to imagine you will stay on this job for years.) So a reassuring answer focuses on your career: you and your husband have decided to postpone children for five years, while you do this work. Or: your career is more important to you than having children. Or: you already have some—and they're nicely taken care of, with school and babysitters, so they'll never keep you away from work.

If you get angry at such a patronizing question, and if you

detect a pattern of hostility (conscious or not), you may decide this employer's not for you. You could just get up and walk out. Or you could continue, for practice—and the off chance you'll have the satisfaction of turning down his job offer.

And if you're a man, the answers tilt the other way, though employers rarely ask men this question. When you have children to support—or plan to—you become a more "responsible" citizen, a steady worker. You can't afford to quit—you *have* to work hard.

THE QUESTION: Are you planning to have children?

MY ANSWER: _____

_____

_____

_____

What Do You Know About What We Do Here?

Outline what you do know—even if it is a bit vague. Then ask a few questions that show you've done *similar* work in the past, and want to see how this compares. For instance, you might ask what kind of customers they concentrate on, how big the budget is, how they handle this or that normal hassle in the business.

Smart questions focus on the problems that *usually* come up. Be ready to say what solutions you've applied before, or what you suggest. The employer understands that you don't know all the details of this business: but an applicant who thinks as if already on the job, getting down to particular tasks, stands out.

If you've talked with customers, workers, or competitors, by all means say whatever flattering things you've heard. Probe for possible difficulties the employer may be facing. Pride, and challenge, those are the reasons you've chosen to come here—not just that you need the cash and any job will do.

THE QUESTION: What do you know about what we do here?

MY ANSWER—AND MY QUESTIONS FOR THE EMPLOYER: _____.

_____

_____

Why Have You Changed Jobs So Often?

Perhaps you were searching for a job you could really enjoy—
and now you've found it. There's no shame in having checked
out a number of possibilities before settling on this particular
job. But go over your master application and figure out exactly:
which jobs led to this one? What unlisted experiences tipped you
off that you like this kind of work? Why do you find it fulfilling?
In other words, develop *proof* that you've actually tested jobs,
rejected others, and chosen this one for a reason. Everyone—
even an employer—likes to feel chosen.

Even if drinking, addiction, divorce, or worse went along with
your job-jumping, focus on the positive. In the old days, you
were searching—but now you know. You want *this* job—and
here's why. You like doing X, Y, and Z. You feel satisfied
when . . . You've discovered you're really good at . . . Don't
apologize: just make sense out of your life.

THE QUESTION: Why have you changed jobs so often?
MY ANSWER: _____

\ _____

_____

_____

Why Do You Want to Be a _____?

This question sounds hostile, as if the employer were implying
you can't do the job. But don't get defensive. Take a breath.
Relax. Think.

"For the money" is the first answer most people think of. Of
course. But is that what an employer wants to hear?

Talk about your values. You've sorted these out now, so you
can mention the ones you share with your future employer. What
has satisfied you the most in similar positions? How can this job
give you pleasure?

Think of a story that sums up the rewards (other than money)
you expect to get from this kind of work—perhaps a time when
you felt gratified after completing some similar task. Give names
and quote what was said. Help the employer imagine what it was
like for you, and why you treasure the memory.

THE QUESTION: Why do you want to be a _____?

MY ANSWER, AND MY STORY ABOUT THE TIME
WHEN . . . _____

_____

_____

_____

_____

Why Haven't You Worked for So Long?

You *have* worked. Maybe nobody was paying you. But unless you've been on vacation you've done something and polished many abilities. Raising children or managing a household takes planning, budgeting, diplomacy, persistence, and hard physical labor. If you were in school, say so; you were improving your usefulness, after all. And if you were making your living illegally, talk about being self-employed.

In fact, "self-employed" covers many sins. Any employer will respect you for trying to start your own business—and sympathize with the difficulties. Better be a failed boss than a vacationer.

THE QUESTION: Why haven't you worked for so long?

MY ANSWER: _____

_____

_____

_____

_____

Why Did You Leave Your Last Job?

You weren't fired. Laid off, maybe—that suggests business slowed down, and your former boss let hundreds go. That wouldn't be your fault.

Perhaps you quit to look for a job that challenged you more. Maybe you were only doing that as a part-time job, and now you want to work full time. Maybe you moved, or went back to school.

Show ambition—you wanted to use more of your abilities, you sought a more important job, like the one you're applying for.

THE QUESTION: Why did you leave your last job?

MY ANSWER: _____

_____

_____

_____

_____

What Did You Think of Your Last Boss?

If you didn't like your last boss, repress your anger. If you didn't care, overcome your indifference. Why?

Your next boss figures you may view him or her the way you did the last boss. If you quarreled with your former employer, and your resentment still shows, the person interviewing you will pick this up. And without your knowing why, you'll be getting the thumbs-down signal.

So remember: basically, you liked your last boss. He or she was demanding, but fair. What else can you bring yourself to say? Grudging compliments, or phrases like "Oh, she was OK," are not enough.

Your praise should also suggest you like to work. Picture a leader: someone who organizes tasks well, delegates authority, judges evenhandedly, sets realistic goals, meets deadlines. A paragon!

THE QUESTION: What did you think of your last boss?

MY ANSWER: _____

_____

_____

_____

_____

Are You Planning More Schooling?

If not, say "No," but suggest that you'd be willing to take extra training if it would help on the job. Think out what that training might be. Figure out where you could take such classes, and when. For hints, see chapter 8, "If You Want More Training."

If you are already enrolled in an evening or weekend school, reassure the employer that these few classes will never interfere with work. Where possible, show how the courses may even help you do your work.

And even if you're just applying to wait on tables while finishing your college program in drama, don't snub the restaurant owner: your future career means a lot to you, but to the boss it's fluff. So act as if the job means more to you than any exam or grade.

THE QUESTION: Are you planning more schooling?

MY ANSWER: _____

_____

_____

_____

_____

What Do You Expect to Be Doing in Five or Ten Years?

Why do they ask? To see if you plan ahead. To check your plans against the job you're applying for: does this position logically lead in that direction? If not, they fear you may quit as soon as they're finished training you.

Go back through the aims you evolved for yourself earlier. Emphasize the ones that this job could help you toward.

THE QUESTION: What do you expect to be doing in five or ten years?

MY ANSWER: _____

_____

_____

_____

Listening and Responding

Listening can help you more than talking, particularly if all you say is what you figured out beforehand. Listening lets you adapt your ideas so the person in front of you can understand them.

"I hear you, I hear you," some people say—but they don't listen. To do more than hear, you need to divide your attention. Part stays within, following your own reaction to the boss, asking "Do I like this person? Am I afraid?" And part flows outside, asking

> What is the boss feeling right now?
> What kind of person is this?
> What upsets this person?
> What does this person want and need?

To find out, you'll have to encourage the boss to speak. Yes, encourage. Even employers find it hard to meet a stranger. You can nod, and hunch forward, muttering agreement. You can ask leading questions, and pursue a topic when the boss peters out. Don't sit there like an unhappy student, bored at the lecture, or the employer will feel hurt. React.

And as the boss talks, you could imagine what kind of supervisor this person would be. Clear? Decisive? Fair? Impatient? Confused? Sympathetic.

When you're evaluating the boss, you put yourself on the same level. This helps you avoid feeling like a servant, peasant, or freshman. You can reject the boss at any time. For instance, if you notice you're getting frightened every time the boss talks about firing people, you might wonder if she scares the workers that way too. Is she a bully? Basically, you have to decide if you like the potential boss.

And if you do, then listen to their tone, see what concerns them. Here are problems you may be able to solve; challenges you like; tasks you've already performed. When you hear anxiety or anger enter a voice, step forward with your sympathy, and then start talking about how you could help.

And keep watching when you talk. Are you rambling? Boring? Exciting? Have you found ideas that wake the boss up? Are you provoking rage, for some reason? If the boss keeps interrupting, take the hint and shut up for a moment.

I'm not suggesting you hide your feelings. In fact, honest

emotion can help you cut through a lot of nonsense. Lying is hard—you get tangled up if the employer pursues a question beyond generalities. Telling the truth is easier (you don't have to memorize all the false data you've thrown out). And real enthusiasm can remind employers of their own reasons for going into the business. You can reinspire a jaded boss.

So when you respond, address the boss's half-stated fears about you—directly. And use particular examples, from your experience. These stories let the boss "see" you at work on the last job; they provide evidence for your claim that you can do the work.

Most applicants talk too much and say too little. Why? They have learned a line, a pitch, and they are just repeating it ten different ways. So, even if you have to take some time to think, give real responses. You can always relate them to your main points, but why protest too much? Stress the way you've worked: give dates, facts, figures. And stop.

The ability to give a short answer to a simple question is so rare you'll stand out from the herd if you say things like "Yes, I've done that for ten years at Willamette Corporation"; or even "I don't know."

But stay tuned. If the employer seems to want more, go on. You prepare long answers *in case* they're wanted. But you can't tell what a boss will want until you've met the person.

If you don't understand a question, ask what it means. You're not in school at the mercy of a tricky teacher. If you haven't thought about a given subject, think about it *before* you start to answer. You'll show the boss you're not just a tape recorder, primed with "good answers"—you're an alert, adaptable, and honest human being. *And* you have a point to make—that you'd be great for this job. But you can only persuade someone to listen to that point if you realize that this interview is first of all a conversation with a real person, and only secondarily your chance to make a sales presentation.

Let's say the interview goes well, then. At the close, if you haven't been offered a job, you may want to prepare for a return engagement—maybe to talk with the boss's boss, or another supervisor, maybe to negotiate terms. So ask, "What happens next?" Suggest the next move yourself. Would the boss like you to come back next week? Should you send in a copy of that report you discussed? Is there another person who should meet you?

And ask, "When will you be making a decision on this?"

Volunteer that you will call back at that time. (Don't ask. You've got a right to call, to find out.)

By defining exactly what you will do next, you show you're prepared to *do* something without being asked. That's business-like, because it helps the boss—and you.

Chapter 23

Right After the Interview: Follow Up

When most people finish an interview, they forget it. Two weeks later, they can't really recall what went on, so they're left stammering when the employer calls, "Just to go over some questions we have." In fact, many people cannot even remember which company this person's the boss of. So they sound a bit blank on the phone—hardly enthusiastic.

Only about one person in eight follows up on an interview— with personal notes, a letter, a phone call. But employers say they're impressed by such follow-through. Why? It shows

- You're thorough. You finish what you start.
- You don't go home and sulk. You keep pushing for what you want.
- You remember what's important to the *employer*, and you address yourself to solving the company's problems.
- You probably will follow through on the job—not letting matters drop until the boss asks what's going on.

So even if you ranked even with other candidates after the initial interview, you can pull ahead of them just by following up.

The first step comes right after your first interview. Don't go right home. Give yourself a break. Go to a restaurant, treat yourself to a drink, and start writing down your impression of the conversation while it's still bright in your memory. You'll use this information later. At the moment, taking notes helps you weigh your chances, estimate what the employer liked and didn't like about you, recall what you should have said—and will point out in your follow-up letter.

So as you sit there sipping, interrogate yourself, and record the answers to questions like these:

- What points did I stress during the interview?
- What seemed important to the boss? In my qualifications, or lack of them; in the company's work.
- What did the boss like about me? Dislike?
- How can I fit into the boss's plans?
- What problems does the boss face?
- How can I help solve those problems?
- What did I forget to mention?
- What's the most important idea for me to emphasize in my letter?

As you write, you can imagine what it would be like working for this employer. If the prospect pleases you, fine; the review will strengthen your impulse to push for the job. But if you notice drawbacks, complaints, suspicions, add those to your paper. But try not to let them stop you from making that extra effort to win a job offer.

Go for every job offer you can. Don't give in to feelings that you're not right for the job, or that you'll be rejected. Persist—in every case. If you start giving up on companies you're unsure about, you'll miss out on a job at a place you like. So form a habit of following up, no matter what you feel; then you can do it easily, almost automatically, when you really *want* the job.

Use your notes to organize a letter to the employer. This is not just a thank you; it's another sales pitch. You may start by thanking the employer for taking so much time with you. But that's just the excuse to reiterate your main selling points.

Focus on two or three problems you can solve, tasks you can definitely carry out. Spell out your experience in those areas again, and add whatever you didn't mention during the interview.

In this way, you refresh the employer's memory of you. A few days after talking with half a dozen candidates, the employer may not be able to distinguish between you and the others. Your letter comes in at the right time to strengthen any positive impressions of you, and to reinforce the ideas you brought up during the original interview. You could even send another copy of your résumé (the employer's got yours around *somewhere*, but this one's in hand). And throw in an appropriate sample of your work.

Here's an example of a follow-up letter.

16 Beecham Street
Berkeley, CA 94707

April 23, 1982

Corporate Systems, Inc.
1623 Broadway
Oakland, CA 94606

Dear Mr. Monroe:

I enjoyed talking with you about your ideas for a new air conditioner. In my ten years working at the Carrier Corporation, I've found my own thinking moving in the same direction, as evidenced by the three patents I've secured. (I enclose the descriptions.)

As a Senior Mechanical Engineer, I've supervised a six-man team in designing and testing some twenty-three new air conditioning products, customized for the purchaser's unique requirements, or government regulations. End users included three chemical labs, four nuclear power plants, and three types of nuclear submarine—all potential markets for the devices you want to develop.

Incidentally, I forgot to mention that I've had six years' experience in creating and following project and team budgets, so I could help in setting up the new financial tracking systems you've been thinking about. We need much more detail than the old hour-by-hour method can give.

I'm excited by the changes you're making at Federal Air, and I'd like to join your team. I'll give you a call Monday afternoon, to talk over any questions you may have. In the meantime, please feel free to give me a call at my office, 8 a.m. to 6 p.m., 525-9217, or at home in the evenings, 523-6654.

Sincerely,

Sarah Williams

Notice that Sarah has included

* Key ideas that will appeal to Mr. Monroe
* Important experience she'd forgotten to mention in the interview
* The exact title of the job she wants
* A specific time when she will call

- Extra copies of her patents, additional evidence of her expertise
- Her phone number (plus another copy of her résumé) so Mr. Monroe can call her anytime
- Explicit statements that she's interested in the job

Here's part of another follow-up letter, from a man who'd been told he wasn't right for the job.

> I'm quite excited by the systems you're developing at Ardmore Foods. My four years' experience with large real-time inventory systems will help me enhance your current system. I'm very familiar with data base interfaces, and I've been a project leader for five years, so I believe I can make sure all the testing goes well.
>
> I know you were a little worried that I've never worked on an IBM 3033. But for four years I've maintained large systems on the IBM 360. And as I showed you, I've helped create a VSAM system similar to the ADF you use. Also, much of my job as a customer representative involved adapting our terminals so they could emulate IBM 3279's, and reprogramming our mini-computers so they could communicate with IBM 3033's.
>
> Let me emphasize my enthusiasm for the direction you're moving in at Ardmore. I agree that the future lies in handheld micros, communicating over the phone lines to the headquarters 3033's. And I'd like to work with your lively team, smoothing the path to that online system. I'll call you on Tuesday.

What this Systems Analyst has done:

- Addressed the boss's worries—directly

- Stressed every key idea mentioned in the interview, showing how he could help

- Showed that he was really interested—even excited

- Turned some of the drawbacks mentioned by the boss (like working for an IBM competitor) into possible advantages

- Set up a time when he can talk with the boss again, just in case the boss is still making up his mind

If the employer indicated he'd be making a decision by Wednesday, call back Wednesday morning. Maybe he's decided to hire you. Maybe he hasn't yet made up his mind. That's your cue to start talking. Go back over the points you made in the letter, saying again how interested you are in the job. Find out if he has any worries about you, and address those. Volunteer to come back in again, "To talk about how I can help on specific projects," as if you'd only been talking general issues before.

Remember, it's hard for most employers to make up their minds: which applicant to choose? By sending a letter, then calling up, you make it easy for the employer to review your qualifications—without struggling to recall which applicant you were. You clarify the boss's picture of you. And you prove you work harder than the others. *Wanting* the job helps distinguish you from other equally qualified applicants. Persisting will get you the nod.

And even if the boss has chosen someone else, you can help yourself a lot by repeating your interest. ("That's too bad. I think you've got a really exciting program going there, and I'd like to be part of it some day.") You leave the door open. You show you're not going away mad. Rather, you take this turndown as a temporary setback.

You'd be surprised how often this approach gets you a second call from the employer, a few days later. "Our first choice turned us down. And we were so impressed with the way you handled our rejection that we'd like you to consider coming to work for us now."

So don't give up. Following up an interview with a thank you does more than satisfy the demands of politeness. It uses courtesy as an excuse to insist on your worth, to display your businesslike attitude, to prove you persist in a friendly way even when knocked down. So your job search doesn't stop after the interview—that's just the halfway mark.

Chapter 24

What to Do When You're Offered a Job

What if you're actually offered a job? Your first impulse will probably be to accept immediately, with a sigh of relief.

That's not a bad idea, if

- You've already thought over all the jobs available and determined that this is the one you want.
- You've already been told exactly what the salary will be, and it's not subject to negotiation.
- You want to start work right away.

Yes, wise old heads will say you should hem and haw, and put off a final decision until you've haggled over salary, pensions, fringe benefits, titles, moving expenses, and vacation schedules. That's true, if you're really debating between two or three offers, or if you're waiting for your favorite firm to come through with the salary you want. But sometimes you just want the job, and you don't care about the details. Fine, take it. That shows you really do value the work more than the cash. And you'll certainly start work from a position of mutual enthusiasm.

But if you're more cautious, you can say something encouraging like, "That sounds very attractive." That doesn't commit you. And you can then sound thoughtful: "I'd like to get some details, then think it over tonight." No one can object to that.

What details? Money, first of all. Start by pointing out that money's not going to be the key factor in your decision. Then go for more.

If possible, move first on salary. Figure out the most and the least they're likely to offer, and then announce that you're looking "in the range" from their middle figures to something slightly more than they can afford. For instance, if you know that other people in this job earn from $23,000 to $30,000, and you gather this company pays about average ($26,500), you should say you're looking for something in the range of $27,000 to $32,000. That way they can offer you $28,000 and you will figure you've gained a thousand, while they feel good having knocked four thousand off your top.

When you state your range, add that, "Everything's negotiable," so you don't get turned down flat if you've asked more than they can swing. Then, if you want the job anyway, you can dicker about titles, desks, assistance, job responsibilities, and trade off salary for better conditions.

If you're challenged, "Why do you deserve so much money?" just go into your sales pitch again. You feel you'll be that valuable to the firm. You can do X, Y, and Z.

- Don't try to justify your demands by listing your expenses. You'll just sound like you can't handle a budget.
- Don't lie about previous earnings. Any smart employer's already checked your references.
- Don't ask a lot just because you dislike the job. (Better look for another job.)

If you've never earned that much before, stake your claim on your worth, and don't get bullied when the employer says, "Have you ever earned that much before?" Just point out that you think you deserve that much, given what you can do for the company—and you're sure the competition can afford it, too.

Disregard most talk about wonderful benefits. Another company in the same business will probably offer the same package.

Do haggle about the time they'd expect you to report. If you don't take a vacation before you go in, you won't get one for a year, in most places. Now's the only time you can negotiate a vacation time, so if you want to coordinate with your spouse's May vacation, argue for that as a condition of employment. Now it's easy for the boss to grant. After you're hired, it's hard, because then you'll be just another employee, with the least seniority of all, waiting in line for something fourteen months later.

Ask about anything that worries you. Is there carpooling? Day care? Can they stand you bringing your baby some days? Raise any doubts now, so you can ponder the boss's reactions overnight.

Then really talk over the offer with your spouse, lover, or friends. Call your support group for advice. Talk to other people in the field: would they consider this a good deal? Ask:

- What else should I pin down *before* accepting?
- Does the money sound good?
- Does the work sound interesting?
- Should I accept?

Don't hold out for other offers unless those employers swear they are about to come up with a dollar figure, and you like their jobs much more than this one. Set them a deadline. Tell the first company exactly when you'll reply to their offer. (Say you are discussing it with your lawyer, accountant, relatives. And emphasize that you really want to sign on—as soon as you've ironed out these little details.)

If you're really debating between two offers, you'll probably want to weight the pluses and minuses of each:

- Which will help your long-range career most?
- Which sounds most interesting right now?
- Which one's drawbacks seem least objectionable?
- Which criteria matter most to you now? (And which company satisfies more?)
    —Money.
    —Fringes.
    —Working conditions.
    —On the job training.
    —Advancement.
    —Location or schedule.
    —Other.
- What's your gut choice?

When you've finally made a decision, call the employer and settle the details. Then accept. But say you'll look forward to seeing the offer in writing. If for some reason they won't do that, and you're not suspicious, then write the letter yourself, accepting their offer and spelling out the terms, and send that by certified mail. The phone offer and acceptance form a valid contract, but the letter's easier to use for proof if you get into a dispute. Don't anticipate an argument, though. If you're really distrustful, don't accept the job.

And when you've signed your acceptance letter, celebrate. Act rich. Go out to dinner. Enjoy yourself. You've finished one of the hardest jobs there is—you've found work.

Jobs Available

Chapter 25

Jobs Available

Here are more than three hundred jobs. The descriptions come from a U.S. Department of Labor catalogue of twenty thousand jobs, the *Dictionary of Occupational Titles*. So not every job shows up here. But this list includes a broad range of jobs in almost every field.

You can browse through the list, looking for work that appeals to you. You can read about jobs you've had—or jobs that are similar—and borrow the descriptions for your own résumé. By examining the numbers in parentheses at the end of each description, you can tell if the job matches your own levels of interest in data, people, and things. (The three-digit code, described in chapter 3, "Clarifying Your Values," codes the complexity of each job as it deals with data, people, and things. The first position refers to data; the second, people; the third, things. A low number means that high skills are needed; a high number suggests that minimal abilities are needed.)

And if you read straight through, you'll get a taste of the amazing variety of work done in this country.

ACCOUNTANT: Directs and coordinates activities of workers engaged in general accounting, or applies principles of accounting to devise and implement system for general accounting: Directs and coordinates activities of workers engaged in keeping accounts and records, or performing such book-keeping activities as recording disbursements, expenses, and tax payments. Prepares individual, division, or consolidated balance sheets to reflect company's assets, liabilities, and capital. Prepares profit and loss statements for specified accounting period. Audits contracts, orders, and vouchers, and prepares reports to substantiate individual transactions prior to settlement. (167)

ACTOR: Portrays role in dramatic production to interpret character or present characterization to audience: Rehearses part to learn lines and cues as directed. Interprets serious or comic role by speech, gesture, and body movement to entertain or inform audience for stage, motion picture, television, radio, or other media production. (047)

ACTUARY: Applies knowledge of mathematics, probability, statistics, principles of finance and business to problems in life, health, social, and casualty insurance, annuities, and pensions: Determines mortality, accident, sickness, disability, and retirement rates; constructs probability tables regarding fire, natural disasters, and unemployment, based on analysis of statistical data and other pertinent information. Designs or reviews insurance and pension plans and calculates premiums. Ascertains premium rates required and cash reserves and liabilities necessary to insure payment of future benefits. Determines equitable basis for distributing surplus earnings under participating insurance and annuity contracts in mutual companies. (167)

ADMINISTRATIVE ASSISTANT: Aids executive in staff capacity by coordinating office services, such as personnel, budget preparation and control, housekeeping, records control, and special management studies: Studies management methods in order to improve workflow, simplify reporting procedures, or implement cost reductions. Analyzes unit operating practices, such as record-keeping systems, forms control, office layout, suggestion systems, personnel and budgetary requirements, and performance standards to create new systems or revise established procedures. Analyzes jobs to delimit position responsibilities for use in wage-and-salary adjustments, promotions, and evaluation of workflow. Studies methods of improving work measurements or performance standards. Coordinates collection and preparation of operating reports, such as time-and-attendance records, terminations, new hires, transfers, budget expenditures, and statistical records of performance data. Prepares reports including conclusions and recommendations for solution of administrative problems. Issues and interprets operating policies. Reviews and answers correspondence. May assist in preparation of budget needs and annual reports of organization. May interview job applicants, conduct orientation of new employees, and plan training programs. May direct services, such as maintenance, repair, supplies, mail, and files. (167)

ADMINISTRATIVE CLERK: Compiles and maintains records of business transactions and office activities of establishment, performing variety of following or similar clerical duties and utilizing knowledge of systems or procedures: Copies data and compiles records and reports. Tabulates and posts data in record books. Computes wages, taxes, premiums, commissions, and payments. Records orders for merchandise or service. Gives information to and interviews customers, claimants, employees, and sales personnel. Receives, counts, and pays out cash. Prepares, issues, and sends out receipts, bills, policies, invoices, statements, and checks. Prepares stock inventory. Adjusts complaints. Operates office machines, such as typewriter, adding, calculating, and duplicating machines. Opens and routes incoming mail, answers correspondence, and prepares outgoing mail. May take dictation. May prepare payroll. May keep books. May purchase supplies. (362)

ADMINISTRATIVE SECRETARY: Keeps official corporation records and executes administrative policies determined by or in conjunction with other officials: Prepares memorandums outlining and explaining administrative procedures and policies to supervisory workers. Plans conferences. Directs preparation of records, such as notices, minutes, and resolutions for stockholders' and directors' meetings. Directs recording of company stock issues and transfers. Acts as custodian of corporate documents and records. Directs preparation and filing of corporate legal documents with government agencies to conform with statutes. In small organizations, such as trade, civic, or welfare associations, often performs publicity work. Depending on organization, works in line or staff capacity.(167)

AERONAUTICAL ENGINEER: Designs, develops, and tests aircraft, space vehicles, surface effect vehicles, and missiles, applying engineering principles and techniques: Designs and develops commercial, military, executive, general aviation or special purpose aircraft; space vehicles, satellites, missiles, scientific probes; or other related hardware or systems. Tests models, prototypes, subassemblies, or production vehicles to study and evaluate operational characteristics and effects of stress imposed during actual or simulated flight conditions. May specialize in design and development of structural components, such as wings, fuselage, rib assemblies, landing gear, or operational control systems. May specialize in analytical programs concerned with ground or flight testing, or development of acoustic, thermodynamic or propulsion systems. May assist in planning technical phases of air transportation systems or other aspects of flight operations, maintenance, or logistics. (061)

AGRICULTURAL ENGINEER: Applies engineering technology and knowledge of biological sciences to agricultural problems concerned with power and machinery, electrification, structures, soil and water conservation, and processing of agricultural products: Develops criteria for design, manufacture, or construction of equipment, structures, and facilities. Designs and uses sensing, measuring, and recording devices and instrumentation to study such problems as effects of temperature, humidity, and light, on plants or animals, or relative effectiveness of different methods of applying insecticides. Designs and directs manufacture of equipment for land tillage and fertilization, plant and animal disease and insect control, and for harvesting or moving commodities. Designs and supervises erection of structures for crop storage, animal shelter, and human dwelling, including light, heat, air-conditioning, water supply, and waste disposal. Plans and directs construction of rural electric-power distribution systems, and irrigation, drainage, and flood-control systems for soil and water conservation. Designs and supervises installation of equipment and instruments used to evaluate and process farm products, and to automate agricultural operations. May conduct radio and television educational programs to provide assistance to farmers, local groups, and related farm cooperatives. Workers are usually designated according to area of specialty or product. (061)

AGRONOMIST: Conducts experiments or investigations in field-crop problems and develops new methods of growing crops to secure more efficient production, higher yield, and improved quality: Plans and carries out breeding studies at experiment stations or farms to develop and improve varieties of field crops, such as cotton, tobacco, or cereal with respect to characteristics, such as yield, quality, adaptation to specific soils or climates, and resistance to diseases and pests. Studies crop production to discover best methods of planting, cultivation, harvesting, and effects of various climatic conditions on crops. Develops methods for control of noxious weeds, crop diseases, and insect pests. May specialize in specific field crop, group of field crops, or specific agronomic problem.(061)

AIR ANALYST: Analyzes samples of air in industrial establishments or other work areas to determine amount of suspended foreign particles and effectiveness of control methods, using dust collectors: Starts dust collector apparatus that draws air through machine and precipitates dust on tubes, plates, electrodes, or in flasks. Weighs or otherwise determines amount of collected particles, such as lead, rock, or coal dust. Compares weight or count of particles with volume of air passed through machine, and computes percentage of concentration per cubic foot of air tested, using mathematical and chemical formulas. Prepares summary of findings for submission to appropriate department. May recommend remedial measures. (261)

AIRPLANE-FLIGHT ATTENDANT: Performs variety of personal services conducive to safety and comfort of airline passengers during flight: Greets passengers, verifies tickets, records destinations, and assigns seats. Explains use of safety equipment, such as seat belts, oxygen masks, and life jackets. Serves previously prepared meals and beverages. Observes passengers to detect signs of discomfort, and issues palliatives to relieve them of ailments, such as airsickness and insomnia. Answers questions regarding performance of aircraft, stopovers, and flight schedules. Performs other personal services, such as distributing reading material and pointing out places of interest. Prepares reports showing place of departure and destination, passenger ticket numbers, meal and beverage inventories, palliatives issued, and lost and found articles. May collect money for meals and beverages. (367)

AIRPLANE PILOT: Pilots airplane to transport passengers, mail, or freight, or for other commercial purposes: Reviews ship's papers to ascertain factors, such as load weight, fuel supply, weather conditions, and flight route and schedule. Orders changes in fuel supply, load, route, or schedule to insure safety of flight. Reads gages to verify that oil, hydraulic fluid, fuel quantities, and cabin pressure are at prescribed levels prior to starting engines. Starts engines and taxies airplane to runway. Sets brakes, and accelerates engines to verify operational readiness of components, such as superchargers, carburetor-heaters, and controls. Contacts control tower by radio to obtain takeoff clearance and instructions. Releases brakes and moves throttles and hand and foot controls to take off and control airplane in flight. Pilots airplane to destination adhering to flight plan and regulations and procedures of Federal Government, company, and airport. Logs information, such as time in flight, altitude flown, and fuel consumed. Must hold Commercial Pilot's Certificate issued by Federal Aviation Administration. (263)

ANESTHESIOLOGIST: Administers anesthetics to render patients insensible to pain during surgical, obstetrical, and other medical procedures: Examines patient to determine degree of surgical risk, and type of anesthesia and sedation to administer, and discusses findings with medical practitioner concerned with case. Positions patient on operating table and administers local, intravenous, spinal, caudal, or other anesthetic according to prescribed medical standards. Institutes remedial measures to counteract adverse reactions or complications. Records type and amount of anesthetic and sedation administered and condition of patient before, during, and after anesthesia. May instruct medical students and other personnel in characteristics and methods of administering various types of anesthetics, signs and symptoms of reactions and complications, and emergency measures to employ. (101)

ANNOUNCER: Announces radio and television programs to audience: Memorizes script, reads, or ad-libs to identify station, introduce and close shows, and announce station breaks, commercials, or public service information. Cues worker to transmit program from network central station or other pick-up points according to schedule. Reads news flashes to keep audience informed of important happenings. May rewrite news bulletin from wire service teletype to fit specific time slot. May describe public event such as parade or convention.May interview guest such as sport or other public personality and moderate panel or discussion show to entertain audience. May keep daily program log. In small stations may perform additional duties such as operating control console or radio transmitter, selling time, or writing advertising copy. May be designated according to media as RADIO ANNOUNCER or TELEVISION ANNOUNCER. When announcing program of local interest may be designated LOCAL ANNOUNCER. When announcing program for transmission over network and affiliated stations may be designated NETWORK ANNOUNCER. May announce in foreign language for international broadcast and be designated ANNOUNCER, INTERNATIONAL BROADCAST. May describe sporting event during game from direct observation or announce sports news received at station for radio or television broadcasting and be designated SPORTS ANNOUNCER. (147)

APPLIANCE REPAIRER: Repairs portable, household electrical appliances, such as fans, heaters, vacuum cleaners, toasters, and flatirons, on assembly line: Refers to inspector's checklist, or defect-symbol marked on appliance, to identify defective or malfunctioning part. Disassembles appliance to remove defective part, using power screwdrivers, soldering iron, and handtools.

Installs new part, and reassembles appliance. Records nature of repair in log or on mechanical counting device. Maintains stock of replacement parts. May determine repair requirements by connecting appliance to power source or examining parts for defects while disassembling. May file or bend parts to remove burs, or to improve alinement and fit. May hold appliance against buffing or polishing wheel to remove scratches from metal surfaces. May touch up paint defects, using brush or spray gun. May be designated according to part repaired as HEATING-ELEMENT REPAIRER; or appliance repaired as ELECTRIC-FRYING-PAN REPAIRER; FOOD-MIXER REPAIRER; TOASTER-ELEMENT REPAIRER; VACUUM-CLEANER REPAIRER. (584)

AQUATIC BIOLOGIST: Studies plants and animals living in water, and environmental conditions affecting them: Investigates salinity, temperature, acidity, light, oxygen content, and other physical conditions of water to determine their relationship to aquatic life. Examines various types of water life, such as plankton, worms, clams, mussels, and snails. May specialize in study of salt water aquatic life, and be designated MARINE BIOLOGIST; or fresh water aquatic life, and be designated LIMNOLOGIST. May specialize in culture, breeding, and raising of squatic life, such as shrimp, lobsters, clams, oysters, or fish, and commercial fish farm operations, and be designated AQUACULTURIST. (061)

ARCHITECT: Provides professional services in research, development, design, construction, alteration, or repair of real property, such as private residences, office buildings, theaters, public buildings, or factories: Consults with client to determine functional and spatial requirements and prepares information regarding design, specifications, materials, equipment, estimated costs, and building time. Plans layout of project and integrates engineering elements into unified design. Prepares scale and full-size drawings and contract documents for building contractors. Furnishes sample recommendations and shop drawing reviews to client. Assists client in obtaining bids and awarding construction contracts. Supervises administration of construction contracts and conducts periodic onsite observation of work in progress. May prepare operating and maintenance manuals, studies, and reports. (061)

ART DIRECTOR: Formulates concepts and supervises workers engaged in executing layout designs for art work and copy to be presented by visual communications media, such as magazines, books, newspapers, television, posters, and packaging: Reviews illustrative material and confers with client or individual responsible for presentation regarding budget, background information, objectives, presentation approaches, styles, techniques, and related production factors. Formulates basic layout design concept and conducts research to select and secure suitable illustrative material, or conceives and assigns production of material and detail to artists and photographers. Assigns and directs staff members to develop design concepts into art layouts and prepare layouts for printing. Reviews, approves, and presents final layouts to client or department head for approval. May perform duties of

GRAPHIC DESIGNER to design art layouts. May mark up, paste up, and finish layouts to prepare layouts for printing. May draw illustrations. May prepare detailed story board showing sequence and timing of story development when producing material for television. May specialize in particular field, media, or type of layout. (031)

ART THERAPIST: Plans and conducts art therapy programs in public and private institutions to rehabilitate mentally ill and physically disabled patients: Confers with members of medically oriented team to determine nature of patient illness. Recommends art therapy program for patients. Devises program and instructs patients in art techniques. Encourages and guides patient participation. Appraises patients' art projects and recovery progress. Reports findings to other members of treatment team and counsels on patient's response until art therapy is discontinued. Maintains and repairs art materials and equipment. (127)

ASSEMBLER, AUTOMOBILE: Assembles automobiles and trucks or automobile and truck components, such as axles, transmissions, bodies, and motors, performing any combination of following tasks: Fits and fastens parts, such as brackets and small body-hardware or subassemblies, such as manifolds, transmissions, engines, and axle units, using handtools or powered handtools. Adjusts brakes, inflates tires, lubricates chassis, and pours in oil or brake fluid. (684)

ASSEMBLER, PRODUCTION: Performs one or more repetitive bench or fine assembly operations to mass-produce products, such as automobile or tractor radiators, blower wheels, refrigerators, or gas stoves: Places parts in specified relationship to each other. Bolts, clips, screws, cements, or otherwise fastens parts together by hand, or using handtools or portable powered tools. May tend machines, such as arbor presses or riveting machine, to perform force fitting or fastening operations on assembly line. May be assigned to different work stations as production needs require. May work on line where tasks vary as different model of same article moves along line. May be specified according to part or product produced. (687)

ASSEMBLER/TESTER, ELECTRONICS: Assembles subassemblies into electronic scale, dynamometer, or other force measuring instruments following specifications, and tests for, diagnoses, and adjusts operating malfunctions: Assembles computer readout printer, scale, and scanner into one unit, using interconnecting cables and handtools. Assembles electronic components, such as frames, chassis boards, resistors, capacitors, circuit breakers, switches, transformers, and condensors into dynamometer or other force measuring instrument, using handtools, soldering iron, bench lathe, and drill press. Measures voltages, using voltmeter, and adjusts voltages to specified value. Varies line voltage, and interprets wave pattern on oscilloscope screen to determine operational accuracy of instrument under varying line voltage conditions. (281)

175

ASTRONOMER: Observes and interprets celestial phenomena and relates research to basic scientific knowledge or to practical problems, such as navigation: Studies celestial phenomena by means of optical, radio, or other telescopes, equipped with such devices as cameras, spectrometers, radiometers, photometers, and micrometers, which may either be on ground or carried above atmosphere with balloons, rockets, satellites, or space probes. Interprets information obtained in terms of basic physical laws. Determines sizes, shapes, brightness, spectra, and motions, and computes positions of sun, moon, planets, stars, nebulae, and galaxies. Calculates orbits of various celestial bodies. Determines exact time by celestial observations, and conducts research into relationships between time and space. Develops mathematical tables giving positions of sun, moon, planets, and stars at given times for use by air and sea navigators. Conducts research on statistical theory of motions of celestial bodies. Analyzes wave lengths of radiation from celestial bodies, as observed in all ranges of spectrum. Studies history, structure, extent, and evolution of stars, stellar systems, and universe. May design new and improved optical, mechanical, and electronics instruments for astronomical research. May specialize in either observational or theoretical aspects of stellar astronomy, stellar astrophysics, interstellar medium, galactic structure, extragalactic astronomy, or cosmology. (067)

ATHLETIC TRAINER: Evaluates physical condition and advises and treats professional and amateur athletes to maintain maximum physical fitness for participation in athletic competition: Prescribes routine and corrective exercises to strengthen muscles. Recommends special diets to build up health and reduce overweight athletes. Massages parts of players' bodies to relieve soreness, strains, and bruises. Renders first aid to injured players, such as giving artificial respiration, cleaning and bandaging wounds, and applying heat and cold to promote healing. Calls PHYSICIAN for injured persons as required. Wraps ankles, fingers, or wrists of athletes in synthetic skin, protecting gauze, and adhesive tape to support muscles and ligaments. Treats chronic minor injuries and related disabilities to maintain athletes performance. May give heat and diathermy treatments as prescribed by health service. Workers are identified according to type of sport. (224)

AUDIOLOGIST: Specializes in diagnostic evaluation of hearing, prevention, habilitative and rehabilitative services for auditory problems, and research related to hearing and attendant disorders: Determines range, nature, and degree of hearing function related to patient's auditory efficiency (communication needs), using electroacoustic instrumentation, such as pure-tone and speech audiometers, and acoustic impedance equipment. Coordinates audiometric results with other diagnostic data, such as educational, medical, social, and behavioral information. Differentiates between organic and nonorganic hearing disabilities through evaluation of total response pattern and use of acoustic tests, such as Stenger and electrodermal audiometry. Plans, directs, conducts, or participates in conservation, habilitative and rehabilitative programs including hearing aid selection and orientation, counseling, guidance, auditory training, speech reading, language habilitation, and speech conservation. May conduct research in physiology, pathology, biophysics, and psychophysics of auditory systems. May design and develop clinical and research procedures and apparatus. May act as consultant to educational, medical, and other professional groups. May teach art and science of audiology and direct scientific projects. May specialize in fields, such as industrial audiology, geriatric audiology, pediatric audiology, and research audiology. (101)

AUDIO-VISUAL PRODUCTION SPECIALIST: Plans and produces audio, visual, and audio-visual material for communication, information, training, and learning purposes: Develops production ideas based on assignment or generates own ideas based on objectives and personal interest. Conducts research or utilizes knowledge and training to determine format, approach, content, level, and media which will be most effective, meet objectives, and remain within budget restrictions. Plans and develops, or directs assistants to develop, preproduction ideas into outlines, scripts, continuity, story boards, and graphics. Executes rough and finished graphics and graphic designs or directs assistants to execute them. Locates and secures settings, properties, effects, and other production necessities. Directs and coordinates activities of assistants and other production personnel during production. May review, evaluate, and direct changes and modifications to material produced independently by other personnel. May set up, adjust, and operate equipment, such as cameras, sound mixers, and recorders during production. May present narration or announcements. May construct and position in place properties, sets, lighting equipment, and other environmental effects. May develop manuals, texts, workbooks, or related materials for use in conjunction with production materials. May conduct training sessions on selection, use, and design of audiovisual materials and operation of presentation equipment. (061)

AUDITOR: Examines and analyzes accounting records of establishment and prepares reports concerning its financial status and operating procedures: Reviews data regarding material assets, net worth, liabilities, capital stock, surplus, income, and expenditures. Inspects items in books of original entry to determine if proper procedure in recording transactions was followed. Counts cash on hand, inspects notes receivable and payable, negotiable securities, and cancelled checks. Verifies journal and ledger entries of cash and check payments, purchases, expenses, and trial balances by examining and authenticating inventory items. Reports to management concerning scope of audit, financial conditions found, and source and application of funds. May make recommendations regarding improving operations and financial position of company. (162)

AUTOMOBILE MECHANIC: Repairs and overhauls automobiles, buses, trucks, and other automotive vehicles: Examines vehicle and discusses with customer or AUTOMOBILE-REPAIR-SERVICE ESTIMATOR; AUTOMO-BILE TESTER; or BUS INSPECTOR nature and extent of damage or malfunction. Plans work procedure, using charts, technical manuals, and

177

experience. Raises vehicle, using hydraulic jack or hoist, to gain access to mechanical units bolted to underside of vehicle. Removes unit, such as engine, transmission, or differential, using wrenches and hoist. Disassembles unit and inspects parts for wear, using micrometers, calipers, and thickness gages. Repairs or replaces parts, such as pistons, rods, gears, valves, and bearings, using mechanic's handtools. Overhauls or replaces carburetors, blowers, generators, distributors, starters, and pumps. Rebuilds parts, such as crankshafts and cylinder blocks, using lathes, shapers, drill presses. (261)

AUTOMOBILE RENTAL CLERK: Rents automobiles to customers at airports, hotels, marinas, and other locations: Talks to customer to determine type of automobile desired and accessories, such as power steering or air-conditioning, location where car is to be picked up and returned, and number of days required. Examines customer's driver's license, and determines amount of deposit required. Quotes cost of rental, based on per-day and per-mile rates. Completes rental contract and obtains customer's signature and deposit, or checks charge-plate number against list of disapproved charge plates. Telephones storage and service area to determine if automobile desired is available and to request delivery of automobile, and to check automobile upon return for damage and to record mileage reading. Computes rental charges based on rental time, miles traveled, type of car rented, taxes, and other incidental expenses incurred. May reconcile cash and rental agreements and charge slips and send them to management. May deliver automobile to customer. May keep log of location of rented automobiles.(477)

AUTOMOBILE SERVICE STATION ATTENDANT: Services automobiles, buses, trucks, and other automotive vehicles with fuel, lubricants, and accessories: Fills fuel tank of vehicles with gasoline or diesel fuel to level specified by customer. Observes level of oil in crankcase and amount of water in radiator, and adds required amounts of oil and water. Adds necessary amount of water to battery, and washes windshield or vehicle. Lubricates vehicle and changes motor oil. Replaces accessories, such as oil filter, air filter, windshield wiper blades, and fan belt. Installs antifreeze and changes spark plugs. Repairs or replaces tires. Replaces lights, and washes and waxes vehicle. Collects cash from customer for purchases and makes change or charges purchases, using customer-charge plate. May adjust brakes. May sell batteries and automobile accessories usually found in service stations. May assist in arranging displays, taking inventories, and making daily reports. (467)

AUTOMOTIVE ENGINEER: Develops improved or new designs for automotive structural members, motors, transmissions, and associated automotive equipment or modifies existing equipment on production vehicles, and directs building, modification, and testing of vehicle: Conducts experiments and tests on existing designs and equipment to obtain data on function of and performance of equipment. Analyzes data to develop new designs for motors, chassis, and other related mechanical, hydraulic, and electro-mechanical components and systems in automotive equipment. Designs components and systems to improve economy and safety of operation, control of emissions, and operational performance at optimum costs. Directs and coordinates building, or modification of, automotive equipment or vehicle to insure conformance with engineering design. Directs testing activities on components and equipment under designated conditions to insure operational performance meets design specifications. Alters or modifies design to obtain specified functional and operational performance. (061)

BAKER: Mixes and bakes ingredients according to recipes to produce breads, pastries, and other baked goods: Measures flour, sugar, shortening, and other ingredients to prepare batters, doughs, fillings, and icings, using scale and graduated containers. Dumps ingredients into mixing-machine bowl or steam kettle to mix or cook ingredients according to specifications. Rolls, cuts, and shapes dough to form sweet rolls, piecrust, tarts, cookies, and related products preparatory to baking. Places dough in pans, molds, or on sheets and bakes in oven or on grill. Observes color of products being baked and turns thermostat or other controls to adjust oven temperature. Applies glaze, icing, other topping to baked goods, using spatula or brush. May specialize in baking one type of product, such as breads, rolls, pies, or cakes. May decorate cakes. May develop new recipes for cakes and icings. (381)

BARTENDER: Mixes and serves alcoholic and nonalcoholic drinks to patrons of bar, following standard recipes: Mixes ingredients, such as liquor, soda, water, sugar, and bitters, to prepare cocktails and other drinks. Serves wine and draught or bottled beer. Collects money for drinks served. Orders or requisitions liquors and supplies. Places bottled goods and glasses to make attractive display. May slice and pit fruit for garnishing drinks. May prepare appetizers, such as pickles, cheese, and cold meats. (474)

BIOCHEMIST: Studies chemical processes of living organisms: Conducts research to determine action of foods, drugs, serums, hormones, and other substances on tissues and vital processes of living organisms. Isolates, analyzes, and identifies hormones, vitamins, allergens, minerals, and enzymes and determines effects on body functions. Examines chemical aspects of formation of antibodies, and conducts research into chemistry of cells and blood corpuscles. Studies chemistry of living processes, such as mechanisims of development of normal and abnormal cells, breathing and digestion, and of living energy changes, such as growth, aging, and death. (061)

BIOLOGIST: Studies origin, relationship, development, anatomy, functions, and other basic principles of plant and animal life. May specialize in research centering around particular plant, animal, or aspect of biology. May collect and analyze biological data to determine environmental effects of present and potential use of land and water areas. May prepare environmental impact reports. May teach. (061)

BIOLOGY SPECIMEN TECHNICIAN: Prepares and embeds in plastic biological specimens of plant and animal life for use as instructional aids:

Selects plant or animal specimen in preserved or dried state. Dissects animal and cleans all matter from skeletal structures. Prepares slices or cross sections of small animals, embryos, or cross sections of animal organs, such as glands, kidneys, hearts, or eyes. Selects, trims, and stains a variety of stalks, flowers, and leaves to show plant structure and systems. Selects different stains to clearly indicate support structure, circulatory system, or other feature of plant or animal. Assembles and positions components of specimen in mold, using pins and holding devices. Mixes polylite plastic or other material and completes embedding by varied molding techniques. Works with plants, animals, mollusks, insects, and other classes of plants and animals. Identifies type and age of specimen, date of preparation, and type of embedding material used. May operate incubator to grow chicken eggs for embryo specimens. May prepare ecological kits which demonstrate polluting conditions in water, soil, or air. (381)

BIOMEDICAL ENGINEER: Conducts research into biological aspects of humans or other animals to develop new theories and facts, or test, prove, or modify known theories of life systems, and to design life-support apparatus, utilizing principles of engineering and bio-behavioral sciences: Plans and conducts research concerning behavioral, biological, psychological, or other life systems. Studies engineering aspects of bio-behavioral systems of humans, utilizing knowledge of electrical, mechanical, chemical, or other engineering principles and knowledge of human anatomy and physiology. Develops mathematical models to simulate human bio-behavoioral systems in order to obtain data for measuring or controlling life processes, utilizing knowledge of computer, graphics, and other related technologies. Designs and develops instruments and devices, such as artificial organs, cardiac pacemakers, or ultrasonic imaging devices, capable of assisting medical or other health-care personnel in observing, repairing, or treating physical ailments or deformities, using knowledge of materials compatible with body tissues, energy exchanges within the body, and instrumentation capable of measuring and controlling body functions. May specialize in design and development of biomedical equipment used by medical facilities and be known as CLINICAL ENGINEER. (061)

BIOMEDICAL EQUIPMENT TECHNICIAN: Inspects, maintains, repairs, calibrates, and modifies electronic, electrical, mechanical, hydraulic, and pneumatic equipment and instruments used in medical therapy, diagnosis, according to schematic and verbal instructions, using handtools and machine tools: Inspects and tests equipment and apparatus, such as blood-gas analyzers, spectrophotometers, radiation monitors, and microscopes, to insure specified functional qualities according to blueprints and written specifications. Examines and tests equipment to determine cause of malfunction or inaccuracy, using manufacturers's schematics, maintenance manuals, and standard and specialized test instruments, such as oscilloscopes and pressure gages. Disassembles equipment to locate malfunctioning components and repairs or replaces defective parts, such as circuit amplifiers, tubes, rotors, bellows, and motors, using handtools or portable power tools. Reassembles equipment and adjusts and calibrates precision components to insure specified operation, using testing and calibrating instrument. Notifies manufacturer or distributor of incorrectable equipment malfunction to arrange for repair by service personnel. Modifies equipment as directed by supervisory personnel performing such duties as adding to or changing original components to meet specific therapeutic or diagnostic requirements. May specialize in repair and maintenance of specific types of bio-medical equipment, such as that used in radiology, nuclear medicine or patient monitoring operations. (261)

BOND CLERK: Performs any combination of following duties to record bonds sold or purchased, deposited for safekeeping, or for collection: Fills out bond purchase applications giving buyer's name, address, beneficiary, and bond number. Receives payment for bonds purchased. Types customer's name and amount and issue of bonds on cash letters and envelopes. Examines bond-transaction documents for compliance with government regulations. Lists government coupons and bonds and sends items to Federal Reserve bank for payment. Totals and proves daily transactions, using adding machine. Processes matured bond coupons for collection. Types and keeps records of tickets for coupons and bonds. Credits or debits customer's accounts to liquidate collection payments. Composes and types or dictates correspondence answering inquiries relative to discrepancies and unpaid items. Cancels paid coupons and bonds, using cancelling machine. May prepare checks to pay bills in settlement of securities transactions and record checks drawn and paid. May compute deferred interest on exchange bonds, using calculator. (362)

BOOKKEEPER: Keeps complete set of records of financial transactions of establishment: Verifies and enters details of transactions as they occur or in chronological order in account and cash journals from items, such as sales slips, invoices, check stubs, inventory records, and requisitions. Summarizes details on separate ledgers, using adding or calculating machine, and transfers data to general ledger. Balances books and compiles reports to show statistics, such as cash receipts and expenditures, accounts payable and receivable, profit and loss, and other items pertinent to operation of business. Calculates employee wages from plant records or timecards and prepares checks or withdraws cash from bank for payment of wages. May prepare withholding, Social Security, and other tax reports. May compute, type, and mail monthly statements to customers. May complete books to or through trial balance. (382)

BOOKKEEPING-MACHINE OPERATOR: Operates bookkeeping machine to record data and to maintain complete set of records of financial transactions of establishment in same manner as BOOKKEEPER: Sorts documents to be posted, such as checks, and debit and credit items. Selects and places bookkeeping form on writing surface of machine and sets carriage. Depresses keys of machine keyboard to record identifying headings and data, and to calculate and post totals, net amounts, and other computations. Verifies entries and summarizes and balances totals to insure accuracy. Prepares periodic trial balances and other statistical information as required. May operate other office machines, such as adding and calculating machines. (382)

BUDGET OFFICER: Directs and coordinates activities of personnel responsible for formulation and presentation of budgets for controlling funds to implement program objectives of governmental organization: Directs compilation of data based on statistical studies and analyses of past and current years to prepare budgets and to justify funds requested. Correlates appropriations for specific programs with appropriations for divisional programs and includes items for emergency funds. Reviews operating budgets periodically to analyze trends affecting budget needs. Consults with unit heads to insure adjustments are made in accordance with program changes in order to facilitate long-term planning. Directs preparation of regular and special budget reports to interpret budget directives and to establish policies for carrying out directives. Prepares comparative analyses of operating programs by analyzing costs in relation to services performed during previous fiscal years and submits reports to director of organization with recommendations for budget revisions. Testifies regarding proposed budgets before examining and fund-granting authorities to clarify reports and gain support for estimated budget needs. Administers personnel functions of budget department, such as training, work scheduling, promotions, transfers, and performance ratings. (117)

BUSINESS MANAGER: Manages financial affairs of entertainers and negotiates with agents and representatives for contracts and appearances: Negotiates with officials of unions, motion picture or television studios, stage productions, or entertainment houses for contracts and financial return to be received for engagements. Promotes client's interests by advising on income, investments, taxes, legal, and other financial matters. Provides liaison between client and representatives concerning contractual rights and obligations to settle contracts. Summarizes statements on periodic basis concerning client's investments, property, and financial status. (117)

BUYER: Purchases merchandise or commodities for resale: Inspects and grades or appraises agricultural commodities, durable goods, apparel, furniture, livestock, or other merchandise offered for sale to determine value and yield. Selects and orders merchandise from showings by manufacturing representatives, growers, or other sellers, or purchases on open market for cash, basing selection on nature of clientele, or demand for specific commodity, merchandise, or other property, utilizing knowledge of various articles of commerce and experience as buyer. Transports purchases or contacts carriers to arrange transportation of purchases. Authorizes payment of invoices or return of merchandise. May negotiate contracts for severance of agricultural or forestry products from land. May conduct staff meetings with sales personnel to introduce new merchandise. May price items for resale. May be required to be licensed by state. May be identified according to type of commodities, merchandise, or goods purchased. (157)

CABLE SPLICER: Splices overhead, underground, or submarine multiple-conductor cables used in telephone and telegraph communication and electric-power transmission systems: Climbs utility poles or towers, utilizes truck-mounted lift bucket, or descends into sewers and underground vaults where cables are located. Cuts lead sheath from installed cable to gain access to defective cable connections, using hacksaw. Cuts and peels lead sheath and insulation from newly-installed cables and conductors preparatory to splicing. Tests (traces or phases-out) each conductor to identify corresponding conductors in adjoining cable sections, according to electrical diagrams and specifications, to prevent incorrect connections between individual communication circuits or electric power circuits, using testlamp or bell system. Cleans, tins, and splices corresponding conductors by twisting ends together or by joining ends with metal clips and soldering each connection. Covers conductors with insulating or fireproofing materials. Fits lead sleeve around cable joint and wipes molten lead into joints between sleeve and cable sheath to produce moisture-proof joint. Fills completed sleeve with insulating oil. (light, heat, & power;) (361)

CABLE TELEVISION LINE TECHNICIAN: Maintains and repairs television antenna cables and equipment: Measures signal strength at amplifiers or at customers' terminal boxes, using field strength meter. Repairs or replaces worn components to insure acceptable signal strength. Climbs utility pole and connects test television set to amplifiers. Observes set to evaluate reception and determine cause of faulty reception. Repairs defective cable systems. Answers customers' inquiries or complaints and explains cost and operation of cable service. (261)

CARPENTER: Constructs, erects, installs, and repairs structures and fixtures of wood, plywood, and wallboard, using carpenter's handtools and power tools, and conforming to local building codes: Studies blueprints, sketches, or building plans for information pertaining to type of material required, such as lumber or fiberboard, and dimensions of structure or fixture to be fabricated. Selects specified type of lumber or other materials. Prepares layout, using rule, framing square, and calipers. Marks cutting and assembly lines on materials, using pencil, chalk, and marking gage. Shapes materials to prescribed measurements, using saws, chisels, and planes. Assembles cut and shaped materials and fastens them together with nails, dowel pins, or glue. Verifies trueness of structure with plumb bob and carpenter's level. Erects framework for structures and lays subflooring. Builds stairs and lays out and installs partitions and cabinet work. Covers subfloor with building pap` to keep out moisture and lays hardwood, parquet, and wood-strip-block floors by nailing floors to subfloor or cementing them to mastic or asphalt base. Applies shock-absorbing, sound deadening, and decorative paneling to ceilings and walls. Fits and installs prefabricated window frames, doors, doorframes, weather stripping, interior and exterior trim, and finish hardware, such as locks, letterdrops, and kick plates. Constructs forms and chutes for pouring concrete. Erects scaffolding and ladders for assembling structures above ground level. May weld metal parts to steel structural members. (381)

CASEWORKER: Counsels and aids individuals and families requiring assistance of social service agency: Interviews clients with problems, such as personal and family adjustments, finances, employment, and physical and mental impairments to determine nature and degree of problem. Secures information, such as physical, psychological, and social factors, contributing to client's situation and evaluates these and client's capacities. Counsels client individually, in family, or in other small groups regarding plans for meeting needs and aids client to mobilize inner capacities and environmental resources to improve social functioning. Helps client to modify attitudes and patterns of behavior by increasing understanding of self, personal problems, and client's part in creating them. Refers clients to community resources and other organizations. Compiles records. May secure supplementary information, such as employment, medical records, or school reports. May determine client's eligibility for financial assistance. May work in collaboration with other professional disciplines. Usually required to have knowledge and skill in casework method acquired through degree program at school of social work. (107)

CASHIER: Performs any combination of following duties to receive funds from customers and employees, to disburse funds, and to record monetary transactions in a business establishment or place of public accommodation: Receives cash or checks from customers and employees in person or by mail. Completes credit-card charge transactions for customers using charge plate. Counts money to verify amounts and issues receipts for funds received. Issues change and cashes checks. Compares totals on cash register with amount of currency in register to verify balances. Endorses checks and lists and totals cash and checks for bank deposit. Prepares bank deposit slips. Withdraws cash from bank accounts and keeps custody of cash fund. Disburses cash and writes vouchers and checks in payment of company expenditures. Posts data to accounts and balances receipts and disbursements. Compiles collection, disbursement, and bank-reconciliation reports. Operates office machines, such as typewriter, calculating, bookkeeping, and check-writing machines. May authorize various plant expenditures and purchases. May prepare payroll and paychecks. (362)

CENTRAL-OFFICE OPERATOR: Operates telephone switchboard to establish or assist customers in establishing local or long-distance telephone connections: Observes signal light on switchboard, plugs cords into trunk-jack, and dials or presses button to make connections. Inserts tickets in calculagraph (time-stamping device) to record time of toll calls. Consults charts to determine charges for pay-telephone calls, and requests coin deposits for calls. May give information regarding subscribers' telephone numbers. Calculates and quotes charges on long-distance calls. May make long-distance connections and be designated LONG-DISTANCE OPERATOR. (462)

CHAUFFEUR: Drives private car as ordered by owner or other passenger and performs other miscellaneous duties: Assists passengers to enter and leave car and holds umbrellas in wet weather. Keeps car clean, polished, and in operating condition. May make minor repairs, such as fixing punctures, cleaning spark plugs, or adjusting carburetor. May assist CARETAKER with heavy work. May groom and exercise pets. (673)

CHECK-PROCESSING CLERK: Examines and processes incoming checks and credit-card-payment coupons in bank: Scans incoming checks for irregularities, such as incorrect dates and missing, altered, and illegible entries. Date-stamps items to record receipt. Photographs checks and coupons for bank copies. Sorts checks by account number and date or type of payment. Compares signatures on checks with signature cards. Verifies that check and coupon amounts are identical. Computes, using adding machine, check totals for each account, compares total with account balance, and notifies supervisor of insufficient funds. Identifies, stamps, and forwards checks listed on stop-payment report and coupons to other bank personnel. May post figures to bank records. May submit checks above specified amount to supervisor for review. (387)

CHEF: Supervises, coordinates, and participates in activities of cooks and other kitchen personnel engaged in preparing and cooking foods in hotel restaurant, cafeteria, or other establishment: Estimates food consumption, and requisitions or purchases foodstuffs. Receives and checks foodstuffs and supplies for quality and quantity. Selects and develops recipes. Supervises personnel engaged in preparing, cooking, and serving meats, sauces, vegetables, soups, and other foods. Cooks or otherwise prepares food according to recipe {Cook}. Cuts, trims, and bones meats and poultry for cooking. Portions cooked foods, or gives instructions as to size of portions and methods of garnishing. Carves meat. May employ, train, and discharge workers. May maintain time and payroll records. May plan menus. (131)

CHEMICAL ENGINEER: Designs equipment and develops processes for manufacturing chemicals and related products utilizing principles and technology of chemistry, physics, mathematics, engineering and related physical and natural sciences: Conducts research to develop new and improved chemical manufacturing processes. Designs, plans layout, and oversees workers engaged in constructing, controlling, and improving equipment to carry out chemical processes on commercial scale. Analyzes operating procedures and equipment and machinery functions to reduce processing time and cost. Designs equipment to control movement, storage, and packaging of solids, liquids, and gases. Designs and plans measurement and control systems for chemical plants based on data collected in laboratory experiments and pilot plant operations. Determines most effective arrangement of unit operations such as mixing, grinding, crushing, heat transfer, size reduction, hydrogenation, distillation, purification, oxidation, polymerization, evaporation, and fermentation, exercising judgement to compromise between process requirements, economic evaluation, operator effectiveness, and physical and health hazards. Directs activities of workers who operate and control such equipment as condensers, absorption and evaporation towers, kilns, pumps, stills, valves, tanks, boilers, compressors, grinders, pipelines, electro-magnets, and centrifuges to effect required chemical or physical change. Performs tests and takes measurements throughout stages of production to determine degree of control over variables such as temperature, density, specific gravity, and pressure. May apply principles of chemical engineering to solve environmental problems. May apply principles of chemical engineering to solve biomedical problems. May develop electro-chemical processes to generate electric currents, using controlled chemical reactions or to produce chemical changes, using electric currents. May specialize in heat transfer and energy conversion, petrochemicals and fuels, materials handling, pharmaceuticals, foods, forest products, or products such as plastics, detergents, rubber, or synthetic textiles. May be designated according to area of specialization. (061)

CHEMICAL ENGINEERING TECHNICIAN: Applies chemical engineering principles and technical skills to assist CHEMICAL ENGINEER in developing, improving, and testing chemical-plant processes, products, and equipment: Prepares charts, sketches, diagrams, flow charts, and compiles and records engineering data to clarify design details or functional criteria of chemical processing and physical operation units. Participates in fabricating, installing, and modifying equipment to insure that critical standards are met. Tests developmental equipment and formulates standard operating procedures. Tests processing equipment and instruments to observe and record operating characteristics and performance of specified design or process. Observes chemical or physical operation processes and recommends modification or change. Observes and confers with equipment operators to insure specified techniques are used. Writes technical reports and submits finding to CHEMICAL ENGINEER. Performs preventive and corrective maintenance of chemical processing equipment. May prepare chemical solutions for use in processing materials, such as synthetic textiles, detergents, and fertilizers following formula. May set up test apparatus. May instruct or direct activities of technical personnel. (261)

CHEMICAL LABORATORY TECHNICIAN: Conducts chemical and physical laboratory tests and makes qualitative and quantitative analyses of materials, liquids, and gases for purposes such as research, development of new products and materials, processing and production methods, quality control, maintenance of health and safety standards, criminology, environmental, and others involving experimental, theoretical or practical application of chemistry and related sciences: Sets up laboratory equipment and instrumentation required for tests, research or process control. Analyzes products, such as food, drugs, plastics, dyes, paints, detergents, paper, petroleum, and other products, to determine strength, stability, purity, and other characteristics of chemical content. Tests ores, minerals, gases, pollutants, and other materials and substances, such as carbon, tungsten, nitrogen, iron, gold, or nickel. Prepares chemical solutions for use in processing materials, such as textiles, detergents, paper, felt, and fertilizers, following standardized formulas or experimental procedures. May work with radioactive and biological materials, radiochemical procedures, emission spectrometry, and other techniques. (261)

CHEMIST: Conducts research, analysis, synthesis, and experimentation on liquid, solid and gaseous materials, substances, and compounds for purposes of product and process development, quality control, quantitative and qualitative analysis, improvement of analytical techniques, methodologies and procedures, and application of new products and instrumentation: Devises new equipment, and develops formulas, processes, techniques, and methods for solution of technical problems. Analyzes organic and inorganic compounds to determine chemical and physical properties, utilizing techniques, such as chromatography, spectroscopy and spectrophotometry. Induces changes in composition of substances by introduction of heat, light, energy, and chemical catalysts. Conducts research on products, such as paints, coatings, plastics, rubber, glass, textiles, metals, resins, adhesives, leather, dyes, detergents, or petroleum. Conducts research into relationship between molecular, chemical, and physical properties of substances and compounds. Confers with scientists and engineers regarding research of solutions to problems, and prepares technical reports for management. Prepares standards and specifications for processes, facilities, products, and tests. (061)

CHEMIST, FOOD: Conducts research and analysis concerning chemistry of foods to develop and improve foods and beverages: Experiments with natural and synthetic materials or by-products to develop new foods, additives, preservatives, antiadulteration agents, and related products. Studies effects of various methods of processing, preservation, and packaging on composition and properties of foods, such as color, texture, aroma, taste, shelf life, and nutritive content. Tests food and beverage samples, such as starch, sugar, cereals, beer, canned and dehydrated food products, meats, vegetables, dairy foods, and other products to insure compliance with food laws, and standards of quality and purity. May perform, or supervise workers performing, quality control tests in food processing, canning, freezing, brewing or distilling. May specialize in particular food or process. (061)

CIRCULATION-SALES REPRESENTATIVE: Promotes and coordinates sale and distribution of newspapers in areas served by franchised wholesale distributors: Surveys urban and suburban areas to determine newspaper sales potential, using statistical tables, and recommends new outlets and locations for newsstands, street-sale racks, and carrier routes. Schedules delivery and distribution of newspapers and regulates size of orders to maintain maximum sales with minimum return of unsold papers. Evaluates dealer sales and assists dealers through sales promotion and training programs. Inspects routes to insure prompt and regular delivery of newspapers to distributors, dealers, carriers, and vending machines. Distributes and explains circulation instructions and changes to distributors and dealers, and investigates and adjusts dealer complaints. Examines and investigates applications for sale or transfer of franchises. Investigates delinquent accounts and makes collections. Instructs drivers, dealers, and carriers in sales techniques to improve sales. Lays out home delivery routes and organizes carrier crews. Analyzes sales statistics to assist management in circulation planning. Reports on sales and activities of competitors. Writes promotional bulletins to notify dealers and carriers of special sales promotions and offers. Arranges for sale of newspapers at special events and sale of special issues and editions in case of important news breaks. (167)

CITY PLANNING AIDE: Compiles data for use by URBAN PLANNER in making planning studies: Summarizes information from maps, reports, field and file investigations, and books. Traces maps and prepares statistical tabulations, computations, charts, and graphs to illustrate planning studies in areas, such as population, transportation, traffic, land use, zoning, proposed subdivisions, and public utilities. Prepares and updates files and records. May answer public inquiries, conduct field interviews, and make surveys of traffic flow, parking, housing, educational facilities, recreation, zoning, and other conditions which affect planning studies. (364)

CIVIL ENGINEER: Plans, designs, and directs construction and maintenance of structures and facilities, such as roads, railroads, airports, bridges, harbors, channels, dams, irrigation projects, pipelines, powerplants, water and sewage systems, and waste disposal units. May perform technical research and utilize computers as aids in developing solutions to engineering problems. May be designated according to specialty or product. (061)

CLEANER, COMMERCIAL OR INSTITUTIONAL: Keeps premises of office building, apartment house, or other commercial or institutional building in clean and orderly condition: Cleans and polishes lighting fixtures, marble surfaces, and trim. May cut and trim grass, and shovel snow, using power equipment or handtools. May deliver messages. May transport small equipment or tools between departments. May set up tables and chairs in auditorium or hall. (687)

CLERK, GENERAL: Performs any combination of following and similar clerical tasks requiring limited knowledge of systems or procedures: Writes or types bills, statements, receipts, checks, or other documents, copying information from one record to another. Proofreads records or forms. Counts, weighs, or measures material. Sorts and files records. Receives money from customers and deposits money in bank. Addresses envelopes or packages by hand or with typewriter or addressograph machine. Stuffs envelops by hand or with envelop stuffing machine. Answers telephone, conveys messages, and runs errands. Stamps, sorts, and distributes mail. Stamps or numbers forms by hand or machine. Copies documents, using office duplicating equipment. (562)

CLERK-TYPIST: Compiles data and operates typewriter in performance of routine clerical duties to maintain business records and reports: Types reports, business correspondence, application forms, shipping tickets, and other matter. Files records and reports, posts information to records, sorts and distributes mail, answers telephone, and performs similar duties. May compute amounts, using adding or calculating machine. (362)

CLOTHES DESIGNER: Designs men's women's, and children's garments, shoes, and handbags: Analyzes trends and predictions, confers with sales and management executives, compares leather, fabrics, and other apparel materials, and integrates findings with personal interests, tastes, and knowledge of design to create new apparel designs. Sketches rough and detailed drawings of apparel and writes specifications describing factors, such as color scheme, construction, and type of material to be used. Confers with and coordinates activities of workers who draw and cut patterns and construct garments to fabricate sample garment. Examines sample garment on and off model and modifies or alters design as necessary to achieve desired effect. May draw garment or shoe pattern, using measuring and drawing instruments. May cut pattern. May construct sample, using standard sewing equipment. May arrange for showing of sample garments at sales meetings or fashion shows. May attend fashion and fabric shows to observe new fashions and materials. May be identified according to specific group designed for as men, women, or children; and areas of specialization, such as sportswear, coats, dresses, suits, lingerie, or swimwear. (061)

COLLECTION CLERK: Notifies or locates customers of delinquent accounts and attempts to secure payment, using postal services, telephone, or personal visit: Mails form letters to customers to encourage payment of delinquent accounts. Confers with customer by telephone in attempt to determine reason for overdue payment, reviewing terms of sales, service, or credit contract with customer. Prepares statements for credit department if customer fails to respond. May order repossession or service disconnection, or turn over account to attorney. May sort, read, answer, and file correspondence. May receive payments and post amount paid to customer's account. May grant extensions of credit. May void sales tickets for unclaimed c.o.d. and lay-away merchandise. May personally interview or respond to correspondence or telephone inquiry from customers regarding delinquent bills, and whether any action taken is correct and whether adjustment of action taken is recommended. May trace customer to new address by inquiring at post office or by questioning neighbors. May attempt to repossess merchandise, such as automobile, furniture, and appliances, when customer fails to make payment. (357)

COMMUNITY ORGANIZATION WORKER: Plans, organizes, and works with community groups concerned with social problems of community: Stimulates, promotes, and coordinates agencies, groups, and individuals to meet identified needs. Studies and assesses strength and weakness of existing resources. Interprets needs, programs, and services to agencies, groups, and individuals involved and provides leadership and assistance. Prepares reports. May assist in budget preparation and presentation. May assist in raising funds. Works in specialized fields, such as aging, juvenile delinquency, urban renewal and redevelopment, and mental and physical health or in public or voluntary coordinating agency, such as community welfare or health council, or combined fund raising and welfare planning council. Usually required to have degree from school of social work. (167)

COMPUTER OPERATOR: Monitors and controls electronic computer to process business, scientific, engineering, or other data, according to operating instructions: Sets control switches on computer and peripheral equipment, such as external memory, data communicating, synchronizing, input, and output recording or display devices, to integrate and operate equipment according to program, routines, subroutines, and data requirements specified in written operating instructions. Selects and loads input and output units with materials, such as tapes or punchcards and printout forms, for operating runs or oversees operators of peripheral equipment who perform these functions. Moves switches to clear system and start operation of equipment. Observes machines and control panel on computer *console* for error lights, verification printouts and error messages, and machine stoppage or faulty output. Types alternate commands into computer console, according to predetermined instructions, to correct error or failure and resume operations. Notifies supervisor of errors or equipment stoppage. Clears unit at end of operating run and reviews schedule to determine next assignment. Records operating and down time. Wires control panels of peripheral equipment. May control computer to provide input or output service for another computer under instructions from operator of that unit. (362)

CONCILIATOR: Mediates and conciliates disputes over negotiations of labor agreements or other labor relations disputes: Promotes use of fact-finding and advisory services to prevent labor disputes and to maintain sound labor relationships. Promotes use of mediation and conciliation services to resolve labor disputes. Advises and counsels parties to solve labor problems. Investigates and mediates labor disputes upon request of any bona fide party, using knowledge of labor law, industry practices, and social policies involved in labor relations. Urges expeditious settlement of negotiations to prevent employee wage loss, to minimize business interruptions, and to achieve labor-management peace. Interrogates parties and clarifies problems to focus discussion on crucial points of disagreement. Assists parties to compromise and settle deadlocked negotiations. Prepares reports of decisions reached or outcome of negotiations. May assist in arranging arbitration. May conduct representation elections according to written consent agreement of concerned parties. May oversee balloting procedures to assist in ratification of labor agreements. (207)

CONSTRUCTION WORKER: Performs any combination of following duties on construction projects, usually working in utility capacity, by transferring from one task to another where demands require worker with varied experience and ability to work without close supervision: Measures distances from grade stakes, drives stakes, and stretches tight line. Bolts, nails, aligns, and blocks up under forms. Signals operators of construction equipment to facilitate alignment, movement, and adjustment of machinery to conform to grade specifications. Levels earth to fine grade specifications, using pick and shovel. Mixes concrete, using portable mixer. Smooths and finishes freshly poured cement or concrete, using float, trowel, or screed. Positions, joins, aligns, and seals pipe sections. Erects scaffolding, shoring, and braces.

Mops, brushes, or spreads paints or bituminous compounds over surfaces for protection. Sprays materials such as water, sand, steam, vinyl, paint, or stucco through hose to clean, coat, or seal surfaces. Applies calking compounds by hand or with calking gun to seal crevices. Grinds, sands, or polishes surfaces, such as concrete, marble, terrazzo, or wood flooring, using abrasive tools or machines. Performs variety of tasks involving dextrous use of hands and tools, such as demolishing buildings, sawing lumber, dismantling forms, removing projections from concrete, mounting pipe hangers, and cutting and attaching insulating material. (664)

CONSULTANT: Consults with client to define need or problem, conducts studies and surveys to obtain data, and analyzes data to advise on or recommend solution, utilizing knowledge of theory, principles, or technology of specific discipline or field of specialization: Consults with client to ascertain and define need or problem area, and determine scope of investigation required to obtain solution. Conducts study or survey on need or problem to obtain data required for solution. Analyzes data to determine solution, such as installation of alternate methods and procedures, changes in processing methods and practices, modification of machines or equipment, or redesign of products of services. Advises client on alternate methods of solving need or problem, or recommends specific solution. May negotiate contract for consulting service. May specialize in providing consulting service to government in field of specialization. May be designated according to field of specialization such as engineering or science discipline, economics, education, labor, or in specialized field of work as health services, social services, or investment services. (167)

CONTRACTOR: Contracts to perform specified construction work in accordance with architect's plans, blueprints, codes, and other specifications: Estimates costs of materials, labor, and use of equipment required to fulfill provisions of contract and prepares bids. Confers with clients to negotiate terms of contract. Subcontracts specialized craft work, such as electrical, structural steel, concrete, and plumbing. Purchases material for construction. Supervises workers directly or through subordinate supervisors.(167)

COOK: Prepares, seasons, and cooks soups, meats, vegetables, desserts, and other foodstuffs for consumption in hotels and restaurants: Reads menu to estimate food requirements and orders food from supplier or procures it from storage. Adjusts thermostat controls to regulate temperature of ovens, broilers, grills, roasters, and steam kettles. Measures and mixes ingredients according to recipe, using variety of kitchen utensils and equipment, such as blenders, mixers, grinders, slicers, and tenderizers, to prepare soups, salads, gravies, desserts, sauces, and casseroles. Bakes, roasts, broils, and steams meats, fish, vegetables, and other foods. Adds seasoning to foods during mixing or cooking, according to personal judgment and experience. Observes and tests food being cooked by tasting, smelling, and piercing with fork to determine that it is cooked. Carves meats, portions food on serving plates, adds gravies, sauces, and garnishes servings to fill orders. May supervise other cooks and kitchen employees. May wash, peel, cut, and shred vegetables and fruits to prepare them for use. May butcher chickens, fish, and shellfish. May cut, trim, and bone meat prior to cooking. May bake bread, rolls, cakes, and pastry. May price items on menu. Usually found in establishments having only a few employees. (361)

COPY WRITER: Writes advertising copy for use by publication or broadcast media to promote sale of goods and services: Consults with sales media and marketing representatives to obtain information on product or service and discuss style and length of advertising copy. Obtains additional background and current development information through research and interview. Reviews advertising trends, consumer surveys, and other data regarding marketing of specific and related goods and services to formulate presentation approach. Writes preliminary draft of copy and sends to supervisor for approval. Corrects and revises copy as necessary. May write articles, bulletins, sales letters, speeches, and other related informative and promotional material. (067)

COSMETOLOGIST: Provides beauty services for customers: Analyzes hair to ascertain condition of hair. Applies bleach, dye, or tint, using applicator or brush, to color customer's hair, first applying solution to portion of customer's skin to determine if customer is allergic to solution. Shampoos hair and scalp with water, liquid soap, dry powder, or egg, and rinses hair with vinegar, water, lemon, or prepared rinses. Massages scalp and gives other hair and scalp-conditioning treatments for hygienic or remedial purposes. Styles hair by blowing, cutting, trimming, and tapering, using clippers, scissors, razors, and blow-wave gun. Suggests coiffure according to physical features of patron and current styles, or determines coiffure from instructions of patron. Applies water or waving solutions to hair and winds hair around rollers, or pin curls and finger-waves hair. Sets hair by blow-dry or natural-set, or presses hair with straightening comb. Suggests cosmetics for conditions, such as dry or oily skin. Applies lotions and creams to customer's face and neck to soften skin and lubricate tissues. Performs other beauty services, such as massaging face or neck, shaping and coloring eyebrows or eyelashes, removing unwanted hair, applying solutions that straighten hair or retain curls or waves in hair, and waving or curling hair. Cleans, shapes, and polishes fingernails and toenails. (271)

COUNSELOR, CAMP: Directs activities of children at vacation camp: Plans activities, such as hikes, cookouts, and campfires, to provide wide variety of camping experiences. Demonstrates use of camping equipment and explains principles and techniques of activities, such as backpacking, nature study, and outdoor cooking, to increase campers' knowledge and competence. Plans and arranges competition in activities, such as team sports or housekeeping, to stimulate campers interest and participation. Demonstrates use of materials and tools to instruct children in arts and crafts. Instruct campers in skills, such as canoeing, sailing, swimming, archery, horseback riding, and animal care, explaining and demonstrating procedures and safety techniques.

Organizes, leads, instructs, and referees games. Enforces camp rules and regulations to guide conduct, maintain discipline, and safeguard health of campers. May be identified according to type of camp activity. (124)

CREDIT ANALYST: Analyzes paying habits of customers who are delinquent in payment of bills and recommends action: Reviews files to select delinquent accounts for collection efforts. Evaluates customer records and recommends that account be closed, credit limit reduced or extended, or collection attempted, based on earnings and savings data, payment history, and purchase activity of customer. Confers with representatives of credit associations and other businesses to exchange information concerning credit ratings and forwarding addresses. Interviews customers in person or by telephone to investigate complaints, verify accuracy of charges, or to correct errors in accounts. (267)

CREDIT AUTHORIZER: Authorizes credit charges against customer's account: Receives charge slip or credit application by mail, or receives information from salespeople or merchants over telephone. Verifies credit standing of customer from information in files, and approves or disapproves credit, based on predetermined standards. May file sales slips in customer's ledger for billing purposes. May prepare credit cards or charge account plates. May keep record of customer's charges and payments and mail charge statement to customer. (367)

CREDIT-CARD-CONTROL CLERK: Compiles, verifies, and files records and forms to control procedures for issuance, blocking (withholding), or renewal of bank credit cards, performing any combination of following duties: Receives shipments of plastic credit-card blanks and verifies totals received against invoices. Assigns consecutive batch numbers to blank cards, using ticket-counting machine, and stores cards in vault. Issues blank cards on requisition to embossing workers for printing of cards and keeps records of batch numbers issued. Receives new or reissued printed cards, verifies number sequence, and compares identifying data on cards with data on application files to detect errors. Compiles lists of cards containing errors and initiates correction forms. Places completed credit cards and bank literature into envelops for mailing. Receives returned cards and reviews correspondence or searches bank records to determine customers' reasons for return. Receives blocking notices from bank officials and places designated cards in hold file. Releases blocked cards upon authorization from bank officials. Destroys inaccurate, mutilated, or expired cards, in presence of witnesses, using scissors. Compiles destroyed-plastics lists and records reasons for destruction, using typewriter. Occasionally verifies customers' account balances to expedite issuance or renewal of cards. Maintains related files and control records. (367)

CREDIT CLERK: Processes applications of individuals applying for loans and credit: Interviews applicant to obtain personal and financial data and fills out application. Calls or writes to credit bureaus, employers, and personal references to check credit and personal references. Verifies credit limit, considering such factors as applicant's assets, credit experience, and personal references, based on predetermined standards. Notifies customer by mail, telephone, or in person of acceptance or rejection of application. May keep record or file of credit transactions, deposits, and payments, and sends letters or confers with customers having delinquent accounts to make payment. May solicit business by sending form letters and brochures to prospective customers. May adjust incorrect credit charges and grant extensions of credit on overdue accounts. May accept payment on accounts. May keep record of applications for loans and credit. May compute interest and payments, using adding and calculating machine. May provide credit information or rating on request to retail stores, credit agencies, or other banks about customer. May check value of customer's collateral, such as securities, held as security for loan. May advise customer by phone or in writing about loan or credit information. May assist customer to fill out loan or credit application. (367)

CREDIT OFFICER: Analyzes dealer applications for lines of credit to insure that financial condition conforms with policies of bank or financial institution and with requirements for discounting of commercial paper, and analyzes branch offices' discounting activities for profitability: Reviews applications with reports on dealer's financial condition, inspection of premises, merchandise on hand, and sales records, to determine if dealer resources meet criteria for establishing lines of credit or extending existing lines of credit. Contacts branch office personnel to obtain any missing documents required for evaluation of application. Approves, rejects, or defers action on application and prepares recommendation on loan request for action by management. Reviews data submitted by branch offices on dealer discounting activities to ascertain trends and profitability of operations. Prepares recommendations on actions to be taken regarding dealer accounts, collection of past due payments, or repossession of merchandise, based on findings. Reviews and approves chargeoff requests. Prepares reports for management on profitability of business with dealer accounts, such as profit and loss statement, repossession statistics, and extent of chargeoff losses. (267)

CURATOR: Directs and coordinates activities of workers engaged in operating exhibiting institution, such as museum, botanical garden, arboretum, art gallery, herbarium, or zoo: Directs activities concerned with instructional, acquisition, exhibitory, safekeeping, research, and public service objectives of institution. Assists in formulating and interpreting administrative policies of institution. Formulates plans for special research projects. Oversees curatorial, personnel, fiscal, technical, research, and clerical staff. Administers affairs of institution by corresponding and negotiating with administrators of other institutions to obtain exchange of loan collections or to exchange information or data, maintaining inventories, preparing budget, representing institution at scientific or association conferences, soliciting support for institution, and interviewing and hiring personnel. Obtains, develops, and organizes new collections to expand and improve educational and research facilities. Writes articles for publication in scientific journals. Consults with board of directors and professional personnel to plan and implement acquisitional, research, display and public service activities of institution. May participate in research activities. (017)

CUSTOMER SERVICE REPRESENTATIVE: Interviews applicants for water, gas, electric, or telephone service: Talks with customers by phone or in person and receives orders for installation, turn-on, discontinuance, or change in services. Fills out contract forms, determines charges for service requested, collects deposits, prepares change of address records, and issues discontinuance orders. May solicit sale of new or additional services. May adjust complaints concerning billing or service rendered, referring complaints of service failures, such as low voltage or low pressure to designated departments for investigation. May specialize in visiting customers at their place of residence to investigate conditions preventing completion of service-connection orders and to obtain contract and deposit when service is being used without contract. (367)

DANCER: Dances alone, with partner, or in group to entertain audience: Performs classical, modern, or acrobatic dances, coordinating body movements to musical accompaniment. Rehearses dance movements. May choreograph own dance. May sing and provide other forms of entertainment. (047)

DECKHAND, FISHING VESSEL: Performs any combination of following duties aboard fishing vessel: Stands lookout, steering, and engine-room watches. Attaches nets, slings, hooks, and other lifting devices to cables, booms, and hoists. Loads equipment and supplies aboard vessel by hand or using hoisting equipment. Signals other workers to move, hoist, and position loads. Rows boats and dinghies and operates skiffs to transport fishers, divers, and sponge hookers and to tow and position nets. Attaches accessories, such as floats, weights, and markers to nets and lines. Pulls and guides nets and lines onto vessel. Removes fish from nets and hooks. Sorts and cleans marine life and returns undesirable and illegal catch to sea. Places catch in containers and stows in hold and covers with salt and ice. Washes deck, conveyors, knives and other equipment, using brush, detergent, and water. Lubricates, adjusts, and makes minor repairs to engines and equipment. Secures and removes vessel's docking lines to and from docks and other vessels. (667)

DECORATOR: Prepares and installs decorations and displays from blueprints or drawings for trade and industrial shows, expositions, festivals, and other special events: Cuts out designs on cardboard, hard board, and plywood, according to motif of event. Constructs portable installations according to specifications, using woodworking power tools. Installs booths, exhibits, displays, carpets, and drapes, as guided by floor plan of building. Arranges installations, furniture, and other accessories in position shown in prepared sketch. Installs decorations, such as flags, banners, festive lights, and bunting, on or in building, street, exhibit halls, and booths, to achieve special effects. Assembles and installs prefabricated parts to reconstruct traveling exhibits from sketch submitted by client, using handtools. (381)

DENTAL ASSISTANT: Assists DENTIST engaged in diagnostic, operative, surgical, periodontal, preventive, orthodonic, removable and fixed prosthdontic, endodontic, and pedodontic procedures during examination and treatment of patients: Provides diagnostic aids including exposing radiographs, taking and recording medical and dental histories, recording vital signs, making preliminary impressions for study casts, and making occlusal registrations for mounting study casts. Performs clinical supportive functions including preparing and dismissing patients; sterilizing and disinfecting instruments and equipment; providing postoperative instructions prescribed by DENTIST; and preparing tray setups for dental procedures. Assists DENTIST in management of medical and dental emergencies. Assists in maintaining patient treatment records and maintaining operatory equipment and instruments. Performs such laboratory procedures as pouring, trimming, and polishing study casts; fabricating custom impression trays from preliminary impressions; cleaning and polishing removable appliances; and fabricating temporary restorations. Provides oral hygiene instruction, such as conducting plaque control program. Performs basic business office procedures, including maintaining appointment control, receiving payment for dental services, and maintaining supply order. (371)

DENTAL HYGIENIST: Performs dental prophylaxis: Removes calcareous deposits, accretions, and stains from teeth by scaling accumulation of tartar from teeth and beneath margins of gums, using rotating brush, rubber cup, and cleaning compound. Applies medicaments to aid in arresting dental decay. Charts conditions of decay and disease for diagnosis and treatment by DENTIST. May expose and develop X-ray film. May make impressions for study casts. May remove sutures and dressings. May administer local anesthetic agents. May place and remove rubber dams, matrices, and temporary restorations. May place, carve, and finish amalgam restorations. May remove excess cement from coronal surfaces of teeth. May specialize in providing clinical services and health education in program designed to improve and maintain oral health of school children. (361)

DENTAL LABORATORY TECHNICIAN: Fabricates and repairs full and partial dentures according to DENTIST'S prescription, using handtools, molding equipment, and bench fabricating machines: Reads prescription and examines models and impressions to determine type of denture to be made or repaired, applying knowledge of oral anatomy and restoration procedures. Positions teeth in wax model in specified plane of *occlusal harmony*. Molds wax around base of teeth and verifies accuracy of occlusion, using articulator. Molds wax over denture setup to form contours of gums, using knives and spatula. Routes workpiece to DENTAL CERAMIST for casting. Removes plastic particles and excess plastic from surfaces of cast dentures, using bench lathe equipped with grinding and buffing wheels. Casts plaster models of dentures to be repaired. Selects and mounts replacement teeth in model to match color and shape of natural or adjacent teeth, using color chart and tooth illustrations. Casts plastic reproductions of gums, using acrylics and molding equipment. Fills cracks and separations in dentures with plastic, using knives and spatula. Rebuilds denture linings to duplicate original thickness, contour, and color according to specifications, using plastic. Cures denture plastic in pressure pot or oven. Tests repaired dentures for accuracy of occlusion, using articulator. Polishes metal, plastic, and porcelain surfaces to specified finish, using grinding and buffing wheels. Bends and solders gold and platinum wire to construct wire frames for dentures, using soldering gun and handtools. May fabricate denture wire, using centrifugal casting machine. May confer with DENTIST to resolve problems in design and setup of dentures. (381)

DIE CUTTER: Operates machine to cut out parts of specified size and shape from materials, such as cardboard, cloth, leather, mica, paper, plastic, or rubber: Places single or multiple layers of material on bed of machine. Turns handwheel to raise or lower head of machine (ram) according to thickness of material or depth of die. Positions one or more cutting dies on material or clamps dies to head of machine and positions material under dies to insure maximum utilization of material. Depresses pedal or moves lever to activate ram that forces die through material. Removes cut parts from die or bed of machine. Measures parts with rule or compares parts with standard to verify conformance to specifications. Stacks parts in storage area according to size and shape. May sharpen cutting edges of dies, using file or hone. (682)

DIE MAKER: Engraves designs onto steel dies used to produce textile printing rollers, using engravers' handtools and machines: Measures dimensions of pattern to be engraved in die, using ruler. Operates engine lathe to turn steel roller down to size according to dimensions of pattern and copper printing roller. Sketches design on steel roller (die) utilizing one of following alternate methods: (1) Lays out reference points on design according to location of one complete pattern repeat, using ruler, dividers, and pencil. Covers design with transparent film and transfers reference points to film, using scriber and magnifying lens. Sketches design colors onto separate sheets of film, using brushes and ink. Examines design to detect errors in scribing and color quality and corrects or alters design, employing knowledge of colors, fabrics to be printed, and engraving and printing techniques. Immerses steel roller in electroplating solution to coat roller with copper. Wraps film around roller, allowing ink in design to react with copper coating to transfer design from film to roller. (2) Computes machine settings required to reproduce straight-line designs on roller, using mathematical tables and formulas. Plots machine settings on graph paper. Mounts steel roller in index-dividing machine and adjusts tracing carriage of machine according to computations on graph paper. Lowers tracing-carriage scriber to surface of roller and moves levers of machine to sketch vertical and horizontal lines on roller. Mounts sketched rollers in *fixture* on worktable and engraves outline of design following sketch lines, using gravers' tools. Cuts or stipples in ground lines as specified, using gravers' and stippling tools. Prints proof print of engraved design on wax paper to verify accuracy of etchings on roller. Removes scratches from and polishes roller die, using polishing lathe. Punches indentations into edges of die to facilitate transfer of design from die to *mill*, using hammer and punch. Controls furnace to harden and temper dies. (281)

DIETITIAN: Plans and directs preparation and service of diets prescribed by PHYSICIAN: Consults medical, nursing, and social service staffs concerning problems affecting patients' food habits and needs. Formulates menus for therapeutic diets based on indicated physiologic and psychologic needs of patients and integrates them with basic institutional menus. Inspects meals served for conformance to prescribed diets and standards of palatability and appearance. Instructs individuals and their families on nutritional principles, dietary plans, food selection, and preparation. May engage in research. May teach nutrition and diet therapy to DIETETIC INTERNS: medical and nursing staff, and students. (127)

DIRECTOR, COMMUNITY ORGANIZATION: Directs activities of organization to coordinate functions of various community health and welfare programs: Organizes and develops planning program to ascertain community requirements and problems in specific fields of welfare work, and to determine agency responsibility for administering program. Surveys functions of member agencies to avoid duplication of efforts and recommends curtailment, extension, modification, or initiation of services. Advises health and welfare agencies in planning and providing services based on community surveys and analyses. Reviews estimated budgets of member agencies. Prepares and release reports, studies, and publications to promote public understanding of and support for community programs. May recruit and train volunteer workers. May organize and direct campaign for solicitation of funds. (117)

DIRECTOR, SOCIAL: Plans and organizes recreational activities and creates friendly atmosphere for guests in hotels and resorts or for passengers on board ship: Greets new arrivals, introduces them to other guests, acquaints them with recreation facilities, and encourages them to participate in group activities. Ascertains interests of group and evaluates available equipment and facilities to plan activities, such as card parties, games, tournaments, dances, musicals, and field trips. Arranges for activity requirements, such as setting up equipment, transportation, decorations, refreshments, and entertainment. Associates with lonely guests and visits those who are ill. May greet and seat guests in dining room. May assist management in resolving guests' complaints. (167)

DIRECTOR, STAGE: Interprets script, directs technicians, and conducts rehearsals to create stage presentation: Confers with PLAYWRIGHT and PRODUCER to discuss script changes. Confers with MANAGER, STAGE, to coordinate production plans. Rehearses cast in individual roles to elicit best possible performance. Suggests changes, such as voice and movement, to develop performance based on script interpretation and using knoweldge of acting techniques. Approves scenic and costume designs, sound, special effects, and choreography. May select cast. (067)

DIRECTOR, TELEVISION: Interprets script, conducts rehearsals, and directs and integrates all audio and video elements of television program: Rehearses cast and establishes pace of program to stay within time requirements. Informs technicians of scenery, lights, props, and other equipment desired. Approves scenery, costumes, choreography, and music. Issues instructions to technicians from control room during telecast to keep them informed of effects desired, such as dissolves, long shots. medium shots, superimpositions, fade-ins or fadeouts. May move controls to integrate material from multisite origins into live program. May direct news and special events programs. May direct program for live broadcast or for electronic video recording. May direct nonbroadcast television presentation, such as program for sales, medical, educational, or industrial purposes. May direct commercials. (067)

DISPLAY DESIGNER: Designs displays, using paper, cloth, plastic, and other material to decorate streets, fairgrounds, buildings, and other places for celebrations, fairs, and special occasions: Confers with client regarding budget, theme, materials, colors, emblem styles, and related factors. Plans display and sketches rough design for client's approval. Selects stock decorations or directs construction according to design concepts. May construct decorations. May direct and supervise workers who put up decorations. May design, draw, paint, or sketch backgrounds and fixtures made of wood, cardboard, paper, plaster, canvas, or other material for use in windows or interior displays. (051)

DRAFTER, CIVIL: Drafts detailed construction drawings, topographical profiles, and related maps and specification sheets used in planning and construction of highways, river and harbor improvements, flood control, drainage, and other civil engineering projects. Plots maps and charts showing profiles and cross-sections, indicating relation of topographical contours and elevations to buildings, retaining walls, tunnels, overhead power-lines, and other structures. Drafts detailed drawings of structures and installations such as roads, culverts, fresh water supply and sewage disposal systems, dikes, wharfs, and breakwaters. Computes volume of tonnage of excavations and fills and prepares graphs and hauling diagrams used in earth-moving operations. May accompany survey crew in field to locate grading markers or to collect data required for revision of construction drawings. (281)

DRAFTER, ELECTRICAL: Drafts electrical equipment, working drawings and wiring diagrams used by construction crews and repairmen who erect, install, and repair electrical equipment and wiring in communications centers, power-plants, industrial establishments, commercial or domestic buildings, or electrical distribution systems. (281)

DRAFTER, ELECTRONIC: Drafts wiring diagrams, schematics, and layout drawings used in manufacture, assembly, installation, and repair of electronic equipment, such as television cameras, radio transmitters and receivers, audioamplifiers, computers, and radiation detectors. Drafts layout and detail drawings of racks, panels, and enclosures. May conduct service and interference studies and prepare maps and charts related to radio and television systems. (281)

EDITOR, FILM: Edits motion picture film, television video tape, and sound tracks: Evaluates and selects scenes in terms of dramatic and entertainment value and story continuity. Trims film segments to specified lengths and reassembles segments in sequence that presents story with maximum effect. Reviews assembled film on screen and makes corrections. Confers with supervisory personnel and others concerning filming of scenes. May specialize in particular field of film editing, such as feature, news, sound, sound effects, or music. (264)

EDITOR, PUBLICATIONS: Formulates policy; plans, coordinates, and directs editorial activities; and supervises workers who assist in selecting and preparing material for publication in magazines, trade journals, house organs, and related publications: Confers with executives, department heads, and editorial staff to formulate policy, coordinate department activities, establish production schedules, solve publication problems, and discuss makeup plans and organizational changes. Determines theme of issue and gathers related material. Writes or assigns staff members or freelance writers to write articles, reports, editorials, reviews, and other material. Reads and evaluates material submitted for publication consideration. Secures graphic material from picture sources and assigns artists and photographers to produce pictures and illustrations. Assigns staff member, or personally interviews individuals and attends gatherings, to obtain items for publication, verify facts, and clarify information. Assigns research and other editorial duties to assistants. Organizes material, plans overall and individual page layouts, and selects type. Marks dummy pages to indicate position and size of printed and graphic material. Reviews final proofs and approves or makes changes. Reviews and evaluates work of staff members and makes recommendations and changes. (037)

EDITORIAL ASSISTANT: Prepares written material for publication, performing any combination of following duties: Reads copy to detect errors in spelling, punctuation, and syntax. Verifies facts, dates, and statistics, using standard reference sources. Rewrites or modifies copy to conform to publication's style and editorial policy and marks copy for typesetter, using standard symbols to indicate how type should be set. Reads galley and page proofs to detect errors and indicates corrections, using standard proofreading symbols. May confer with authors regarding changes made to manuscript. May select and crop photographs and illustrative materials to conform to space and subject matter requirements. May prepare page layouts to position and space articles and illustrations. May write or rewrite headlines, captions, columns, articles, and stories according to publication requirements. May initiate or reply to correspondence regarding material published or being considered for publication. May read and evaluate submitted manuscripts and be designated MANUSCRIPT READER. (267)

ELECTRICAL ENGINEER: Conducts research and development activities concerned with design, manufacture, and testing of electrical components, equipment, and systems; applications of equipment to new uses; and manufacture, construction, and installation of electrical equipment, facilities, and systems: Designs electrical components of equipment, and equipment, used in generation of electric power or products and systems utilizing electrical energy for commercial, domestic, and industrial purposes. Designs and directs activities of engineering personnel engaged in fabrication of test control apparatus and equipment, and in establishment of methods, procedures, and conditions for testing equipment. Develops applications of controls, instruments, and systems to new commercial, domestic, and industrial uses. Directs activities concerned with manufacture, construction, installation, and operational testing to insure conformance of equipment and systems with functional specifications and customer requirements. May direct and coordinate operation, maintenance, and repair activities of field installations of equipment and systems. May specialize in application of electrical principles and technology to specific areas of discipline, such as electrical energy generation, transmission, and distribution systems, instrumentation, control, and protective devices; products as appliances, generators, transformers, relays, switches, motors, and electro-mechanical devices, or area of work as manufacture, applications, construction, or installation. (061)

ELECTRICIAN: Plans layout, installs, and repairs wiring, electrical fixtures, apparatus, and control equipment: Plans new or modified installations to minimize waste of materials, provide access for future maintenance, and avoid unsightly, hazardous, and unreliable wiring, consistent with specifications and local electrical codes. Prepares sketches showing location of wiring and quipment, or follows diagrams or blueprints, insuring that concealed wiring is installed before completion of future walls, ceilings, and flooring. Measures, cuts, bends, threads, assembles, and installs electrical conduit, using such tools as hacksaw, pipe threader, and conduit bender. Pulls wiring through conduit, assisted by ELECTRICIAN HELPER. Splices wires by stripping insulation from terminal leads with knife or pliers, twisting or soldering wires together, and applying tape or terminal caps. Connects wiring to lighting fixtures and power equipment, using handtools. Installs control and distribution apparatus, such as switches, relays, and circuit-breaker panels, fastening in place with screws or bolts, using handtools and power tools. Connects power cables to equipment, such as electric range or motor, and installs grounding leads. Tests continuity of circuit to insure electrical compatibility and safety of components, using testing instruments, such as ohmmeter, battery and buzzer, and oscilloscope. Observes functioning of installed equipment or system to detect hazards and need for adjustments, relocation, or replacement. (261)

ELECTRONICS ASSEMBLER: Assembles electronic components, sub-assemblies, and systems by any one or combination of following methods: Reads work orders, follows production drawings and sample assemblies, and receives verbal instructions regarding duties to be performed. Positions and alines parts in specified relationship to each other in *jig, fixture,* or other holding device, using tweezer, vacuum probe, or hand instruments. (1) Tends machines or uses handtools and power tools to crimp, stake, bolt, rivet, weld, solder, cement, press fit, or perform similar operation to secure parts in place. (2) Mounts assembled components such as transformers, resistors, capacitors, integrated circuits, and sockets on chassis, panel, or printed circuit board. (3) Connects component lead wires to printed-circuit or routes and connects wires between individual component leads and other components, connectors, terminals, and contact points using soldering, welding, thermocompression, or related bonding procedures. (4) Installs finished assemblies or subassemblies in cases and cabinets. (5) Assembles and attaches functional and cosmetic hardware such as caps, clamps, and knobs to assemblies using handtools and power tools. (6) Performs intermediate assembly tasks such as potting, encapsulating, cleaning, coating, epoxy bonding, curing, stamping, etching, impregnating, and color coding parts and assemblies. (7) Tends machines which press or shape component parts such as contacts, shells, and insulators. (8) Tends automatic assembly equipment which joins components and parts. (9) Winds capacitors on manual or automatic winding equipment. (10) Adjusts or trims material from components such as capacitors and potentiometers to change electronic characteristic to specification measured by electronic test instrument. (11) Performs on-line go-not-go testing and inspection using magnifying devices, fixed and moveable measuring instruments, and electronic test equipment to insure parts and assemblies meet production specifications and are free from defects. May perform assembly operations under microscope or other magnifying device. Specific titles may be assigned which designate product, subcomponent, equipment used, or processes. (684)

ELECTRONICS ENGINEER: Conducts research and development activities concerned with design, manufacture, and testing of electronic components, products, and systems, and in development of applications of products to commercial, industrial, medical, military, and scientific uses: Designs electrical circuits, electronic components, and integrated systems, using ferroelectric, nonlinear, dielectric, phosphor, photo-conductive, and thermoelectric properties of materials. Designs and directs engineering personnel in fabrication of test control apparatus and equipment, and determines procedures for testing products. Develops new applications of electrical and dielectric properties of metallic and non-metallic materials used in components, and in application of components to products or systems. May direct field operation and maintenance activities of electronic installations. May evaluate operational systems and recommend design modifications to eliminate causes of malfunctions or changes in system requirements. May specialize in development of electronic principles and technology in fields, such as telecommunications, telemetery, aerospace guidance, missile propulsion control, countermeasures, acoustics, nucleonic instrumentation, industrial controls and measurements, high-frequency heating, laboratory techniques, computers, electronic data processing and reduction, teaching aids and techniques, radiation detection, encephalography, electron optics, and bio-medical research. (061)

ELECTRONICS TECHNICIAN: Applies electronic theory, principles of electrical circuits, electrical testing procedures, engineering mathematics, physics, and related knowledge to lay out, build, test, troubleshoot, repair, and modify developmental and production electronic equipment, such as computers, missile-control instrumentation, and machine tool numerical controls: Discusses layout and assembly problems with ELECTRONICS ENGINEER and draws sketches to clarify design details and functional criteria of electronic units. Assembles experimental circuitry (breadboard) or complete prototype model according to engineering instructions, technical manuals, and knowledge of electronic systems and components and their functions. Recommends changes in circuitry or installation specifications to simplify assembly and maintenance. Sets up standard test apparatus or contrives test equipment and circuitry, and conducts functional, operational, environmental, and life tests to evaluate performance and reliability of prototype or production model. Analyzes and interprets test data. Adjusts, calibrates, alines, and modifies circuitry and components and records effects on unit performance. Writes technical reports and develops charts, graphs, and schematics to describe and illustrate systems operating characteristics, malfunctions, deviations from design specifications, and functional limitations for consideration by professional engineering personnel in broader determinations affecting systems design and laboratory procedures. (161)

ELECTRONICS TESTER: Performs a variety of electronic, mechanical, and electromechanical tests on electronic systems, subassemblies, and parts to insure unit functions according to specifications or to determine cause of unit failure, using full range of electronic test instruments: Reads test schedule, workorders, test manuals, performance specifications, wiring diagrams, and schematics to ascertain testing procedure and equipment to be used. Performs functional tests of systems, subassemblies and parts under specified environmental conditions, such as temperature change, vibration, pressure, and humidity, using devices such as temperature cabinets, shake-test machines, and centrifuges. Calibrates test instruments according to specifications. Connects unit to be tested to equipment, such as signal generator, frequency meter, or spectrum analyzer. Reads dials that indicate electronic characteristics, such as voltage, frequency, distortion, inductance, and capacitance. Compares results with specifications and records test data or plots test results on graph. Traces circuits of defective units, using knowledge of electronic theory and electronic test equipment to locate defects, such as shorts or faulty components. Replaces defective wiring and components, using handtools and soldering iron or records defects on tag attached to unit and returns it to production department for repair. May examine switches, dials, and other hardware for conformance to specifications. May verify dimensions of pins, shafts, and other mechanical parts, using calipers, vernier gages, and micrometers. May operate X-ray equipment to verify internal assembly and alinement of parts according to specifications. May calibrate unit to obtain specified dial reading of characteristics, such as frequency or inductance. (281)

ELECTRONICS WORKER: Performs one or combination of duties to clean, trim, or prepare components or parts for assembly by other workers: Receives work directions from supervisor or reads work order for instructions regarding work to be performed. Cleans and deglosses parts, using various cleaning devices, solutions, and abrasives. Trims flashing from molded or cast parts, using cutting tool or file. Applies primers, plastics, adhesives, and other coatings to designated surfaces, using applicators, such as spray guns, brushes, or rollers. Fills shells, caps, cases, and other cavities with plastic encapsulating fluid or dips parts in fluid to protect, coat, and seal them (ENCAPSULATOR). Prepares wires for assembly by measuring, cutting, stripping, twisting, tinning, and attaching contacts, lugs, and other terminal devices, using a variety of hand and power tools and equipment, such as wire strippers, crimping presses, soldering irons, and welders [WIREWORKER]. Positions and fastens together parts, such as transformer laminates, glass tube laminates, electron tube mounts and cages, variable capacitor rotors and stators, paper loudspeaker cones, and shells and cases for various other components, using handtools and power tools. Charges rectifier plates, using current generating device. Prints identifying information on component shells, using silk screen, transfer press, or electro etch printing devices or equipment. Moves parts and finished components to designated areas of plant to supply assemblers or prepare for shipping or storage. Loads and unloads parts from ovens, baskets, pallets, and racks. Disassembles and reclaims parts, using heating equipment and handtools. Maintains records of production. May load mold with wound resistor forms and pour molten metal into mold to encase resistors. (687)

EMERGENCY MEDICAL TECHNICIAN: Administers first-aid treatment to and transports sick or injured persons to medical facility, working as member of emergency medical team: Responds to instructions from emergency medical dispatcher and drives specially equipped emergency vehicle to specified location. Monitors communication equipment to maintain contact with dispatcher. Removes or assists in removal of victims from scene of accident or catastrophe. Determines nature and extent of illness or injury, or magnitude of catastrophe, to establish first aid procedures to be followed or need for additional assistance, basing decisions on statements of persons involved, examination of victim or victims, and knowledge of emergency medical practice. Administers prescribed first-aid treatment at site of emergency, or in specially equipped vehicle, performing such activities as application of splints, administration of oxygen or intravenous injections, treatment of minor wounds or abrasions, or administration of artificial resuscitation. Communicates with professional medical personnel at emergency treatment facility to obtain instructions regarding further treatment and to arrange for reception of victims at treatment facility. Assists in removal of victims from vehicle and transfer of victims to treatment center. Assists treatment center admitting personnel to obtain and record information related to victims' vital statistics and circumstances of emergency. Maintains vehicles and medical and communication equipment and replenishes first-aid equipment and supplies. May assist in controlling crowds, protecting valuables, or performing other duties at scene of catastrophe. May assist professional medical personnel in emergency treatment administered at medical facility. (374)

EMPLOYMENT CLERK: Interviews applicants for employment and processes application forms: Interviews applicants to obtain information, such as age, marital status, work experience, education, training, and occupational interest. Informs applicants of company employment policies. Refers qualified applicants to employing official. Types letters to references indicated on application, or telephones agencies, such as credit bureaus and finance companies. Files applications forms. Compiles and types reports for supervisors on applicants and employees from personnel records. May review credentials to establish eligibility of applicant in regard to identification and naturalization. May telephone or write applicant to inform of acceptance or rejection for employment. May administer aptitude, personality, and interest tests. (362)

EMPLOYMENT INTERVIEWER: Interviews job applicants to select persons meeting employer qualifications: Reviews completed application and evaluates applicant's work history, education and training, job skills, salary desired, and physical and personal qualifications. Records additional skills, knowledges, abilities, interests, test results, and other data pertinent to classification, selection, and referral. Searches files of job orders from employers and matches applicant's qualifications with job requirements and employer specifications, utilizing manual file search, computer matching services, or employment service facilities. Informs applicant about job duties and responsibilities, pay and benefits, hours and working conditions, company and union policies, promotional opportunities, and other related information. Refers selected applicant to interview with person placing job order according to policy of school, agency, or company. Keeps for future reference records of applicants not immediately selected or hired. May perform reference and background checks. May refer applicant to vocational counseling services. May test or arrange for skills, intelligence, or psychological testing of applicant. May engage in research or follow-up activities to evaluate selection and placement techniques, by conferring with management and supervisory personnel. May specialize in interviewing and referring certain types of personnel, such as professional, technical, managerial, clerical, and other types of skilled or unskilled workers. (267)

ENGINEERING ANALYST: Conducts logical analyses of scientific, engineering, and other technical problems and formulates mathematical models of problems for solution by digital computer: Analyzes assigned problem, such as optimal design configuration of ballistic missile or computer system for industrial process control. Consults with engineering or scientific personnel to refine definition of project and prepare mathematical simulation of physical system under study. Searches library for applicable mathematical formulations and data pertinent to problem. Prepares mathematical model of problem area, such as set of partial differential equations to relate constants, and variables, restrictions, alternatives, objectives, and their numerical parameters, and inserts relevant data. Reduces problem to computer-processable form, utilizing knowledge of numerical analysis. Confers with originator of problem, using knowledge of subject sciences and their language, to discuss adequacy and applicability of computer output or need for reformulation of model. Prepares reports. May use small scale analog or keyboard input digital computer to assist in or test parts of model formulation. (067)

ENVIRONMENTAL ANALYST: Conducts research studies to develop theories or methods of abating or controlling sources of environmental pollutants, utilizing knowledge of principles and concepts of various scientific and engineering disciplines: Determines data collection methods to be employed in research projects and surveys. Plans and develops research models, using knowledge of mathematical, statistical, and physical science concepts and approaches. Identifies and analyzes sources of pollution to determine their effects. Collects and synthesizes data derived from pollution emission measurements, atmospheric monitoring, meteorological and minerological information, and soil or water samples. Prepares graphs, charts, and statistical models from synthesized data, using knowledge of mathematical, statistical, and engineering analysis techniques. Analyzes data to assess pollution problems, establish standards, and develop approaches for control of pollution. (081)

ESTIMATOR: Prepares cost estimates for manufacturing of products, construction projects, or services requested to aid management in bidding on or determining price of product or service: Compiles list of type of materials, tool or *fixture*, or equipment requirements, utilizing knowledge of products to be manufactured, services to be performed, or type of structure to be built, using blueprints and specifications. Itemizes tools, fixtures, or equipment to be manufactured by company or purchased from outside sources. Computes cost estimates for materials, purchased equipment, subcontracted work, production activities and requirements, and labor. May conduct special studies to develop and establish standard hour and related cost data or effect cost reductions. May consult with personnel of other departments relating to cost problems. May specialize according to particular service performed, type of product produced, or phase of work in which involved, as tool and fixture costs, production costs, construction costs, or material costs. (267)

FACULTY MEMBER: Conducts college or university courses for undergraduate or graduate students: Teaches one or more subjects, such as economics, chemistry, law, or medicine, within a prescribed curriculum. Prepares and delivers lectures to students. Compiles bibliographies of specialized materials for outside reading assignments. Stimulates class discussions. Compiles, administers, and grades examinations, or assigns this work to others. Directs research of other teachers or graduate students working for advanced academic degrees. Conducts research in particular field of knowledge and publishes findings in professional journals. Performs related duties, such as advising students on academic and vocational curricula, and acting as adviser to student organizations. Serves on faculty committee providing professional consulting services to government and industry. May be designated according to faculty rank in traditional hierarchy as determined by institution's estimate of scholarly maturity. (227)

FARMER, FIELD CROP: Plants, cultivates, and harvests specialty crops, such as alfalfa, cotton, hops, peanuts, mint, sugarcane, and tobacco, applying knowledge of growth characteristics of individual crop, and soil, climate, and market conditions: Determines number and kind of employees to be hired, acreage to be tilled, and varieties and quantities of plants to be grown. Selects and purchases plant stock and farm machinery, implements, and supplies. Decides when and how to plant, cultivate, and irrigate plants and harvest crops, applying knowledge of plant culture. Attaches farm implements, such as plow, disc, and seed drill to tractor and drives tractor in fields to till soil and plant and cultivate crops. Drives and operates farm machinery to spray fertilizers, herbicides, and pesticides and haul harvested crops. Hires, assigns duties to, and oversees activities of farm workers. Demonstrates and explains farm work techniques and safety regulations to new workers. Maintains employee and financial records. Arranges with buyers for sale and shipment of crop. May install irrigation system(s) and irrigate fields. May set poles and string wires and twine on poles to form trellises. May lubricate, adjust, and make minor repairs on farm machinery, implements, and equipment, using mechanic's handtools and work aids. May plant seeds in cold-frame bed with cloth or glass to protect seedlings from weather. May transplant seedlings in rows, by hand or using transplanter machine. May grade and package crop for marketing. (161)

FASHION COORDINATOR: Promotes new fashions and coordinates promotional activities, such as fashion shows, to induce consumer acceptance: Studies fashion and trade journals, travels to garment centers, attends fashion shows, and visits manufacturers and merchandise markets to obtain information on fashion trends. Consults with buying personnel to gain advice regarding type of fashions store will purchase and feature for season. Advises publicity and display departments of merchandise to be publicized. Selects garments and accessories to be shown at fashion shows. Provides information on current fashions, style trends, and use of accessories. May contract with models, musicians, caterers, and other personnel to manage staging of shows. May conduct teenage fashion shows and direct activities of store-sponsored club for teenagers. (167)

FIELD ENGINEER: Installs and repairs electronic equipment, such as computer, radar, missile-control, and communication systems, in field installations: Consults with customer to plan layout of equipment. Directs workers to install equipment according to manufacturer's specifications. Operates system to demonstrate equipment and to train workers in service and repair techniques, using standard test instruments and handtools. Analyzes malfunctions in operational equipment and interprets maintenance manuals, using knowledge of equipment and electronics, to train workers in repair procedures. Consults with manufacturer's engineering personnel to determine solutions to unusual problems in system operation and maintenance. May instruct workers in electronic theory. May supervise workers in testing, tuning, and adjusting equipment to obtain optimum operating conditions. May install and maintain equipment for customers. (261)

FIELD-SERVICE ENGINEER: Investigates performance reports of company manufactured aircraft, space vehicles, missiles or related systems and recommends design changes to eliminate causes of operational or service difficulties: Inspects malfunctioning vehicle to determine cause and required repairs or rework. Writes instructions for and expedites repair work. Performs preflight inspections of repaired vehicle to insure work is completed according to specifications. Analyzes performance reports from customers and field representatives and recommends design or systems changes. May prepare service handbooks and bulletins based on field investigations, engineering changes, and overall knowledge of product. May take photographs, or make sketches or drawings, to illustrate faulty equipment, repair or design change, or other recommendations regarding maintenance logistics, engineering design, or systems configuration. (167)

FILE CLERK: Files correspondence, cards, invoices, receipts, and other records in alphabetical or numerical order, or according to subject matter, phonetic spelling, or other system: Reads incoming material and sorts according to file system. Places material in file cabinet, drawers, boxes, or in special filing cases. Locates and removes material from files when requested. Keeps records of material removed, stamps material received, traces missing file folders, and types indexing information on folders. May enter data on records. May be designated according to subject matter filed as CHANGE-OF-ADDRESS CLERK; SUBSCRIPTION CLERK; to material filed as ADDRESSOGRAPH-PLATE-FILE CLERK; FILE CLERK, CORRESPONDENCE; FILE CLERK, DRAWINGS; FILE CLERK, STENCILS. May file according to phonetic spelling and be designated FILE CLERK, SOUNDEX SYSTEM. (362)

FIRE FIGHTER: Controls and extinguishes fires, protects life and property, and maintains equipment as volunteer or employee of city, township, or industrial plant: Responds to fire alarms and other emergency calls. Selects hose nozzle, depending on type of fire, and directs stream of water or chemicals onto fire. Positions and climbs ladders to gain access to upper levels of buildings or to assist individuals from burning structures. Creates openings in buildings for ventilation or entrance, using ax, chisel, crowbar, electric saw, core cutter, and other power equipment. Protects property from water and smoke by use of waterproof salvage covers, smoke ejectors, and deodorants. Administers first aid and artificial respiration to injured persons and those overcome by fire and smoke. Communicates with superior during fire, using portable two-way radio. Inspects buildings for fire hazards and compliance with fire prevention ordinances. Performs assigned duties in maintaining apparatus, quarters, buildings, equipment, grounds, and hydrants. Participates in drills, demonstrations, and courses in hydraulics, pump operation and maintenance, and firefighting techniques. May fill fire extinguishers in institutions or industrial plants. May issue forms to building owners listing fire regulation violations to be corrected. May drive and operate firefighting vehicles and equipment. (364)

FIRE LOOKOUT: Locates and reports forest fires and weather phenomena from remote fire-lookout station: Maintains surveillance from station to detect evidence of fires and observe weather conditions. Locates fires on area map, using azimuth sighter and known landmarks, estimates size and characteristics of fire, and reports findings to base camp by radio or telephone. Observes instruments and reports daily meteorological data, such as temperature, relative humidity, wind direction and velocity, and type of cloud formations. Relays messages from base camp, mobile units, and law enforcement and governmental agencies relating to weather forecasts, fire hazard conditions, emergencies, accidents, and location of crews and personnel. Explains state and federal laws, timber company policies, fire hazard conditions, and fire prevention methods to visitors of forest. Maintains records and logbooks. (367)

FLIGHT ENGINEER: Makes preflight, inflight, and postflight inspections, adjustments, and minor repairs to insure safe and efficient operation of aircraft: Inspects aircraft prior to takeoff for defects, such as fuel or oil leaks and malfunctions in electrical, hydraulic, or pressurization systems according to preflight checklist. Verifies passenger and cargo distribution and amount of fuel to insure that weight and balance specifications are met. Monitors control panel to verify aircraft performance, and regulates engine speed according to instructions of AIRPLANE PILOT, COMMERCIAL. Makes inflight repairs, such as replacing fuses, adjusting instruments, and freeing jammed flight control cables, using handtools, or takes emergency measures to compensate for failure of equipment, such as autopilot, wing heaters, and electrical and hydraulic systems. Monitors fuel gages and computes rate of fuel consumption. Keeps log of fuel consumption and engine performance. Records malfunctions which were not corrected during flight and reports needed repairs to ground maintenance personnel. May perform repairs upon completion of flight. Must be licensed by Federal Aviation Administration. (261)

FOOD TECHNOLOGIST: Applies scientific and engineering principles in research, development, production technology, quality control, packaging, processing, and utilization of foods: Conducts basic research, and new product research and development of foods. Develops new and improved methods and systems for food processing, production, quality control, packaging, and distribution. Studies methods to improve quality of foods, such as flavor, color, texture, nutritional value, convenience, or physical, chemical, and microbiological composition of foods. Develops food standards, safety and sanitary regulations, and waste management and water supply specifications. Tests new products in test kitchen and develops specific processing methods in laboratory pilot plant, and confers with process engineers, flavor experts, and packaging and marketing specialists to resolve problems. May specialize in one phase of food technology, such as product development, quality control, or production inspection, technical writing, teaching, or consulting. May specialize in particular branch of food technology, such as cereal grains, meat and poultry, fats and oils, seafood, animal foods, beverages, dairy products, flavors, sugars and starches, stabilizers, preservatives, colors, and nutritional additives, and be identified according to branch of food technology. (081)

FOREIGN-SERVICE OFFICER: Represents interests of United States Government and citizens by conducting relations with foreign nations and international organizations; protecting and advancing political, economic, and commercial interests overseas; and rendering personal services to Americans abroad and to foreign nationals traveling to the United States: Manages and administers diplomatic or consular post abroad. Conveys views of United States government to host government. Reports political and other developments in host country to superior or Secretary of State. Analyzes basic economic data, trends, and developments in host country or region. Advances trade by alerting United States businessmen to potential foreign trade and investment opportunities. Provides medical, legal, familial, and traveling advice and assistance to United States citizens. Issues passports to Americans and visas to foreigners wishing to enter the United States. Offers notarial services and assistance on benefit programs to Americans and eligible foreigners. Determines eligibility of persons to be documented as United States citizens. Takes testimony abroad for use in United States courts. May negotiate agreements between host and United States governments. May recommend how American policy can help improve foreign economic conditions. May coordinate American economic assistance programs. May serve in Washington, D.C. as counterpart to colleagues in the field, relating foreign service administrative needs to Department of State or United States Information Agency. May disseminate information overseas about the United States and its policies by engaging in cultural and educational interaction through United States Information Agency. (117)

FORESTER: Manages and develops forest lands and their resources for economic and recreational purposes: Plans and directs projects in forestation and reforestation. Maps forest areas, estimates standing timber and future growth, and manages timber sales. Plans cutting programs to assure continuous production of timber. Conducts research in methods of cutting and removing timber with minimum waste and damage, and methods of processing wood for various uses. Directs suppression of forest fires and conducts fire-prevention programs. Plans campsites and recreation centers, and directs construction and maintenance of cabins, fences, telephone lines, and roads. Assists in planning and carrying out projects for control of floods, soil erosion, tree diseases, and insect pests in forests. Advises on forestry problems and conducts educational programs on care of forests. May participate in environmental studies and prepare variety of environmental reports. (061)

FOREST WORKER: Performs variety of tasks to reforest and protect timber tracts and maintain forest facilities, such as roads and campsites: Plants tree seedlings in specified pattern, using mattock, planting hoe, or dibble. Cuts out diseased, weak, or undesirable trees, and prunes limbs of young trees to deter knot growth, using handsaw, powersaw, and pruning tools. Fells trees, clears brush from fire breaks, and extinguishes flames and embers to suppress forest fires, using chainsaw, shovel, and engine-driven or hand pumps. Clears and piles brush, limbs, and other debris from roadsides, fire trails, and camping areas, using ax, mattock, or brush hook. Sprays or injects trees, brush, and weeds with herbicides, using hand or powered sprayers or tree injector tool. Erects signs and fences, using posthole digger, shovel, tamper or other handtools. Replenishes firewood and other supplies, and cleans kitchens, restrooms, and campsites or recreational facilities. Holds measuring tape or survey rod, carries and sets stakes, clears brush from sighting line, and performs related tasks to assist forest survey crew. (687)

FRAMER: Installs mirrors or pictures in wooden, plastic, or metal frames, performing any combination of following tasks: Assembles frames from precut material and glues, nails, screws, or staples material together, using clamps, handtools, and power tools. Places glass, picture, or mirror into frame. Inserts wooden strips between mirror and frame or covers mirror edge with stripping to secure mirror in position. Positions backing, such as corrugated paper or cardboard, over back of picture or mirror. Staples backing to frame or locates and marks points on backing where hangers are to be placed, using ruler and pencil. Drills holes with portable electric drill and bolts or screws hangers to mirror backing. Places mirror backing in frame and attaches backing to mirror frame, using clips, screws, staples, and handtools. Bolts wings to frame to form border of shadowbox mirrors. May mount picture on mat before framing. May perform all operations of cutting, shaving, and drilling to prepare frame parts from stock molding according to customer or company specifications. May pack mirrors or pictures for shipment. (684)

FUND RAISER: Plans fund-raising programs for charities or other causes and writes to, telephones, or visits individuals or establishments to solicit funds: Compiles and analyzes information about potential contributors to develop mailing or contact list and to plan selling approach. Writes, telephones, or visits potential contributors and persuades them to contribute funds by explaining purpose and benefits of fund-raising program. Takes pledges or funds from contributors. Records expenses incurred and contributions received. May organize volunteers and plan social functions to raise funds. May prepare fund-raising brochures for mail-solicitation programs. (157)

FURNITURE ASSEMBLER: Assembles wooden parts or assemblies to form sections, frames, or complete articles of furniture: Trims joints to fit, using handtools. Blows dust from mortises and areas to be glued, using airhose. Spreads glue on surfaces to be joined by drawing wood across roller partially submerged in glue, by using brush dipped in glue, or by using glue-filled squeeze bottle. Knocks connecting parts together with mallet or compresses assembled parts in clamp until glue has dried. Wipes excess glue from joints with rag. Drills holes and drives screws into parts to join parts or to reinforce glued joints, using power drill and screwdriver. Attaches glue blocks, metal braces, corner blocks, drawer guides, tops, molding, shelves, dust bottoms, back panels, or skids with nails, screws, glue, or staples, using handtools and power tools. Inspects and verifies accuracy of assembled article for conformance to specified standards, using square and tape measure. Smooths irregular joints with rasp and sandpaper, and levels chair legs, using circular leveling saw. May drill holes and attach hardware, such as drawer guides, drawer locks, catches, and latches, using power drill and handtools. May slide drawers in and out to test ease of movement, and adjust ill-fitting drawers, using handtools. May be designated according to part or article assembled. (684)

GENERAL PRACTITIONER: Attends to variety of medical cases in general practice: Examines patients, utilizing stethoscope, sphygomanometer, and other instruments. Orders or executes various tests, analyses, and X-rays to provide information on patient's condition. Analyzes reports and findings of tests and of examination, and diagnoses condition. Administers or prescribes treatments and drugs. Inoculates and vaccinates patients to immunize them from communicable diseases. Promotes health by advising patients concerning diet, hygiene, and methods for prevention of disease. Provides prenatal care to pregnant women, delivers babies, and provides postnatal care to mother and infant. Reports births, deaths, and outbreak of contagious diseases to governmental authorities. May make house and emergency calls to attend to patients unable to visit office or clinic. May conduct physical examinations of insurance company applicants to determine health and risk involved in insuring applicant. (101)

GEOLOGIST: Studies composition, structure, and history of earth's crust: Examines rocks, minerals, and fossil remains to identify and determine sequence of processes affecting development of earth. Applies knowledge of chemistry, physics, biology, and mathematics to explain these phenomena and to help locate mineral, geothermal, and petroleum deposits and underground water resources. Studies ocean bottom. Applies geological knowledge to engineering problems encountered in construction projects, such as dams, tunnels, and large buildings. Studies fossil plants and animals to determine their evolutionary sequence and age. Prepares geologic reports and maps, interprets research data, and recommends further study or action. (061)

GRAPHIC DESIGNER: Designs art and copy layouts for material to be presented by visual communications media, such as books, magazines, newspapers, television, and packaging: Studies illustrations and photographs to plan presentation of material, product, or service. Determines size and arrangement of illustrative material and copy, selects style and size of type, and arranges layout based upon available space, knowledge of layout principles, and esthetic design concepts. Draws sample of finished layout and presents to ART DIRECTOR for approval. Prepares notes and instructions for workers who assemble and prepare final layouts for printing. Reviews final layout and suggests improvements as needed. May prepare illustrations or rough sketches of material according to instructions of client or supervisor. May prepare series of drawings to illustrate sequence and timing of story development for television production. May mark up, paste up, and assemble final layouts to prepare layouts for printer. May specialize in particular field, medium, or type of layout. (061)

GROUNDSKEEPER: Maintains grounds of industrial, commercial, or public property, performing combination of following tasks: Cuts lawns, using hand mower or power mower. Trims and edges around walks, flower beds, and walls, using clippers and edging tools. Prunes shrubs and trees to shape and improve growth, using shears. Sprays lawn, shrubs, and trees with fertilizer or insecticide. Rakes and burns leaves and cleans or sweeps up litter, using spiked stick or broom. Shovels snow from walks and driveways. Spreads salt on public passage ways. Plants grass, flowers, trees, and shrubs. Waters lawn and shrubs during dry periods, using hose or by activating fixed or portable sprinkler system. Repairs fences, gates, walls, and walks, using carpentry and masonry tools. Paints fences and outbuildings. Cleans out drainage ditches and culverts, using shovel and rake. Depending on size and nature of employing establishment, uses tractor equipped with attachments, such as mowers, lime- or fertilizer-spreaders, and lawn roller. May perform variety of laboring duties, common to type of employing establishment, when yard work is completed. (684)

GROUP WORKER: Organizes and leads groups, such as senior citizens, children, and street gangs, in activities that meet interests of individual members: Develops recreational, physical education, and cultural programs for various age groups. Demonstrates and instructs participants in activities, such as active sports, group dances and games, arts, crafts, and dramatics. Organizes current-events discussion groups, conducts consumer problem surveys, and performs similar activities to stimulate interest in civic responsibility. Promotes group work concept of enabling members to develop their own program activities through encouragement and leadership of membership discussions. Consults with other community resources regarding specific individuals, and makes referral when indicated. Keeps records. May recruit, train, and supervise paid staff and volunteers. Employed in settings such as community center, neighborhood or settlement house, hospital, institution for children or aged, youth centers, and housing projects. (164)

213

GUARD, SECURITY: Guards industrial or commercial property against fire, theft, vandalism, and illegal entry, performing any combination of the following duties: Patrols, periodically, buildings and grounds of industrial plant or commercial establishment, docks, logging camp area, or worksite. Examines doors, windows, and gates to determine that they are secure. Warns violators of rule infractions, such as loitering, smoking, or carrying forbidden articles, and apprehends or expels miscreants. Inspects equipment and machinery to ascertain if tampering has occurred. Watches for and reports irregularities, such as fire hazards, leaking water pipes, and security doors left unlocked. Observes departing personnel to guard against theft of company property. Sounds alarm or calls police or fire department by telephone in case of fire or presence of unauthorized persons. Permits authorized persons to enter property. (667)

GUIDE: Arranges transportation and other accommodations for groups of tourists, following planned itinerary, and escorts groups during entire trip, within single area or at specified stopping points of tour: Makes reservations on ships, trains, and other modes of transportation, and arranges for other accommodations, such as baggage handling, dining and lodging facilities, and recreational activities, using communication media, such as cable, telegraph, or telephone. Accompanies tour group and describes points of interest. May assist tourists to plan itinerary, obtain travel certificates, such as visas, passports, and health certificates, and convert currency into travelers' checks or foreign moneys. (167)

HAIR STYLIST: Specializes in dressing hair according to latest style, period, or character portrayal, following instructions of patron or script: Questions patron or reads instructions of MAKE-UP ARTIST or script to determine hairdressing requirements. Studies facial features of patron or performing artist and arranges, shapes, and trims hair to achieve desired effect, using fingers, combs, barber scissors, hair-waving solutions, hairpins, and other accessories. Dyes, tints, bleaches, or curls or waves hair as required. May create new style especially for patron. May clean and style wigs. (271)

HEALTH OFFICER: Investigates reported cases of communicable diseases and advises exposed persons to obtain medical treatment and to prevent further spread of disease: Locates and interviews exposed person, using information obtained from records of state or local public health departments and from individual already under treatment for communicable disease. Advises person to obtain treatment from private physician or public health clinic. May take blood sample to assist in identifying presence of disease in suspected victim. Questions exposed person to obtain information concerning other persons who may have received exposure. Conducts follow-up interviews with patients and suspected carriers. Writes report of activities and findings. Visits physicians, laboratories, and community health facilities to stimulate reporting of cases and to provide information about government-sponsored health programs concerning immunization efforts, VD control, mosquito abatement, and rodent control. (167)

HOME ATTENDANT: Cares for elderly, convalescent, or handicapped persons in patient's home, performing any combination of the following tasks: Changes bed linens, washes and irons patient's laundry, and cleans patient's quarters. Purchases, prepares, and serves food for patient and other members of family, following special prescribed diets. Assists patients into and out of bed, automobile, or wheelchair, to lavatory, and up and down stairs. Assists patient to dress, bathe, and groom self. Massages patient and applies preparations and treatments, such as liniment or alcohol rubs and heat-lamp stimulation. Administers prescribed oral medications under written direction of physician or as directed by home care nurse. Accompanies ambulatory patients outside home, serving as guide, companion, and aide. Entertains patient, reads aloud, and plays cards or other games with patient. Performs variety of miscellaneous duties as requested, such as obtaining household supplies and running errands. May maintain records of services performed and of apparent condition of patient. May visit several households to provide daily health care to patients. (377)

HOME ECONOMIST: Organizes and conducts consumer education service or research program for equipment, food, textile, or utility company, utilizing principles of home economics: Advises homemakers in selection and utilization of household equipment, food, and clothing, and interprets homemakers' needs to manufacturers of household products. Writes advertising copy and articles of interest to homemakers, tests recipes, equipment, and new household products, conducts radio and television homemakers' programs, and performs other public relations and promotion work for business firms, newspapers, magazines, and radio and television stations. Advises individuals and families on home management practices, such as budget planning, meal preparation, and energy conservation. Teaches improved homemaking practices to homemakers and youths through educational programs, demonstrations, discussions, and home visits. May engage in research in government, private industry, and colleges and universities to explore family relations or child development, develop new products for home, discover facts on food nutrition, and test serviceability of new materials. (121)

HOST/HOSTESS, RESTAURANT: Supervises and coordinates activities of dining room personnel to provide fast and courteous service to patrons: Schedules dining reservations and arranges parties or special services for diners. Greets guests, escorts them to tables, and provides menus. Adjusts complaints of patrons. Assigns work tasks and coordinates activities of dining room personnel to insure prompt and courteous service to patrons. Inspects dining room serving stations for neatness and cleanliness, and requisitions table linens and other dining room supplies for tables and serving stations. May interview, hire and discharge dining room personnel. May train dining room employees. May schedule work hours and keep time records of dining room workers. May assist in planning menus. May act as [CASHIER]. (137)

HOTEL CLERK: Performs any combination of following duties for guests of hotel, motel, motor lodge, or condominium-hotel: Registers and assigns rooms to guests. Issues room key and escort instructions to BELLHOP. Date-stamps, sorts, and racks incoming mail and messages. Transmits and receives messages, using equipment, such as telegraph, telephone, Teletype, and switchboard. Answers inquiries pertaining to hotel services; registration of guests; and shopping, dining, entertainment, and travel directions. Keeps records of room availability and guests' accounts. Computes bill, collects payment, and makes change for guests. Makes and confirms reservations. May sell tobacco, candy, and newspapers. May post charges, such as room, food, liquor, or telephone, to cashbooks, by hand or by machine. May make restaurant, transportation, or entertainment reservation, and arrange for tours. May deposit guest's valuables in hotel safe or safe-deposit box. May order complimentary flowers or champagne for honeymoon couples or special guests. May rent dock space at marina hotel. (362)

HOUSE CLEANER: Performs any combination of the following tasks to maintain hotel premises in clean and orderly manner: Moves and arranges furniture. Turns mattresses. Hangs draperies. Dusts venetian blinds. Polishes metalwork. Prepares sample rooms for sales meetings. Arranges decorations, apparatus, or furniture for banquets and social functions. Collects soiled linens for laundering, and receives and stores linen supplies in linen closet. Performs other duties as described under CLEANER. May deliver television sets, ironing boards, baby cribs, and roll-away beds to guests rooms. May clean swimming pool with vacuum. May remove debris. May clean driveway and garage areas. (687)

HOUSE WORKER, GENERAL: Performs any combination of the following duties in keeping private home clean and orderly, in cooking and serving meals, and in rendering personal services to family members: Plans meals and purchases foodstuffs and household supplies. Prepares and cooks vegetables, meats, and other foods according to employer's instructions or following own methods. Serves meals and refreshments. Washes dishes and cleans silverware. Oversees activities of children, assisting them in dressing and bathing. Cleans furnishings, floors, and windows, using vacuum cleaner, mops, broom, cloths, and cleaning solutions. Changes linens and makes beds. Washes linens and other garments by hand or machine, and mends and irons clothing, linens, and other household articles, using hand iron or electric ironer. Performs additional duties, such as answering telephone and doorbell, and feeding pets. Is usually only worker employed. (474)

IMPORT-EXPORT AGENT: Coordinates activities of international traffic division of import-export agency and negotiates settlements between foreign and domestic shippers: Plans and directs flow of air and surface traffic moving to overseas destinations. Supervises workers engaged in receiving and shipping freight, documentation, waybilling, assessing charges, and collecting fees for shipments. Negotiates with domestic customers, as intermediary for foreign customers, to resolve problems and arrive at mutual agreements. Negotiates with foreign shipping interests to contract for reciprocal freight-handling agreements. May examine invoices and shipping manifests for conformity to tariff and customs regulations. May contact customs officials to effect release of incoming freight and resolve customs delays. May prepare reports of transactions to facilitate billing of shippers and foreign carriers. (117)

INFORMATION SCIENTIST: Designs information system to provide management or clients with specific data from computer storage, utilizing knowledge of electronic data processing principles, mathematics, and computer capabilities: Develops and designs methods and procedures for collecting, organizing, interpreting, and classifying information for input into computer and retrieval of specific information from computer, utilizing knowledge of symbolic language and optical or pattern recognition principles. Develops alternate designs to resolve problems in input, storage, and retrieval of information. May specialize in specific field of information science, such as scientific or engineering research, or in specific discipline, such as business, medicine, education, aerospace, or library science. (067)

INTERIOR DESIGNER: Plans, designs, and furnishes interior environments of residential, commercial, and industrial buildings: Confers with client to determine architectural preferences, purpose and function of environment, budget, types of construction, equipment to be installed, and other factors which affect planning, interior environments. Integrates findings with knowledge of interior design and formulates environmental plan to be practical, esthetic, and conducive to intended purposes, such as raising productivity, selling merchandise, or improving life style of occupants. Advises client on interior design factors, such as space planning, layout and utilization of furnishings and equipment, color schemes, and color coordination. Renders design ideas in form of paste ups, drawings, or illustrations, estimates material requirements and costs, and presents design to client for approval. Selects or designs and purchases furnishings, art works, and accessories. Subcontracts fabrication, installation, and arrangement of carpeting, fixtures, accessories, draperies, paint and wall coverings, art work, furniture, and related items. May plan and design interior environments for boats, planes, buses, trains, and other enclosed spaces. May specialize in particular field, style, or phase of interior design. (051)

JANITOR: Keeps hotel, office building, apartment house, or similar building in clean and orderly condition and tends furnace, air conditioner, and boiler to provide heat, cool air, and hot water for tenants, performing any combination of following duties: Sweeps and mops or scrubs hallways and stairs. Regulates flow of fuel into automatic furnace or shovels coal into hand-fired furnace. Empties tenants' trash and garbage containers. Maintains building, performing minor and routine painting, plumbing, electrical wiring, and other related maintenance activities, using handtools. Replaces air conditioner filters. Cautions tenants regarding complaints about excessive noise, disorderly conduct, or misuse of property. Notifies management concerning need for major repairs or additions to lighting, heating, and ventilating equipment. Cleans snow and debris from sidewalk. Mows lawn, trims shrubbery, and cultivates flowers, using handtools and power tools. Posts signs to advertise vacancies and shows empty apartments to prospective tenants. (664)

KEYPUNCH OPERATOR: Operates alphabetic and numeric keypunch machine, similar in operation to electric typewriter, to transcribe data from source material onto punchcards, paper or magnetic tape, or magnetic cards, and to record accounting or statistical data for subsequent processing by automatic or electronic data processing equipment: Attaches skip bar to machine and previously punched program card around machine drum to control duplication and spacing of constant data. Loads machine with decks of tabulating punchcards, paper or magnetic tape, or magnetic cards. Moves switches and depresses keys to select automatic or manual duplication and spacing, select alphabetic or numeric punching, and transfer cards or tape through machine stations. Depresses keys to transcribe new data in prescribed sequence from source material into perforations on card, or as magnetic impulses on specified locations on tape or card. Inserts previously processed card into card gage to verify registration of punches. Observes machine to detect faulty feeding, positioning, ejecting, duplicating, skipping, punching, or other mechanical malfunctions and notifies supervisor. Removes jammed cards, using prying knife. May tend machines that automatically sort, merge, or match punchcards into specified groups. (582)

LABORATORY TESTER: Performs laboratory tests according to prescribed standards to determine chemical and physical characteristics or composition of solid, liquid, or gaseous materials and substances for purposes such as quality control, process control, product development, or determining conformity to specifications: Sets up, adjusts and operates laboratory equipment and instrumentation, such as microscopes, centrifuge, agitators, viscosimeter, chemical balance scales, spectrophotometer, colorimeter, and other equipment. Tests liquids and materials used as ingredients in adhesives, cement, propellants, lubricants, refractories, synthetic rubber, plastics, paint, paper, cloth, and other products for such qualities as purity, stability, viscosity, density, absorption, burning rate, and melting or flash point. Tests solutions used in processes, such as anodizing, waterproofing, cleaning, bleaching, and pickling, for chemical strength, specific gravity, or other specification. Tests materials for presence and content of elements or substances, such as hydrocarbons, manganese, natural grease, tungsten, sulfur, cyanide, ash, or dust, or other impurities. Tests samples of manufactured products to verify conformity to specifications. Records tests results on standardized forms and writes test reports describing procedures used. May prepare graphs and charts. Cleans and sterilizes laboratory equipment. May prepare chemical solutions according to standard formulas. May add chemicals or raw materials to process solutions or product batches to correct deviations from specifications. (261)

LABORER, GENERAL, MACHINE: Performs any combination of following tasks to assist in machine shop activities: Loads and unloads materials, parts, or products onto or from pallets, skids, conveyors, or trucks manually or using hoist. Delivers metal parts or stock to designated work areas for machining, using electric pallet mover, hoist, or overhead crane. Lifts metal part or stock onto machine, manually or using hoist, and secures it on machine table, in chuck, or holding fixture, using wrenches, to assist in setting up machine. Feeds metal parts or stock into automatic metal working machines and removes machined part from machine after prescribed period of time or at end of machining cycle. Adds coolant to reservoirs of machines and lubricates machine parts and ways, using grease gun and oilcan. Reclaims cutting and lubricating oils from machines by pumping oil from machine reservoir into barrel, dumping oil from barrel into centrifugal separator that removes metal chips and dirt from oil, and drains clean oil from separator into containers. Removes metal chips and shavings from surfaces of machines, using rag or airhose, and wipes surfaces of machines with rag to remove excess oil. Cleans around work areas, using broom and shovel. Separates metal shavings, chips, and scrap materials from trash and places them in bins for resale. May remove burs or excess metal from machined parts, using files, sandpaper, emery cloth, or grinding machine. (684)

LABORER, PETROLEUM REFINERY: Performs any combination of following tasks in refinery: Digs ditches, builds dikes and levees, and fills holes with earth, rock, sand, and asphalt gravels, using pick and shovel. Smooths ground surfaces and roadways, using hand tamper. Cleans refining equipment. Removes debris from roadways and work areas, and sprays and hoes weeds. Shovels sand and gravel off vehicles and dumps or shovels cement and sand into mixers. Mixes and pours cement and transports cement to forms with wheelbarrow. Unloads materials, such as tools, equipment, sacks of cement, sand, catalyst, salt, and lime, and oil barrels from freight cars and trucks, manually or with handtruck; and stacks barrels and sacks for storage. Uncrates equipment and parts, such as fractionating or treating towers and bubble trays, using pry bar and hammer, and installs bubble caps, using wrenches. Rips open sacks and dumps chemicals and catalysts into mixing, treating, or storage tanks. Dopes pipelines to prevent corrosion, using doping pot and tar. Changes hoist cables, and rigs chain hoists, rope blocks, power winches, and gin poles used to move or raise equipment. Skims-oil from cooling water in water boxes. (687)

LABORER, STORES: Performs any combination of following tasks to receive, store, and distribute material, tools, equipment, and products within establishments: Reads production schedule, customer order, work order, shipping order or requisition to determine items to be moved, gathered, or distributed. Conveys materials and items from receiving or production areas to storage or to other designated areas by hand, handtruck, or electric handtruck. Sorts and places materials or items on racks, shelves, or in bins according to predetermined sequence, such as size, type, style, color, or product code. Sorts and stores perishable goods in refrigerated rooms. Fills requisitions, work orders, or requests for materials, tools, or other stock items and distributes items to production workers or assembly line. Assembles customer orders from stock and places orders on pallets or shelves, or conveys orders to packing station or shipping department. Marks materials with identifying information, using stencil, crayon, or other marking device. Opens bales, crates, and other containers, using handtools. Records amounts of materials or items received or distributed. Weighs or counts items for distribution within plant to insure conformance to company standards. Arranges stock parts in specified sequence for assembly by other workers. May prepare parcels for mailing. May maintain inventory records. (687)

LANDSCAPE GARDENER: Plans and executes small-scale landscaping operations and maintains grounds and landscape of private and business residences: Participates with LABORER, LANDSCAPE in preparing and grading terrain, applying fertilizers, seeding and sodding lawns, and transplanting shrubs and plants, using manual and power-operated equipment. Plans lawns, and plants and cultivates them, using gardening implements and power-operated equipment. Plants new and repairs established lawns, using seed mixtures and fertilizers recommended for particular soil type and lawn location. Locates and plants shrubs, trees, and flowers selected by property owner or those recommended for particular landscape effect. Mows and trims lawns, using hand mower or power mower. Trims shrubs and cultivates gardens. Cleans grounds, using rakes, brooms, and hose. Sprays trees and shrubs, and applies supplemental liquid and dry nutrients to lawn and trees. May dig trenches and install drain tiles. May make repairs to concrete and asphalt walks and driveways. (161)

LAUNDRY OPERATOR: Receives, marks, washes, finishes, checks, and wraps articles in laundry performing any combination of following tasks: Classifies and marks incoming laundry with identifying code number, by hand or using machine. Tends washing machine, extractor, and tumbler to clean and dry laundry. Finishes laundered articles, using hand iron, pressing machine, or feeds and folds flatwork on flatwork ironing machine. Sorts laundry and verifies count on laundry ticket. May perform related tasks, such as mending torn articles, using sewing machine or by affixing adhesive patches. May wrap articles. (684)

LAWYER: Conducts criminal and civil lawsuits, draws up legal documents, advises clients as to legal rights, and practices other phases of law: Gathers evidence in divorce, civil, criminal, and other cases to formulate defense or to initiate legal action. Represents client in court, and before quasi-judicial or administrative agencies of government. May act as trustee, guardian, or executor. May teach college courses in law. May specialize in particular phase of law. (107)

LEGAL SECRETARY: Prepares legal papers and correspondence of legal nature, such as summonses, complaints, motions, and subpoenas. May review law journals and other legal publications to identify court decisions peritnent to pending cases and submit articles to company officials. (362)

LIBRARIAN: Maintains library collections of books, serial publications, documents, audiovisual, and other materials, and assists groups and individuals in locating and obtaining materials: Furnishes information on library activities, facilities, rules, and services. Explains and assists in use of reference sources, such as card or book catalog or book and periodical indexes to locate information. Describes or demonstrates procedures for searching catalog files. Searches catalog files and shelves to locate information. Issues and receives materials for circulation or for use in library. Assembles and arranges displays of books and other library materials. Maintains reference and circulation materials. Answers correspondence on special reference subjects. May compile list of library materials according to subject or interests. May select, order, catalog, and classify materials. (127)

LIBRARY ASSISTANT: Compiles records, sorts and shelves books, and issues and receives library materials, such as books, films, and phonograph records: Records identifying data and due date on cards by hand or using photographic equipment to issue books to patrons. Inspects returned books for damage, verifies due-date, and computes and receives overdue fines. Reviews records to compile list of overdue books and issues overdue notices to borrowers. Sorts books, publications, and other items according to classification code and returns them to shelves, files, or other designated storage area. Locates books and publications for patrons. Issues borrower's identification card according to established procedures. Files cards in catalog drawers according to system. Repairs books, using mending tape and paste and brush. Answers inquiries of nonprofessional nature on telephone and in person and refers persons requiring professional assistance to LIBRARIAN. (367)

LITERARY AGENT: Markets clients' manuscripts to editors, publishers, and other buyers: Reads and appraises manuscripts and suggests revisions. Contacts prospective purchaser of material, basing selection upon knowledge of market and specific content of manuscript. Negotiates contract between publisher and client. Usually works on commission basis. (117)

LOAN OFFICER: Examines, evaluates, authorizes or recommends approval of customer applications for lines or extension of lines of credit, commercial loans, real estate loans, consumer credit loans, or credit card accounts: Reviews loan application for completeness. Analyzes applicant's financial status, credit, and property evaluation to determine feasibility of granting loan request. Corresponds with or interviews applicant or creditors to resolve questions regarding application. Approves loan within specified limits or refers loan to loan committee for approval. Completes loan agreement on accepted loans. May supervise loan personnel. May handle foreclosure proceedings. May analyze potential loan markets to develop prospects for loans. May buy and sell contracts, loans, or real estate by negotiating terms of transaction and drawing up requisite documents. May be designated according to type of loan concerned with as MORTGAGE-LOAN OFFICER. May solicit and negotiate conventional or government backed loans on commission basis and be known as MORTGAGE-LOAN AGENT. (267)

LOCKER-ROOM ATTENDANT: Assigns dressing room facilities, locker space or clothing containers, and supplies to patrons of athletic or bathing establishment: Issues dressing room or locker key. Receives patron's clothing-filled container, furnishes claim check, places container on storage shelf or rack, and returns container upon receipt of claim check. Issues athletic equipment, bathing suit, or supplies, such as soap and towels. May arrange for valet services, such as clothes pressing and shoeshining. May collect soiled linen and perform cleaning tasks, such as mopping dressing room floors and washing shower room walls. May collect fees for use of facilities, equipment, or supplies. May pack athletic uniforms and equipment for individual or team out-of-town sporting events. (677)

MACHINE REPAIRER, MAINTENANCE: Repairs and maintains, according to blueprints and other specifications, production machinery and equipment, such as lathes, drill presses, and broaching, milling, and screw machines, using handtools, power tools, and precision-measuring instruments: Inspects and listens to sounds of machines and equipment to locate causes of trouble. Dismantles machines and equipment, relines spindles, adjusts clutches, replaces worn bearing and other parts, and repairs defective parts, using handtools. Measures, cuts, threads, and replaces air and waterlines, using handtools. Assembles machines and equipment and starts them to test their operations. May repair broken parts, using brazing, soldering, and welding equipment. May set up and operate metalworking tools, such as lathe, drill press, or grinder, to make and repair parts. (281)

MACHINIST: Sets up and operates machine tools, and fits and assembles parts to make or repair metal parts, mechanisms, tools, or machines, applying knowledge of mechanics, shop mathematics, metal properties, and layout and machining procedures: Studies specifications, such as blueprint, sketch, damaged part, or description of part to be replaced, to determine dimensions and tolerances of piece to be machined, sequence of operations, and tools, materials, and machines required. Measures, marks, and scribes dimensions and reference points to lay out stock for machining. Sets up and operates metal-removing machines, such as lathe, milling machine, shaper, or grinder, to machine parts to specifications. Verifies conformance of workpiece to specifications, using measuring instruments. Positions and secures workpiece in holding device, such as chuck or collet, or on surface plate or worktable with such devices as vises, V-blocks, and angle plates, and uses handtools, such as files, scrapers, and wrenches, to fit and assemble parts to assemblies or mechanisms. Verifies dimensions and alinement with measuring instruments, such as micrometers, height gages, and gage blocks. May operate mechanism or machine, observe operation, or test with inspection equipment, to diagnose malfunction of machine or to test repaired machine. May perform flame cutting and arc or gas welding operations, when required. May develop specifications from general description and draw or sketch product to be made. (280)

MAIL CARRIER: Sorts mail for delivery and delivers mail on established route: Inserts mail into slots of mail rack to sort for delivery. Delivers mail to residences and business establishments along route. Completes delivery forms, collects charges, and obtains signature on receipts, for delivery of specified types of mail. Enters changes of address in route book and readdresses mail to be forwarded. (367)

MAIL CLERK: Sorts incoming mail for distribution and dispatches outgoing mail: Opens envelopes by hand or machine. Stamps date and time of receipt on incoming mail. Sorts mail according to destination and type, such as returned letters, adjustments, bills, orders, and payments. Readdresses undeliverable mail bearing imcomplete or incorrect address. Examines outgoing mail for appearance and seals envelopes by hand or machine. Stamps outgoing mail by hand or with postage meter. May fold letters or circulars and insert into envelopes. May distribute and collect mail. May weigh mail to determine that postage is correct. May keep record of registered mail. May address mail, using addressing machine. (587)

MAINTENANCE MACHINIST: Sets up and operates variety of machine tools, and fits and assembles parts to fabricate or repair machine tools and maintain industrial machines, applying knowledge of mechanics, shop mathematics, metal properties, layout, and machining procedures: Observes and listens to operating machines or equipment to diagnose malfunction and determine need for adjustment or repair. Studies blueprint, sketch, machine part, or specifications to determine type and dimensions of metal stock required. Measures, marks, and scribes dimensions and reference points on metal stock surfaces, using such measuring and marking devices as calibrated ruler, micrometer, caliper, and scriber. Dismantles machine or equipment, using handtools, such as wrench and screwdriver, to examine parts for defect or to remove defective part. Substitutes new part or repairs or reproduces part from various kinds of metal stock, using handtools, such as scraper, file, and drill, and machine tools, such as lathe, milling machine, shaper, borer, and grinder. Assembles and starts machine to verify correction of malfunction. Maintains and lubricates machine tools and equipment, using handtools, ladder, and lubricants. May weld broken structural parts, using arc or gas welding equipment. May repair or replace faulty wiring, switches, or relays. (280)

MAINTENANCE MECHANIC: Repairs and maintains, in accordance with diagrams, sketches, operation manuals, and manufacturer's specifications, machinery and mechanical equipment, such as engines, motors, pneumatic tools, conveyor systems, and production machines and equipment, using handtools, power tools, and precision-measuring and testing instrument: Observes mechanical devices in operation and listens to their sounds to locate causes of trouble. Dismantles devices to gain access to and remove defective parts, using hoists, cranes, handtools, and power tools. Examines form and texture of parts to detect imperfections. Inspects used parts to determine changes in dimensional requirements, using rules, calipers, micrometers, and other measuring instruments. Adjusts functional parts of devices and control instruments, using handtools, levels, plumb bobs, and straightedges. Repairs or replaces defective parts, using handtools and power tools. Installs special functional and structural parts in devices, using handtools. Starts devices to test their performance. Lubricates and cleans parts. May set up and operate lathe, drill press, grinder, and other metalworking tools to make and repair parts. May initiate purchase order for parts and machines. May repair electrical equipment. (281)

MAINTENANCE MECHANIC, TELEPHONE: Installs, tests, and repairs communication equipment, such as public address and intercommunication systems, wired burglar alarms, switchboards, telegraphs, telephones, and related apparatus, including coin collectors, telephone booths, and switching keys, using schematic diagrams, testing devices, and handtools: Installs equipment according to layout plans and connects units with inside and outside service wires. Maintains equipment and analyzes operational malfunctioning with testing devices, such as oscilloscopes, generators, meters, and electric bridges to locate and diagnose nature of defect, and ascertain repairs to be made. Examines mechanism and disassembles components to replace, clean, adjust or repair parts, wires, switches, relays, circuits, or signaling units, using handtools. Operates and tests equipment to insure elimination of malfunction. May climb poles to install or repair outside service lines. May repair cables, lay out plans for new equipment, and estimate material required. (281)

MANAGEMENT TRAINEE: Performs assigned duties, under close direction of experienced personnel, to gain knowledge and experience required for promotion to management positions: Receives training and performs duties in departments, such as credit, customer relations, accounting, or sales to become familiar with line and staff functions and operations and management viewpoints and policies that affect each phase of business. Observes and studies techniques and traits of experienced workers in order to acquire knowledge of methods, procedures, and standards required for performance of departmental duties. Workers are usually trained in functions and operations of related or allied departments to facilitate transferability between departments and to provide greater promotional opportunities. (167)

MANAGER, CUSTOMER SERVICES: Directs and coordinates customer service activities of establishment to install, service, maintain, and repair durable goods, such as machines, equipment, major appliances, or other items sold, leased, or rented with service contract or warranty: Reviews customer requests for service to ascertain cause for service request, type of malfunction, and customer address. Determines manhours, number of personnel, and parts and equipment required for service call, utilizing knowledge of product, typical malfunctions, and service procedures and practices. Prepares schedules for service personnel, assigns personnel to routes or to specific repair and maintenance work according to workers' knowledge, experience, and repair capabilities on specific types of products. Arranges for transportation of machines and equipment to customer's location for installation or from customer's location to shop for repairs that cannot be performed on premises. Keeps records of work hours and parts utilized, and work performed for each service call. Requisitions replacement parts and supplies. May contact service personnel over radio-telephone to obtain or give information and directions regarding service or installation activities. Workers are designated according to type of customer service managed or product serviced. (167)

MANAGER, DEPARTMENT: Directs and coordinates, through subordinate supervisory personnel, departmental activities and functions in commercial, industrial, or service establishment, utilizing knowledge of department functions and company policies, standards, and practices: Reviews and analyzes reports, records, and directives, and confers with supervisory personnel to obtain data required for planning department activities, such as new departmental commitments, status of work in progress, and problems encountered. Assigns, or delegates responsibility for specific work or functional activities and dissemination of policy to supervisory personnel. Gives work directions, resolves problems, prepares work schedules, and sets deadlines to insure completion of operational functions. Coordinates activities of department with inter-related activities of other departments to insure optimum efficiency and economy. Prepares reports and records on departmental activities for management. Evaluates current procedures and practices for accomplishing activities and functions of department to develop and implement alternate methods designed for improvement of work. Workers are designated according to department functions or activities or by type of department managed unless specifically described elsewhere. (167)

MANAGER, FAST FOOD: Manages franchised or independent fast food or wholesale prepared food establishment: Directs, coordinates, and participates in preparation of, and cooking, wrapping or packing types of food served or prepared by establishment, collecting of money from in-house or take-out customers, or assemblying food orders for wholesale customers. Coordinates activities of workers engaged in keeping business records, collecting and paying accounts, ordering or purchasing supplies, and delivery of foodstuffs to wholesale or retail customers. Interviews, hires, and trains personnel. May contact prospective wholesale customers, such as mobile food vendors, vending machine operators, bar and tavern owners, and institutional personnel, to promote sale of prepared foods, such as doughnuts, sandwiches, and specialty food items. May establish delivery routes and schedules for supplying wholesale customers. Workers are usually classified according to type or name of franchised establishment or type of prepared foodstuff retailed or wholesaled. (137)

MANAGER, HOTEL OR MOTEL: Manages hotel or motel to insure efficient and profitable operation: Establishes standards for personnel administration and performance, service to patrons, room rates, advertising, publicity, credit, food selection and service, and type of patronage to be solicited. Plans dining room, bar, and banquet operations. Allocates funds, authorizes expenditures, and assists in planning budgets for departments. Hires person-

225

nel. Delegates authority and assigns responsibilities to department heads. In small motels or hotels, processes reservations and adjusts guests' complaints. (117)

MANAGER, OFFICE: Coordinates activities of clerical personnel in establishment or organization: Analyzes and organizes office operations and procedures, such as typing, bookkeeping, preparation of payrolls, flow of correspondence, filing, requisition of supplies, and other clerical services. Evaluates office production, revises procedures, or devises new forms to improve efficiency of workflow. Establishes uniform correspondence procedures and style practices. Formulates procedures for systematic retention, protection, retrieval, transfer, and disposal of records. Plans office layouts and initiates cost reduction programs. Reviews clerical and personnel records to insure completeness, accuracy, and timeliness. Prepares activities reports for guidance of management. Prepares employee ratings and conducts employee benefit and insurance programs. Coordinates activities of various clerical departments or workers within department. (167)

MANAGER, RETAIL STORE: Manages retail store engaged in selling specific line of merchandise, as groceries, meat, liquor, apparel, jewelry, or furniture; related lines of merchandise, as radios, televisions, and household appliances; or general line of merchandise, performing following duties personally or supervising employees performing duties: Plans and prepares work schedules and assigns employees to specific duties. Formulates pricing policies on merchandise according to requirements for profitability of store operations. Coordinates sales promotion activities and prepares, or directs workers preparing, merchandise displays and advertising copy. Supervises employees engaged in, or performs, sales work, taking of inventories, reconciling cash with sales receipts, keeping operating records, or preparing daily record of transactions for ACCOUNTANT. Orders merchandise or prepares requisitions to replenish merchandise on hand. Insures compliance of employees with established security, sales, and record keeping procedures and practices. Workers managing retail stores are classified according to specific line of merchandise sold, as women's apparel or furniture; related lines of merchandise, as camera and photographic supplies, or gifts, novelties, and souvenirs; type of business, as mail order establishment or auto supply house; or general line of merchandise carried, as sporting goods, drugs and sundries, or variety store. (167)

MANUFACTURER'S SERVICE REPRESENTATIVE: Installs and repairs machinery or equipment in customer's establishment, following blueprints and manufacturer's instructions, and utilizing knowledge of mechanical, hydraulic, and electrical machinery: Consults with personnel in engineering department to resolve problems of machine design to avoid construction problems in customer's establishment. Studies blueprints and observes tryout of machine in manufacturer's plant to become familiar with machine operation. Operates machine through trial run at customer's establishment to insure that quality and rate of production meet specifications, and trains customer's personnel in adjusting, maintaining, and repairing machinery or equipment. Consults with customer about deviations of machine operation from original specifications and explains reasons for changes. Repairs or supervises repair of worn or defective machinery or equipment in customer's plant. May be designated according to type, size, or trade name of machines, tools, or equipment serviced. (261)

MANUFACTURING ENGINEER: Directs and coordinates manufacturing processes in industrial plant: Determines space requirements for various functions and plans or improves production methods including layout, production flow, tooling and production equipment, material, fabrication, assembly methods, and manpower requirements. Communicates with planning and design staffs concerning product design and tooling to assure efficient production methods. Estimates production times and determines optimum staffing for production schedules. Applies statistical methods to estimate future manufacturing requirements and potential. Approves or arranges approval for expenditures. Reports to management on manufacturing capacities, production schedules, and problems to facilitate decision-making. (167)

MARKET RESEARCH ANALYST: Researches market conditions in local, regional, or national area to determine potential sales of product or service: Establishes research methodology and designs format for data gathering, such as surveys, opinion polls, or questionaires. Examines and analyzes statistical data to forecast future marketing trends. Gathers data on competitors and analyzes prices, sales, and methods of marketing and distribution. Collects data on customer preferences and buying habits. Prepares reports and graphic illustrations of findings. (067)

MASSEUR/MASSEUSE: Massages customers and administers other body-conditioning treatments for hygienic or remedial purposes: Applies alcohol, lubricants, or other rubbing compounds. Massages body, using such techniques as kneading, rubbing, and stroking flesh, to stimulate blood circulation, relax contracted muscles, facilitate elimination of waste matter, or to relieve other conditions, using hands or vibrating equipment. Administers steam or dry heat, ultraviolet or infrared, or water treatments on request of customer or instructions of PHYSICIAN. May give directions to clients in activities, such as reducing or remedial exercises. May examine client and recommend body conditioning activities or treatments. May record treatments furnished to customers. (374)

MATERIAL COORDINATOR: Coordinates and expedites flow of material, parts, and assemblies within or between departments in accordance with production and shipping schedules or department supervisors' priorities: Reviews production schedules and confers with department supervisors to determine material required or overdue, and to locate material. Requisitions material and establishes delivery sequences to departments according to job order priorities and anticipated availability of material. Arranges for in-plant transfer of materials to meet production schedules. Arranges with department supervisors for repair and assembly of material and its transportation to various departments. Examines material delivered to production departments to verify if type specified. May monitor and control movement of material and parts along conveyor system, using remote-control panelboard. May compute amount of material needed for specific job orders, applying knowledge of product and manufacturing processes and using adding machine. May compile report of quantity and type of material on hand. May move or transport material from one department to another, using handtruck or industrial truck. May compile perpetual production records in order to locate material. (167)

MATERIAL HANDLER: Loads, unloads, and moves materials within or near plant, yard, or worksite, performing any combination of the following duties: Reads work order or follows oral instructions to ascertain materials or containers to be moved. Opens containers, using steel cutters, crowbar, clawhammer, or other handtools. Loads and unloads materials onto or from pallets, trays, racks, and shelves by hand. Loads materials into vehicles and installs strapping, bracing, or padding to prevent shifting or damage in transit, using handtools. Conveys materials to or from storage or worksites to designated area, using handtruck, electric dolly, wheelbarrow, or other device. Secures lifting attachments to materials and conveys load to destination, using hand-operated crane or hoist, or signals crane or hoisting operators to move load to destination. Counts, weighs, and records number of units of materials moved or handled on daily production sheet. Attaches identifying tags or labels to materials or marks information on cases, bales, or other containers. Loads truck. Stacks or assembles materials into bundles and bands bundles together, using banding machine and clincher. Clamps sections of portable conveyor together or places conveyor sections on blocks or boxes to facilitate movement of materials or products. Removes samples of materials, labels with identifying information, and takes samples to laboratory for analysis. Lifts heavy objects by hand or using power hoist, and cleans work area, machines, and equipment, using broom, rags, and cleaning compounds to assist machine operators. Makes simple adjustments or repairs, such as realining belts or replacing rollers, using handtools. Assembles crates to contain products, such as machines or vehicles, using handtools and precut lumber. Shovels loose materials such as sand, gravel, metals, plastics, or chemicals into machine hoppers or into vehicles and containers, such as wheelbarrows, scrap truck, or barrels. May occasionally operate industrial truck or electric hoist to assist in loading or moving materials and products. (687)

MECHANIC, FIELD AND SERVICE: Inspects, tests, and adjusts jet, prop jet, and propeller driven airplanes during and between test flights, following specifications: Opens engine throttle to full power and examines powerplant to detect excess vibration and leaks in engine parts, such as tubing connections and carburetors. Observes instruments to determine that factors, such as fuel and oil pressures, acceleration, and temperatures, meet specifications. Performs functional test of systems, such as landing gear and loors, rigging and controls, fuel, heating, ventilating, and pressurization, for conformance to specifications. Calibrates compasses and other directional equipment. Accompanies airplane on test and acceptance flights to make in-flight adjustments to controls. Records in log, during flights, work to be performed in shop or field to prepare airplane for delivery. Replaces malfunctioning parts, using handtools, portable power tools, precision measuring instruments, and testing equipment. Workers may specialize in testing specific systems, such as hydraulic, electrical power, and structural. (281)

MECHANICAL ENGINEER: Plans and designs mechanical or electromechanical products or systems, and directs and coordinates operation and repair activities: Designs products or systems, such as instruments, controls, engines, machines, and mechanical, thermal, hydraulic, or heat transfer systems, utilizing and applying knowledge of engineering principles [DESIGN ENGINEER, PRODUCTS]. Plans and directs engineering personnel in fabrication of test control apparatus, and equipment, and development of methods and procedures for testing products or systems [TEST ENGINEER]. Directs and coordinates construction and installation activities to insure conformance of products and systems with engineering design and customer specifications. Coordinates operation, maintenance, and repair activities to obtain optimum utilization of machines and systems. May evaluate field installations and recommend design modifications to eliminate malfunctions or changes in machine or system function. May specialize in one specific field of mechanical engineering discipline, such as heat transfer, hydraulics, electro-mechanics, controls and instrumentation, nuclear systems, tooling, air-conditioning and refrigeration; or in types of products, as machines, propulsion systems, machinery and mechanical equipment; or in type of work performed as steam or gas generation and distribution, steam plant engineering, or system planning. (061)

MEDICAL LABORATORY TECHNICIAN: Performs routine tests in medical laboratory for use in treatment and diagnosis of disease: Prepares tissue samples for PATHOLOGIST. Takes blood samples. Executes such laboratory tests as urinalysis and blood counts. Makes quantitative and qualitative chemical and biological analyses of body specimens, under supervision of MEDICAL TECHNOLOGIST or laboratory director. (381)

MEDICAL RECORD CLERK: Compiles, verifies, and files medical records of hospital or clinic patients and compiles statistics for use in reports and surveys: Prepares folders and maintains records of newly admitted patients. Reviews contents of patients' medical record folders, assembles into standard order, and files according to established procedure. Reviews inpatient and emergency room records to insure presence of required reports and PHYSICIANS' signatures, and routes incomplete records to appropriate personnel for completion or prepares reports of incomplete records to notify administration. Checks list of discharged patients to insure receipt of all current records. Compiles daily and periodic statistical data, such as admissions, discharges, deaths, births, and types of treatment rendered. Records diagnoses and treatments, including operations performed, for use in completing hospital insurance billing forms. May maintain death log. May type and process birth certificates. May assist other workers with coding of records. May make copies of medical records, using duplicating equipment. (362)

MEDICAL TECHNOLOGIST: Performs chemical, microscopic, serologic, hematologic, immunohematologic, parasitic, and bacteriologic tests to provide data for use in treatment and diagnosis of disease: Receives specimens for laboratory, or obtains such body materials as urine, blood, pus, and tissue directly from patient, and makes quantitative and qualitative chemical analyses. Cultivates, isolates, and identifies pathogenic bacteria, parasites, and other micro-organisms. Cuts, stains, and mounts tissue sections for study by PATHOLOGIST. Performs blood tests for transfusions, studies morphology of blood. Groups or types blood and cross-matches that of donor and recipient to ascertain compatibility. Engages in medical research to further control and cure disease. May calibrate and use equipment designed to measure glandular and other bodily activity. (361)

METALLURGIST, PHYSICAL: Investigates and conducts experiments concerned with physical characteristics, properties, and processing of metals to develop new alloys, applications, and methods of commercially fabricating products from metals: Conducts microscopic, X-ray, X-ray diffraction, and spectroscopic studies of metals and alloys, such as steel, cast iron, and nonferrous alloys, to determine their physical characteristics, such as crystal structure, dispersion of alloy particles through basic metal, and presence of impurities, fractures, and other defects in metal samples. Develops melting, hot-working, cold-working, and heat-treating processes to obtain desired characteristics, such as ductility, malleability, elongation ability, durability, and hardness. Tests alloys in tension, compression, impact, bending, or fatigue devices to study physical characteristics for manufacturing purposes or determine compliance with manufacturing specifications and standards. Consults with engineers and officials to develop methods of manufacturing alloys at minimum costs. May specialize in particular area of physical metallurgy, such as development of improved techniques and materials, for use in production of pressed metallic-powder products. (061)

METEOROLOGIST: Analyzes and interprets meteorological data gathered by surface and upper-air stations, satellites, and radar to prepare reports and forecasts for public and other users: Studies and interprets synoptic reports, maps, photographs, and prognostic charts to predict long and short range weather conditions. Issues weather information to media and other users over teletype machine or telephone. Prepares special forecasts and briefings for those involved in air and sea transportation, agriculture, fire prevention, and air-pollution control. Issues hurricane and severe storm warnings. May direct forecasting services at weather station. May conduct basic or applied research in meteorology. May establish and staff observation stations. (062)

MODEL: Models garments, such as dresses, coats, underclothing, swimwear, and suits, for garment designers, BUYERS, sales personnel, and customers: Dresses in sample or completed garments. Stands, turns, and walks to demonstrate features, such as garment quality, style, and design, to observers at fashion shows, private showings, and retail establishments. May inform prospective purchasers as to model, number, and price of garments and department where garment can be purchased. May select own accessories. May be designated according to size of garment modeled. May model for PHOTOGRAPHER. (667)

MOTION-PICTURE PROJECTIONIST: Sets up and operates motion picture projection and sound-reproducing equipment to produce coordinated effects on screen: Inserts film into top magazine reel of projector. Threads film through picture aperture of projector, around pressure rollers, sprocket wheels, and sound drum or magnetic sound pickup on film, and onto spool that automatically takes up film slack. Regulates projection light and adjusts sound-reproducing equipment. Monitors operation of machines and transfers operation from one machine to another without interrupting flow of action on screen. Rewinds broken end of film onto reels by hand to minimize loss of time. Inspects and rewinds projected films for another showing. Repairs faulty sections of film. Operates stereopticon (magic lantern) or other special-effects equipment to project picture slides on screen. Cleans lenses, oils equipment, and makes minor repairs and adjustments. (362)

MUSICIAN, INSTRUMENTAL: Plays musical instrument as soloist or as member of musical group, such as orchestra or band, to entertain audience: Studies and rehearses music to learn and interpret score. Plays from memory or by following score. May transpose music to play in alternate key. May improvise. May compose. May play instrument to signal activity, such as flag raising, post time, or arrival of dignitaries at sporting or other events. (041)

NURSE AIDE: Assists in care of hospital patients, under direction of nursing and medical staff: Answers signal lights and bells to determine patients' needs. Bathes, dresses, and undresses patients. Serves and collects food trays and feeds patients requiring help. Transports patients to treatment units, using wheelchair or wheeled carriage, or assists them to walk. Drapes patients for examinations and treatments, and remains with patients, performing such duties as holding instruments and adjusting lights. Dusts and cleans patients' rooms. Changes bed linen, runs errands, directs visitors, and answers telephone. Takes and records temperature, pulse and respiration rates, and food and liquid intake and output, as directed. May apply compresses and hot water bottles. May clean, sterilize, store, prepare, and issue dressing packs, treatment trays, and other supplies. May prepare patients for delivery and clean delivery room. May bathe, weigh, dress, and feed newborn babies. May clean, sterilize, and assemble into packs supplies and instruments used in surgery, and maintain cleanliness and order of operating rooms. (674)

NURSE, GENERAL DUTY: Renders general nursing care to patients in hospital, infirmary, sanitarium, or similar institution: Administers prescribed medications and treatments in accordance with approved nursing techniques. Prepares equipment and aids PHYSICIAN during treatments and examinations of patients. Observes patient, records significant conditions and reactions, and notifies supervisor or PHYSICIAN of patient's condition and reaction to drugs, treatments, and significant incidents. Takes temperature, pulse, blood pressure, and other vital signs to detect deviations from normal and determine progress of patient. May rotate among various clinical services of institution, such as obstetrics, surgery, orthopedics, outpatient and admitting, pediatrics, psychiatry, and tuberculosis. May prepare rooms, sterile instruments, equipment, and supplies, and handing, in order of use, to assist SURGEON or OBSTETRICIAN in operations and deliveries. May make beds, bathe and feed patients, and assist in their rehabilitation. May serve as leader for group of personnel rendering nursing care to number of patients. (374)

NURSE, LICENSED PRACTICAL: Cares for ill, injured, convalescent, and handicapped persons in hospitals, clinics, private homes, sanitariums, and similar institutions: Takes and records temperature, blood pressure, and pulse and respiration rate. Dresses wounds, gives enemas, douches, alcohol rubs, and massages. Applies compresses, ice bags, and hot water bottles. Observes patients and reports adverse reactions to medical personnel in charge. Administers specified medication, and notes time and amount on patients' charts. Assembles and uses such equipment as catheters, tracheotomy tubes, and oxygen suppliers. Performs routine laboratory work, such as urinalysis. Sterilizes equipment and supplies, using germicides, sterilizer, or autoclave. Prepares food trays and feeds patients. Records food and fluid intake and output. Bathes, dresses, and assists patients in walking and turning. Cleans rooms, makes beds, and answers patients' calls. Washes and dresses bodies of deceased persons. Must pass state board examination and be licensed. May assist in delivery, care, and feeding of infants. (374)

NURSE PRACTITIONER: Provides general medical care and treatment to assigned patients in facilities, such as clinics, health centers, or public health agency, working with PHYSICIAN: Performs physical examinations and preventive health measures within prescribed guidelines. Orders, interprets, and evaluates diagnostic tests to identify and assess patient's clinical problems and health care needs. Records physical findings, and formulates plan and prognosis, based on patient's condition. Discusses case with PHYSICIAN and other health professionals to assure observation of specified practice. Submits health care plan and goals of individual patients for periodic review and evaluation by PHYSICIAN. Recommends drugs or other forms of treatment, such as physical therapy, inhalation therapy, or related therapeutic procedures. May refer patients to PHYSICIAN for consultation or to specialized health resources for treatment. May determine when patient has recovered and release patient. Where state law permits, may engage in independent practice. (264)

OCCUPATIONAL THERAPIST: Plans, organizes, and conducts occupational therapy program in hospital, institution, or community setting to facilitate rehabilitation of mentally, physically, or emotionally handicapped: Plans program involving activities, such as manual arts and crafts, practice in function, prevocational, vocational, and homemaking skills and activities of daily living, and participation in sensorimotor, educational, recreational, and social activities designed to help patients regain physical or mental functioning or adjust to handicaps. Consults with other members of rehabilitation team to select activity program consistent with needs and capabilities of each patient and to coordinate occupational therapy with other therapeutic activities. Selects constructive activities suited to individuals physical capacity, intelligence level, and interest to upgrade patient to maximum independence, prepare patient for return to employment, assist in restoration of functions, and aid in adjustment to disability. Teaches patients skills and techniques required for participation in activities and evaluates patients' progress. Designs and constructs special equipment for patient and suggests adaptations of patient's work-living environment. Requisitions supplies and equipment. Lays out materials for patients' use and cleans and repairs tools at end of sessions. May conduct training programs or participate in training medical and nursing students and other workers in occupations therapy techniques and objectives. May design, make, and fit adaptive devices, such as splints and braces, following medical prescription. (121)

OFFICE-MACHINE SERVICER: Repairs and services office machines, such as adding, accounting, and calculating machines, and typewriters, using handtools, power tools, micrometers, and welding equipment: Operates machines to test moving parts and to listen to sounds of machines to locate causes of trouble. Disassembles machine and examines parts, such as gears, guides, rollers, and pinions for wear and defects, using micrometers. Repairs, adjusts, or replaces parts, using handtools, power tools, and soldering and welding equipment. Cleans and oils moving parts. May give instructions in operation and care of machines to machine operators. May assemble new machines. (281)

OPERATIONS-RESEARCH ANALYST: Conducts analyses of management and operational problems and formulates mathematical or simulation models of problem for solution by computers or other methods: Analyzes problem in terms of management information and conceptualizes and defines problem. Studies information and selects plan from competitive proposals that affords maximum probability of profit or effectiveness in relation to cost or risk. Prepares model of problem in form of one or several equations that relates constants and variables, restrictions, alternatives, conflicting objectives and their numerical parameters. Defines data requirements and gathers and validates information applying judgment and statistical tests. Specifies manipulative or computational methods to be applied to model. Performs validation and testing of model to insure adequacy, or determines need for reformulation. Prepares reports to management defining problem, evaluation, and possible solution. Evaluates implementation and effectiveness of research. May design, conduct, and evaluate experimental operational models where insufficient data exists to formulate model. May specialize in research and preparation of contract proposals specifying competence of organization to perform research, development, or production work. May develop and apply time and cost networks, such as Program Evaluation and Review Techniques (PERT), to plan and control large projects. May work in association with engineers, scientists, and management personnel in business, government, health, transportation, energy, manufacturing, environmental sciences, or other technologies. (067)

OPTOMETRIST: Examines eyes to determine visual efficiency and performance, diseases, or other abnormalities by means of instrumentation and observation, and prescribes corrective procedures: Conserves, improves, and corrects vision through use of lenses, prisms, vision therapy, visual training, and control of visual environment. Examines patients for visual pathology or ocular manifestations of systemic disease, and refers those with pathological conditions to medical practitioner for further diagnosis and treatment. May specialize in treatment of children with learning problems, vision of aged, rehabilitation of partially sighted, or environmental vision. May specialize in vision training, vision therapy, vision development, contact lenses, or low vision aids. May conduct research, instruct in college or university, act as consultant, or work in public health field. (101)

ORDERLY: Performs any combination of following duties, as directed by nursing and medical staff, to care for hospitalized patients: Bathes patients and gives alcohol rubs. Cleans and shaves hair from skin area of operative cases. Measures and records intake and output of liquids, and takes and records temperature, and pulse and respiration rate. Gives enemas. Carries meal trays to patients. Lifts patients onto and from bed, and transports patients to hospital areas, such as operating and X-ray rooms, by rolling bed, or using wheelchair or wheeled stretcher. Sets up equipment, such as oxygen tents, portable X-ray machines, and overhead irrigation bottles. Places anesthesia equipment near operating table, and assists in holding patient on table during administration of anesthetic. Sets up bone fracture equipment and assists PHYSICIAN in putting on casts and braces. Maintains supply of hospital clothing for attending PHYSICIANS. Makes beds and collects soiled linen. Cleans rooms and corridors. Bathes deceased patients, accompanies body to morgue, and places personal belongings in mortuary box. May administer catheterizations and bladder irrigations. May accompany discharged mental patients home, or those transferred to other institutions. (674)

PACKAGER, HAND: Packages materials and products manually, performing any combination of following duties: Cleans packaging containers. Lines and pads crates and assembles cartons. Obtains and sorts product. Wraps protective material around product. Starts, stops, and regulates speed of conveyor. Inserts or pours product into containers or fills containers from spout or chute. Weighs containers and adjusts quantity. Nails, glues, or closes and seals containers. Labels containers, container tags, or products.

Sorts bundles or filled containers. Packs special arrangements or selections of product. Inspects materials, products, and containers at each step of packaging process. Records information, such as weight, time, and date packaged. (587)

PACKAGER, MACHINE: Tends machine that performs one or more packaging functions, such as filling, marking, labeling, tying, packing, or wrapping containers: Starts machine and observes operation to detect malfunctions of machine. Stops machine and reports malfunction to supervisor. Makes minor adjustments or repairs, such as opening valves, changing forming and cutting dies, setting guides, or clearing away damaged products of containers. Inspects filled container to insure that product is packaged according to specifications. May feed product to conveyors, hoppers, or other feeding devices, and unload packaged product. May replenish packaging supplies, such as wrapping paper, plastic sheet, boxes, cartons, glue, ink, or labels. May mount supplies on spindles or place supplies in hopper or other feeding devices. May position and hold container in machine and press pedal or button or move lever to clean, glue, label, sew, or staple container. May cut stencils and stencil information on container, such as lot number or shipping destination. May tally number of units of product packaged or record information, such as size, weight, and type of products packaged. (685)

PACKER, AGRICULTURAL: Packs agricultural produce, such as bulbs, fruits, nuts, eggs, and vegetables, for storage or shipment, performing any combination of following duties: Lines box, barrel, basket, carton, or crate with treated paper, cardboard, excelsior, or prepared padding, or inserts paper trays or separators in container. Places rows of produce in layers in containers, and inserts excelsior, shredded cellophane, or paper trays after each layer and over top layer of produce, or scoops produce into container. Wraps produce in treated paper, foil, or plastic film wrap before placing produce in container. Packs exposed top layer of produce, arranging produce in successive rows in container. Positions basket liner upside down over ring of produce on pallet and fills basket liner with specified amount of produce. Places basket upside down over filled liner on pallet. Pushes basket and pallet over conveyor rollers onto table of turning frame, clamps basket and pallet in place, and moves lever to turn basket upright. Fits lid on container and nails, wires, or tapes in place. Stamps grade, brand, and date of packing on container. Washes and trims produce, such as lettuce and carrots, preparatory to packing, working in warehouse or on harvesting machine in the field. Sorts produce according to size, color, and grade before packing. (687)

PAINTER, ARTIST: Paints variety of original subject material, such as landscapes, portraits, still lifes, and abstracts, using watercolors, oils, acrylics, tempera, or other paint medium: Conceives and develops ideas for painting, based on assignment, personality, interests, and knowledge of painting methods and techniques. Applies color medium to canvas or other surface, using brushes, pallet knives, and various other artist's tools and equipment. Integrates and develops visual elements, such as line, space, mass, color, and perspective to produce desired effect. May make preliminary sketch of painting. May coat finished painting with varnish or other preservative. May paint in particular style, such as realism, impressionism, naturalism, or regionalism. May specialize in particular media, or subject material. (061)

PAINTER, CONSTRUCTION: Applies coats of paint, varnish, stain, enamel, or lacquer to decorate and protect interior or exterior surfaces, trimmings, and fixtures of buildings, and other structures: Smooths surfaces, using sandpaper, brushes, or steel wool and removes old paint from surfaces, using paint remover, scraper, wire brush, or blowtorch to prepare surfaces for painting. Fills nail holes, cracks, and joints with putty, plaster, or other filler. Selects premixed paints, or mixes required portions of pigment, oil, and thinning and drying substances to prepare paint that matches specified colors. Paints surfaces, using brushes, spray gun, or paint rollers. Simulates wood grain, marble, brick, or tile effects. Applies paint with cloth, brush, sponge, or fingers to create special effects. Erects scaffolding or sets up ladders to perform tasks above ground level. (381)

PAINTER, SIGN: Designs, lays out, and paints letters and designs to create signs, using measuring and drawing instruments, brushes, and handtools: Reads work orders to determine type of sign specified, work procedures, and materials required. Sketches design on paper, using drawing instruments, such as angles, rulers, and shading pencils. Lays out design on plastic, silk, or tin to prepare stencil, or on paper to draw *pounce I* pattern, using measuring and drawing instruments. Sketches or follows pattern to draw design or lettering onto objects, such as billboards and trucks, using stencils and measuring and drawing instruments. Brushes paint, lacquer, enamel, or japan over stencil, or paints details, background, and shading to fill in outline or sketch of sign. (381)

PAINTER, SPRAY: Sprays surfaces of machines, manufactured products, or working area with protective or decorative material, such as paint, enamel, glaze, *gel-coat*, or lacquer, using spray gun: Cleans grease and dirt from product, using materials, such as lacquer thinner, turpentine, soap, and water. Applies masking tape over parts and areas that are not to be coated [MASKER]. Fills cavities and dents with putty to attain smooth surface. Selects and mixes coating liquid to produce desired color, according to specifications, using paddle or mechanical mixer. Pours coating liquid into spray container and connects gun to airhose, using wrenches. Turns sprayer valves and nozzle to regulate width and pressure of spray, according to knowledge of painting technique. Pulls trigger and directs spray onto work surface to apply prime or finish coat. Coats areas inaccessible to hand sprayer, using brush. Cleans spraying equipment and brushes with solvent. May heat and spray wax onto products after they are tested. May use acid, wire brush, or steel wool to remove rust from metal. (684)

PARALEGAL: Researches law, investigates facts, and prepares documents to assist LAWYER: Researches and analyzes law sources such as statutes, decisions, legal articles, treaties, constitutions, and legal codes to prepare legal documents such as briefs, pleadings, appeals, wills, contracts, deeds, and trust instruments for review, approval, and use by attorney. Appraises and inventories real and personal property for estate planning. Investigates facts and law of case to determine causes of action and to prepare case accordingly. Files pleadings with court clerk. Prepares affidavits of documents and maintains document file. Delivers or directs delivery of subpoenas to witnesses and parties to action. May direct and coordinate activities of law office employees. May prepare office accounts and tax returns. May specialize in litigation, probate, real estate, or corporation law. May search patent files to ascertain originality of patent application and be designated PATENT CLERK. (267)

PAROLE OFFICER: Engages in activities related to conditional release of juvenile or adult offenders from correctional institutions: Establishes relationship with offenders and familiarizes self with offender's social history prior to and during institutionalization. Participates in formulation and development of release plan. Provides treatment supervision of offenders upon release by conducting a plan of regular treatment and interviews. Helps parolee to secure necessary education or employment and refers parolee to social resources of community that can aid in rehabilitation. Attempts to involve families of parolees in helping to solve problems of adjustment. Evaluates parolee's progress on follow-up basis. May return parolee to institution or secure appropriate remedial action by paroling authority where necessary. Employed by correctional institution or parole agency. Usually required to have knowledge and skill in casework methods acquired through degree program at school of social work. (167)

PERSONNEL CLERK: Compiles and keeps personnel records: Records data for each employee, such as address, weekly earnings, absences, amount of sales or production, supervisory reports on ability, and date of and reason for termination. Compiles and types reports from employment records. Files employment records. Searches employee files and furnishes information to authorized persons. May operate calculating machine. May administer and score aptitude, personality, and interest tests. May fill out and explain bonding application required by company. May prepare and file reports of accidents and injuries at industrial establishment and be designated as ACCIDENT-REPORT CLERK. (362)

PETROLEUM ENGINEER: Analyzes technical and cost factors to plan methods to recover maximum oil and gas in oil-field operations, utilizing knowledge of petroleum engineering and related technologies: Examines map of subsurface oil and gas reservoir locations to recommend placement of wells to maximize economical production from reservoir. Evaluates probable well production rate during natural or stimulated-flow production phases. Recommends supplementary processes to enhance recovery involving stimu-

237

lation of flow by use of processes, such as pressurizing or heating in subsurface regions. Analyzes recommendations of reservoir engineering specialist for placement of well in oil field. Develops well drilling plan for management approval, specifying factors including drilling time, number of special operations, such as directional drilling, and testing, and material requirements and costs including well casing and drilling muds. Provides technical consultation during drilling operations to resolve problems such as bore directional change, unsatisfactory drilling rate or invasion of subsurface water in well bore. Advises substitution of drilling mud compounds or tool bits to improve drilling conditions. Inspects well to determine that final casing and tubing installations are completed. Plans oil and gas field recovery containers, piping, and treatment vessels to receive, remove contaminants, and separate oil and gas products flowing from well. Monitors production rate of gas or oil from established wells and plans rework process to correct well production, such as repacking of well bore and additional perforation of subsurface sands adjacent to well bottom. (018)

PHARMACIST: Compounds and dispenses medications, following prescriptions issued by PHYSICIAN; DENTIST; or other authorized medical practitioner: Weighs, measures, and mixes drugs and other medicinal compounds, and fills bottles or capsules with correct quantity and composition of preparation. Dispenses nonprescription medication to public. Advises self-diagnosing and self-medicating patients, or provides information on potential drug interactions, potential adverse drug reactions, and elements of patient's history which might bear on prescribing decision when in advisory capacity to PHYSICIAN. Advises patient regarding storage for prescription medication. Assures that patient understands prescribed instructions. Answers patient's questions regarding prescription medication. Stores and preserves biologicals, vaccines, serums, and other drugs subject to deterioration, utilizing refrigeration and other methods. Orders and maintains supply of drugs, chemicals, and other pharmaceutical stock. Insures specified quantity and potency of materials for medical use. May act as consultant to civic groups and health practitioners on matters pertaining to pharmacy. May assay medications to determine identity, purity, and strength. (161)

PHOTOCOPYING-MACHINE OPERATOR: Tends duplicating machine to reproduce handwritten or typewritten matter: Places original copy on glass plate in machine. Places blank paper on loading tray. Sets control switch for number of copies. Presses button to start machine which transfers image of original copy onto blank paper by photographic and static electricity process. May clean and repair machine. May receive payment for duplicate copies. Important variables may be indicated by trade name of machine tended. (685)

PHOTOGRAPHER: Photographs subjects using still cameras, color or black-and-white film, and a variety of photographic accessories: Selects and assembles equipment according to subject material, anticipated conditions, and knowledge of function and limitations of various types of cameras, lenses, films, and accessories. Views subject and setting and plans composition, camera position, and camera angle to produce desired effect. Arranges subject material, poses subject, or maneuvers into position to take candid photo. Estimates or measures light level, using light meter or creates artificial lighting with flash units, lights, and lighting equipment. Adjusts lens aperture and shutter speed based on combination of factors, such as lighting, depth of field, subject motion, and film speed. Determines subject to lens distance, using tape measure, range finder, ground glass, or reflex viewing system to adjust focus. Positions camera and trips shutter to expose film. May calculate variables, such as exposure time, exposure interval, filter effect; and color temperature using tables, standard formulas, and mechanical or electronic measuring instruments. May make adjustments to camera, lens, or equipment to compensate for factors, such as distorted perspective and parallax. May be required to have detailed knowledge of use and characteristics of various types of film, including specialty films, such as infrared. May design, build, arrange, or secure properties and settings to be used as background for subject material. May direct activities of other workers. May mix chemicals, process film and photographic paper, and make contact and enlarged prints. May spot and retouch prints and negatives. May conceive and plan photographic sequence for effective presentation. May specialize in particular type of photography, such as illustrative, fashion, architectural, or portrait, and be designated accordingly. (062)

PHYSICAL THERAPIST: Plans and administers medically prescribed physical therapy treatment programs for patients to restore function, relieve pain, and prevent disability following disease, injury, or loss of body part, working at hospital, rehabilitation center, nursing home, home-health agency, or in private practice: Reviews and evaluates PHYSICIANS's referral (prescription) and patient's medical records to determine physical therapy treatment required. Performs patient tests, measurements, and evaluations, such as range-of-motion and manual-muscle tests, gait and functional analyses, and body-parts measurements, and records and evaluates findings to aid in establishing or revising specifics of treatment programs. Plans and prepares written treatment program based on evaluation of available patient data. Administers manual therapeutic exercises to improve or maintain muscle function, applying precise amounts of manual force and guiding patient's body parts through selective patterns and degrees of movement. Instructs, motivates, and assists patients in nonmanual exercises, such as active regimens, isometric, and progressive-resistive, and in functional activities, such as ambulation, transfer, and daily-living activities, using weights, pulleys, exercise machines, mats, steps, and inclined surfaces, and assistive and supportive devices, such as crutches, canes, parallel bars, orthoses, and prostheses. Administers treatments involving application of physical agents, such as light, heat, water, and electricity, using equipment such as hydrotherapy tanks and whirlpool baths, moist packs, ultraviolet and infrared lamps, low-voltage generators, and diathermy and ultrasound machines; evaluates effects of treatments at various intensities and durations and adjusts treatments to achieve maximum benefit. Administers massage, applying deep and superficial massage techniques. Administers traction to relieve neck and back pain, using intermittent and static traction equipment. Records patient treatment response, and progress. Instructs patient and family in physical therapy procedures to be continued at home. Evaluates, fits, and adjusts prosthetic and orthotic devices and recommends modifications to ORTHOTIST. Confers with PHYSICIAN and other health practitioners to obtain additional patient information, suggest revisions in treatment program, and integrate physical therapy treatment with other aspects of patient health care. (121)

PHYSICAL THERAPY AIDE: Prepares patients for physical therapy treatments, assists PHYSICAL THERAPIST or PHYSICAL THERAPIST ASSISTANT during administration of treatments, and administers routine treatments: Assists patients to dress, undress, and put on and remove assistive and supportive devices, such as braces, splints, and slings, prior to and after treatments. Secures patients into or onto therapy equipment. Supports, turns, and stabilizes patients to assist PHYSICAL THERAPIST (medical ser.) or PHYSICAL THERAPIST ASSISTANT (medical ser.) to administer treatments, tests, and evaluations. Administers routine treatments, such as hydrotherapy, hot and cold packs, and paraffin bath. Safeguards, motivates, and assists patients practicing exercises and functional activities. Observes patients during treatments and reports signs of fatigue, distress, or other problems. Transports patients to and from treatment area and transfers patients between conveyances and treatment equipment, using transfer techniques appropriate to patients' conditions. Changes linens and arranges treatment supplies and equipment according to standard procedure or written or oral instructions. Cleans work area and equipment after treatment. Prepares hydrotherapy equipment at appropriate temperature and adds disinfectant solutions. Performs miscellaneous clerical and related duties, such as answering telephone, taking messages, running errands, delivering messages, and filing patient records. May record treatment given and equipment used. May inventory and requisition supplies and equipment. May adjust fit of supportive and assistive devices for patients, as instructed. May be assigned to specific type of treatment or patient service and be designated PHYSICAL THERAPY AIDE, HYDROTHERAPY; PHYSICAL THERAPY AIDE, TRANSPORT. (354)

PHYSICIST: Conducts research into phases of physical phenomena, develops theories and laws on basis of observation and experiments, and devises methods to apply laws and theories of physics to industry, medicine, and other fields: Performs experiments with masers, lasers, cyclotrons, betatrons, telescopes, mass spectrometers, electron microscopes, and other equipment to observe structure and properties of matter, transformation and propagation of energy, relationships between matter and energy, and other physical phenomena. Describes and expresses observations and conclusions in mathematical terms. Devises procedures for physical testing of materials. Conducts instrumental analyses to determine physical properties of materials. May specialize in one or more branches of physics and be designated PHYSICIST, ACOUSTICS; PHYSICIST, ASTROPHYSICS; PHYSICIST, ATOMIC, ELECTRONIC AND MOLECULAR; PHYSICIST, CRYOGEN-

ICS; PHYSICIST, ELECTRICITY AND MAGNETISM; PHYSICIST, FLUIDS. Additional titles: PHYSICIST, LIGHT AND OPTICS; PHYSICIST, NUCLEAR; PHYSICIST, PLASMA; PHYSICIST, SOLID EARTH; PHYSICIST, SOLID STATE; PHYSICIST, THERMODYNAMICS. (061)

PHYSIOLOGIST: Conducts research on cellular structure and organ-system functions of plants and animals: Studies growth, respiration, circulation, excretion, movement, reproduction, and other functions of plants and animals under normal and abnormal conditions. Performs experiments to determine effects of internal and external environmental factors on life processes and functions, using microscope, X-ray equipment, spectroscope, and other equipment. Studies glands and their relationship to bodily functions. May specialize in physiology of particular body area, function, or system. May specialize in physiology of animals and be designated ANIMAL PHYSIOLOGIST; of plants and be designated PLANT PHYSIOLOGIST; of human organisms and be designated MEDICAL PHYSIOLOGIST. (061)

PLASTERER: Applies coats of plaster to interior walls, ceilings, and partitions of buildings, to produce finished surface, according to blueprints, architect's drawings, or oral instructions, using handtools and portable power tools: Directs workers to mix plaster to desired consistency and to erect scaffolds. Spreads plaster over lath or masonry base, using trowel, and smooths plaster with darby and float to attain uniform thickness. Applies scratch, brown, or finish coats of plaster to wood, metal, or board lath successively. Roughens undercoat with scratcher (wire or metal scraper) to provide bond for succeeding coats of plaster. Creates decorative textures in finish coat by marking surface of coat with brush and trowel or by spattering it with small stones. May install lathing. May mix mortar. May install guide wires on exterior surface of buildings to indicate thickness of plaster to be applied. May install precast ornamental plaster pieces by applying mortar to back of pieces and pressing pieces into place on wall or ceiling. (361)

PLUMBER: Assembles, installs, and repairs pipes, fittings, and fixtures of heating, water, and drainage systems, according to specifications and plumbing codes: Studies building plans and working drawings to determine work aids required and sequence of installations. Inspects structure to ascertain obstructions to be avoided to prevent weakening of structure resulting from installation of pipe. Locates and marks position of pipe and pipe connections and passage holes for pipes in walls and floors, using ruler, spirit level, and plumb bob. Cuts openings in walls and floors to accommodate pipe and pipe fittings, using handtools and power tools. Cuts and threads pipe, using pipe cutters, cutting torch, and pipe-threading machine. Bends pipe to required angle by use of pipe-bending machine or by placing pipe over block and bending it by hand. Assembles and installs valves, pipe fittings, and pipes composed of metals, such as iron, steel, brass, and lead, and nonmetals, such as glass, vitrified clay, and plastic, using handtools and power tools. Joins pipes by use of screws, bolts, fittings, solder, plastic solvent, and calks joints. Fills pipe system with water or air and reads pressure gages to determine whether system is leaking. Installs and repairs plumbing fixtures, such as sinks, commodes, bathtubs, water heaters, hot water tanks, garbage disposal units, dishwashers, and water softeners. Repairs and maintains plumbing, by replacing washers in leaky faucets, mending burst pipes, and opening clogged drains. May weld holding fixtures to steel structural members. (381)

POLICE OFFICER: Patrols assigned beat on foot, using motorcycle or patrol car, or on horseback to control traffic, prevent crime or disturbance of peace, and arrest violators: Familiarizes self with beat and with persons living in area. Notes suspicious persons and establishments and reports to superior officer. Reports hazards. Disperses unruly crowds at public gatherings. Renders first aid at accidents and investigates causes and results of accident. Directs and reroutes traffic around fire or other disruption. Inspects public establishments requiring licenses to insure compliance with rules and regulations. Warns or arrests persons violating animal ordinances. Issues tickets to traffic violators. Registers at police call boxes at specified interval or time. Writes and files daily activity report with superior officer. May drive patrol wagon or police ambulance. May notify public works department of location of abandoned vehicles to tow away. May accompany parking meter personnel to protect money collected. (263)

POLLUTION-CONTROL TECHNICIAN: Conducts tests and field investigations to obtain data for use by environmental, engineering, and scientific personnel in determining sources and methods of controlling pollutants in air, water, and soil, utilizing knowledge of agriculture, chemistry, meteorology, and engineering principles and applied technologies: Conducts chemical and physical laboratory and field tests according to prescribed standards to determine characteristics or composition of solid, liquid, or gaseous materials and substances, using pH meter, chemicals, autoclaves, centrifuge, spectrophotometer, microscope, analytical instrumentation, and chemical laboratory equipment. Collects samples of gases from smokestacks, and collects other air samples and meteorological data to assist in evaluation of atmospheric pollutants. Collects water samples from streams and lakes, or raw, semiprocessed or processed water, industrial waste water, or water from other sources to assess pollution problem. Collects soil, silt, or mud to determine chemical composition and nature of pullutants. Prepares sample for testing, records data, and prepares summaries and charts for review. Sets monitoring equipment to provide flow of information. Installs, operates, and performs routine maintenance on gas and fluid flow systems, chemical reaction systems, mechanical equipment, and other test instrumentation. May operate fixed or mobile monitoring or data collection station. May conduct bacteriological or other tests related to research in environmental or pollution control activity. May collect and analyze engine exhaust emissions to determine type and amount of pollutants. May specialize in one phase or type of environmental pollution or protection and be identified according to specialty. (261)

POST OFFICE CLERK: Performs any combination of following tasks in post office: Sells postage stamps, postal cards, and stamped envelopes. Issues money orders. Registers and insures mail and computes mailing costs of letters and parcels. Places mail into pigeonholes of mail rack, or into bags, according to state, address, name of person, organization, or other scheme. Examines mail for correct postage and cancels mail, using rubber stamp or canceling machine. Weighs parcels and letters on scale and computes mailing cost based on weight and destination. Records daily transactions. Receives complaints concerning mail delivery, mail theft, and lost mail, completes and routes appropriate forms for investigation. Answers questions pertaining to mail regulations or procedures. Posts circulars on bulletin board for public information; distributes public announcements; and assists public in complying with other federal agency requirements, such as registration of aliens. May drive motorcycle or light truck to deliver special delivery letters. (367)

PRINTER: Sets up and operates printing presses, plate-making equipment, and paper-cutting, drilling, and folding machines, to print and produce items, such as decorative box wrappers, direct-mail advertising pieces, office forms, menus, and weekly house organ in business or industrial establishment: Duplicates negative on photographically sensitized metal plates, using exposure frame. Sponges exposed plates with chemical solutions to develop image and washes plate, using water and sponge. Sets metal type in chase by hand. Mounts lithographic plate on cylinder of offset printing press and mounts type on cylinder of cylinder press or flatbed letterpress. Loads stock in feeder magazine of press. Turns screws to adjust paper feed guides. Fills ink and moisture reservoirs and starts press to print sample sheet. Examines sample sheet to determine printing defects, such as off-level areas, variations in ink volume, register slippage, indications of offsetting, and color register. Adjusts press controls, inking fountains, and automatic feeders, and repacks cylinder overlay to equalize off-level areas as required. Operates press to print production run. Sets up and operates power shear to cut sheets of paper or cardboard to specified dimensions. Operates paper-drilling machine to punch or drill holes in printed paper. Operates automatic sheet folder to fold printed sheets or multi-page items. Places cardboard sheet on top of specified number of office forms and spreads glue along one edge of stock to make pads. Maintains and repairs presses and machines, using handtools. May operate vertical process camera to produce paper offset printing plates by photo-direct method. May repair office addressing, duplicating, and mailing equipment operated by other workers. (380)

PRINTMAKER: Conceives and develops drawings and other art work and prepares printmaking medium used to print fine arts graphics: Determines printmaking method, such as recessed (intaglio), raised (relief), or flat (lithograph), which will be most effective to reproduce conceived art work. Renders art work on stone, metal, wood, linoleum, or other material, using various tools, procedures, and processes to etch, engrave, carve, paint, draw, or perform some similar operation, utilizing knowledge of art and printing to prepare image capable of being transferred. Inks surface of medium and transfers image to paper, using hand or machine press. Examines proofs and makes corrections to art work, if necessary. Approves and signs final proof. May prepare preliminary sketches. May use photographic or silk screen process to produce image. May use any suitable textured surface for print-making medium. May use more than one process on single graphic. May print entire edition or instruct other workers to print it. May teach printmaking. (061)

PROBATION OFFICER: Engages in activities related to probation of juvenile or adult offenders: Determines which juvenile cases fall within jurisdiction of court and which should be adjusted informally or referred to other agencies. May release children to parents or authorize detention pending preliminary hearing. Conducts prehearing or presentence investigations of adults and juveniles by interviewing offender, family, and others concerned. Prepares social history for court. Interprets findings and suggests plan of treatment. Arranges for placement or clinical services if ordered by court and works with offender on probation according to treatment plan toward discharge from probation. Evaluates probationer's progress on follow-up basis. Secures remedial action if necessary, by court. May specialize in working with either juvenile or adult offenders, or both. May be administratively attached to court or to separate agency serving court. Usually required to have knowledge and skill in casework methods acquired through degree program at school of social work. (167)

PROCESS SERVER: Serves court orders and processes, such as summonses and subpoenas: Receives papers to be served from magistrate, court clerk, or attorney. Locates person to be served, using telephone directories, state, county, and city records, or public utility records, and delivers document. Records time and place of delivery. May deliver general messages and documents between courts and attorneys. (367)

PROCUREMENT CLERK: Compiles information and records to prepare purchase orders for procurement of material for industrial firm, governmental agency, or other establishment. Verifies nomenclature and specifications of purchase requests. Searches inventory records or warehouse to determine if material on hand is in sufficient quantity. Consults catalogs and interviews suppliers to obtain prices and specifications. Types or writes invitation-of-bid forms and mails forms to supplier firms or for public posting. Writes or types purchase order and sends copy to supplier and department originating request. Compiles records of items purchased or transferred between departments, prices, deliveries, and inventories. Confers with suppliers concerning late deliveries. May compare prices, specifications, and delivery dates and award contract to bidders or place orders with suppliers or mail-order firms. May compute total cost of items purchased, using calculating machine. May classify priority regulations. May verify bills from suppliers with bids and purchase orders and approve for payment. (367)

PRODUCER: Plans and coordinates various aspects of radio and television programs: Interviews and selects SCREEN WRITERS and cast principals from staff members or outside talent. Obtains costumes, props, music, and other equipment or personnel to complete production. Outlines program to be produced to SCREEN WRITERS and evaluates finished script. Suggests changes in script to meet management or other requirements. Coordinates audio work, scenes, music, timing, camera work, and script. Gives instructions to staff to schedule and conduct rehearsals and develop and coordinate details to obtain desired production. Reviews production to insure objectives are attained. May represent television network acting as liaison to independent producer of television series produced for network broadcast. May review budget and expenditures for programs for conformance to budgetary restrictions. (117)

PROGRAMMER, BUSINESS: Converts symbolic statements of administrative data or business problems to detailed logical flow charts for coding into computer language: Analyzes all or part of workflow chart or diagram representing business problem by applying knowledge of computer capabilities, subject matter, algebra, and symbolic logic to develop sequence of program steps. Confers with supervisor and representatives of departments concerned with program to resolve questions of program intent, output requirements, input data acquisition, extent of automatic programming and coding use and modification, and inclusion of internal checks and controls. Writes detailed logical flow chart in symbolic form to represent work order of data to be processed by computer system, and to describe input, output, and arithmetic and logical operations involved. Converts detailed logical flow chart to language processable by computer [PROGRAMMER, DETAIL]. Devises sample input data to provide test of program adequacy. Prepares block diagrams to specify equipment configuration. Observes or operates computer to test coded program, using actual or sample input data. Corrects program errors by such methods as altering program steps and sequence. Prepares written instructions (run book) to guide operating personnel during production runs. Analyzes, reviews, and rewrites programs to increase operating efficiency or adapt to new requirements. Compiles documentation of program development and subsequent revisions. May specialize in writing programs for one make and type of computer. (162)

PROGRAMMER, CHIEF, BUSINESS: Plans, schedules, and directs preparation of programs to process business data and solve business-oriented problems by the use of electronic data processing equipment: Consults with managerial and systems analysis personnel to clarify program intent, indicate problems, suggest changes, and determine extent of automatic programming and coding techniques to use. Assigns, coordinates, and reviews work of programming personnel. Develops own programs and routines from work flow charts or diagrams. Consolidates segments of program into complete sequence of terms and symbols. Breaks down program and input data for successive computer passes, depending on such factors as computer storage capacity and speed, extent of peripheral equipment, and intended use of output data. Analyzes test runs on computer to correct or direct correction of coded program and input data. Revises or directs revision of existing programs to increase operating efficiency or adapt to new requirements. Compiles documentation of program development and subsequent revisions. Trains subordinates in programming and program coding. Prescribes standards of terminology and symbology to simplify interpretation of programs. Collaborates with computer manufacturers and other users to develop new programming methods. Prepares records and reports. (167)

PROGRAM MANAGER: Manages program to insure that implementation and prescribed activities are carried out in accordance with specified objectives: Plans and develops methods and procedures for implementing program, directs and coordinates program activities, and exercises control over personnel responsible for specific functions or phases of program. Selects personnel according to knowledge and experience in area with which program is concerned, such as social or public welfare, education, economics, or public relations. Confers with staff to explain program and individual responsibilities for functions and phases of program. Directs and coordinates personally, or through subordinate managerial personnel, activities concerned with implementation and carrying out objectives of program. Reviews reports and records of activities to insure progress is being accomplished toward specified program objective and modifies or changes methodology as required to redirect activities and attain objectives. Prepares program reports for superiors. Controls expenditures in accordance with budget allocations. (167)

PROJECT DIRECTOR: Plans, directs, and coordinates activities of designated project to insure that aims, goals, or objectives specified for project are accomplished in accordance with prescribed priorities, time limitation, and funding conditions: Reviews project proposal or plan to ascertain time frame and funding limitations, and to determine methods and procedures for accomplishment of project, staffing requirements, and allotment of funds to various phases of project. Develops staffing plan, and establishes work plan and schedules for each phase of project in accordance with time limitations and funding. Recruits, or requests assignment of, personnel according to staffing plan. Confers with staff to outline project plans, designate personnel who will have responsibilities for phases of project, and establish scope of authority. Directs and coordinates activities of project through delegated subordinates and establishes budget control system for controlling expenditures. Reviews project reports on status of each phase and modifies schedules, as required. Prepares project status reports for management. Confers with project personnel to provide technical advice and to assist in solving problems. May coordinate project activities with activities of government regulatory agencies or other governmental agencies. (117)

PROPERTY CLERK: Receives, stores, records, and issues money, valuables, and other articles seized as evidence, removed from prisoner, or recovered, lost, or stolen property: Prepares record of articles and valuables received including description of article, name of owner (if known), name of police officer from whom received, and reason for retention. Issues property being retained as evidence to officer at time of trial upon receipt of authorization. Telephones owners or mails letters to notify owners upon proof of ownership. Returns property to released prisoners. Prepares list of articles required by law to be destroyed and destroys narcotics and drugs (upon authorization) in presence of official witnesses. Sends alcoholic beverages to state liquor commission. Lists and sends unclaimed or confiscated money to auditor's office. Sends unclaimed and illegal weapons for official destruction. Prepares inventory of unclaimed articles for possible sale at auction or donation to charitable organization. (367)

PSYCHIATRIC AIDE: Assists mentally ill patients, working under direction of nursing and medical staff: Accompanies patients to shower rooms, and assists them in bathing, dressing, and grooming. Accompanies patients to and from wards for examination and treatment, and administers prescribed medications. Assists patients in becoming accustomed to hospital routine and encourages them to participate in social and recreational activities, such as visiting, sports, and dramatics, to promote rehabilitation. Observes patients to ensure that none wanders from grounds. Feeds patients or attempts to persuade them to eat, and notes reasons for rejection of food. Observes patients to detect unusual behavior, and aids or restrains them to prevent injury to themselves or other patients. May escort patients off grounds for medical or dental treatment, to library for selection of reading materials, and to church services, motion pictures, or athletic contests. May clean rooms, ward furnishings, walls, and floors, using water, detergents, and disinfectants. May change bed linens. (377)

PSYCHIATRIST: Studies, diagnoses, and treats mental, emotional, and behavioral disorders: Organizes data concerning patient's family, personal (medical and mental) history, and onset of symptoms obtained from patient, relatives, and other sources, such as NURSE, GENERAL DUTY, and SOCIAL WORKER, PSYCHIATRIC. Examines patient to determine general physical condition, following standard medical procedures. Orders laboratory and other special diagnostic tests and evaluates data obtained. Determines nature and extent of mental disorder, and formulates treatment program. Treats or directs treatment of patient, utilizing somatic, group, and milieu therapy, and variety of psychotherapeutic methods and medications. (107)

PSYCHOLOGIST, CLINICAL: Diagnoses or evaluates mental and emotional disorders of individuals, and administers programs of treatment: Interviews patients in clinics, hospitals, prisons, and other institutions, and studies medical and social case histories. Observes patients in play or other situations, and selects, administers, and interprets intelligence, achievement, interest, personality, and other psychological tests to diagnose disorders and formulate plans of treatment. Treats psychological disorders to effect improved adjustments utilizing various psychological techniques, such as milieu therapy, psychodrama, and play therapy. Selects approach to use in individual therapy, such as directive, nondirective, and supportive therapy, and plans frequency, intensity, and duration of therapy. May collaborate with PSYCHIATRISTS and other specialists in developing treatment programs for patients. May instruct and direct students serving psychological internships in hospitals and clinics. May develop experimental designs and conduct research in fields of personality development and adjustment, diagnosis, treatment, and prevention of mental disorders. May serve as consultant to social, educational, welfare, and other agencies on individual cases or in evaluation, planning, and development of mental health programs. May specialize in behavior problems and therapy, crime and delinquency, group therapy, individual diagnosis and therapy, mental deficiency, objective tests, projective techniques, or speech pathology. (107)

PSYCHOLOGIST, COUNSELING: Provides individual and group counseling services in universities and colleges, schools, clinics, rehabilitation centers, Veterans Administration hospitals, and industry, to assist individuals in achieving more effective personal, social, educational, and vocational development and adjustment: Collects data about individual through use of interview, case history, and observational techniques. Selects and interprets psychological tests designed to assess individual's intelligence, aptitudes, abilities, and interests, applying knowledge of statistical analysis. Evaluates data to identify causes of problem of individuals and to determine advisability of counseling or referral to other specialists or institutions. Conducts counseling or therapeutic interviews to assist individual to gain insight into personal problems, define goals, and plan action reflecting interests, abilities, and needs. Provides occupational, educational, and other information to enable individual to formulate realistic educational and vocational plans. Follows up results of counseling to determine reliability and validity of treatment used. May engage in research to develop and improve diagnostic and counseling techniques. May administer and score psychological tests. (107)

PUBLIC-RELATIONS REPRESENTATIVE: Plans and conducts public relations program designed to create and maintain favorable public image for employer or client: Plans and directs development and communication of information designed to keep public informed of employer's programs, accomplishments, or point of view. Arranges for public-relations efforts in order to meet needs, objectives, and policies of individual, special interest group, business concern, nonprofit organization, or governmental agency, serving as in-house staff member or as outside counsultant. Prepares and distributes fact sheets, news releases, photographs, scripts, motion pictures, or tape recordings to media representatives and other persons who may be interested in learning about or publicizing employer's activities or message. Purchases advertising space and time as required. Arranges for and conducts public-contact programs designed to meet employer's objectives, utilizing knowledge of changing attitudes and opinions of consumers, clients, employees, or other interest groups. Promotes goodwill through such publicity efforts as speeches, exhibits, films, tours, and question/answer sessions. Represents employer during community projects and at public, social, and business gatherings. May specialize in researching data, creating ideas, writing copy, laying out artwork, contacting media representatives, or representing employer directly before general public. May specialize in one type of public-relations effort, such as fund-raising campaigns or political issues. (067)

RADIO MECHANIC: Tests and repairs radio transmitting and receiving equipment in accordance with diagrams and manufacturer's specifications, using handtools and electrical measuring instruments: Examines equipment for damaged components and loose or broken connections and wires. Replaces defective components and parts, such as tubes, condensers, transformers, resistors, and generators, using handtools. Solders or tightens loose connections and cleans and lubricates motor generators. Tests equipment for factors such as power output, frequency power, noise level, audio quality, and dial calibration, using oscilloscopes, radio frequency and watt meters, ammeters, voltmeters, and tube testers. Tests batteries with hydrometer and ammeter and charges batteries. Inserts plugs into receptacles and bolts or screws leads to terminals to connect radios and equipment to power source, using handtools. Turns setscrews to adjust receivers for sensitivity and transmitters for maximum output. Required to have Federal Communications Commission Radiotelephone Operator's license. May install, test, adjust, modify, and repair intercommunication systems. (018)

REAL-ESTATE AGENT: Coordinates activities of real-estate department of company and negotiates acquisition and disposition of properties in most beneficial manner: Supervises staff engaged in preparing lease agreements, recording rental receipts, and performing other activities necessary to efficient management of company properties, or in performing routine research on zoning ordinances and condemnation considerations. Directs appraiser to inspect properties and land under consideration for acquisition, and recommends acquisition, lease, disposition, improvement, or other action consistent with best interest of company. Authorizes or requests authorization for maintenance of company properties not under control of operating departments, such as dwellings, hotels, or commissaries. Evaluates and promotes industrial-development potential of company properties. Negotiates contracts with sellers of land and renters of properties. (117)

RECEPTIONIST: Receives callers at establishment, determines nature of business, and directs callers to destination: Obtains caller's name and arranges for appointment with person called upon. Directs caller to destination and records name, time of call, nature of business, and person called upon. May issue visitor's pass when required. May make future appointments and answer inquiries. May perform variety of clerical duties and other duties pertinent to type of establishment. May collect and distribute mail and messages. (367)

REPORTER: Collects and analyzes information about newsworthy events to write news stories for publication or broadcast: Receives assignment or evaluates leads and news tips to develop story idea. Gathers and verifies factual information regarding story through interview, observation, and research. Organizes material, determines slant or emphasis, and writes story according to prescribed editorial style and format standards. May monitor police and fire department radio communications to obtain story leads. May take photographs to illustrate stories. May appear on television program when conducting taped or filmed interviews or narration. May give live reports from site of event or mobile broadcast unit. May transmit information to NEWSWRITER for story writing. May specialize in one type of reporting, such as sports, fires, accidents, political affairs, court trials, or police activities. (267)

RESERVATIONS AGENT: Makes and confirms reservations for passengers on scheduled airline flights: Arranges reservations and routing for passengers at request of TICKET AGENT or customer, using timetables, airline manuals, reference guides, and tariff book. Types requested flight number on keyboard of on-line computer reservation system and scans screen to determine space availability. Telephones customer or TICKET AGENT to advise of changes in flight plan or to cancel or confirm reservation. May maintain advance or current inventory of available passenger space on flights. May advise load control personnel and other stations of changes in passenger itinerary to control space and insure utilization of seating capacity on flights. (367)

SAFETY INSPECTOR: Inspects machinery, equipment, and working conditions in industrial or other setting to insure compliance with occupational safety and health regulations: Inspects machines and equipment for accident-prevention devices. Observes workers to determine use of prescribed safety equipment, such as glasses, helmets, goggles, respirators, and clothing. Inspects specified areas for fire-prevention equipment and other safety and first-aid supplies. Tests working areas for noise, toxic, and other hazards, using decibel meter, gas detector, and light meter. Prepares report of findings with recommendations for corrective action. Investigates accidents to ascertain causes for use in recommending preventive safety measures and developing safety program. May demonstrate use of safety equipment. (264)

SALES AGENT, INSURANCE: Sells insurance to new and present clients, recommending amount and type of coverage based on analysis of prospect's circumstances: Compiles lists of prospective clients to provide leads for additional business. Contacts prospects and explains features and merits of policies offered, utilizing persuasive sales techniques. Calculates and quotes premium rates for recommended policies, using adding machine and rate books. Calls on policyholders to deliver and explain policy, to suggest additions or changes in insurance program, or to make changes in beneficiaries. May collect weekly or monthly premiums from policyholders and keep record of payments. Must have license issued by state. (257)

SALES AGENT, SECURITIES: Buys and sells stocks and bonds for individuals and organizations as representative of stock brokerage firm, applying knowledge of securities, market conditions, government regulations, and financial circumstances of customers: Gives information and advice regarding stocks, bonds, market conditions, and history and prospects of various corporations to prospective customers, based on interpretation of data from securities reports, financial periodicals, and stock-quotation-viewer screen, and persuades customers to buy or sell specific securities according to their financial needs. Records and transmits buy or sell orders to trading division in accordance with customer's wishes. Calculates and records cost of transaction for billing purposes, using quotations received during transmittal of order. Develops portfolio (list) of selected investments for customer. Compiles list of prospective customers and telephones prospects to obtain additional business. Must have broker's license issued by state. (157)

SALES CLERK, FOOD: Obtains or prepares food items requested by customers in retail food stores, such as groceries, produce, bakery goods, meat and fish, and totals customer bill, receives payment, and makes change: Sets up displays on counters, shelves, or in bins. Fills customer order, performing such duties as obtaining items from shelves, freezers, coolers, bins, tables, or containers, cleaning poultry, scaling and trimming fish, slicing meat or cheese, using slicing machine, or preparing take-out sandwiches and salads. Weighs items, such as produce, meat, and poultry to determine price. Lists and totals prices, using paper and pencil, adding machine, or cash register, and informs customer of total price of purchases. Receives money from cutomers for purchases, and makes change. Bags or wraps purchases for customers. Cleans shelves, bins, tables, and coolers as necessary. Stamps, marks, or tags price on merchandise. Stocks shelves, coolers, counter, bins, tables, freezers, containers, or trays with new merchandise. May make deliveries to customers' homes or places of business on foot or using vehicle. (477)

SALESPERSON, AUTOMOBILES: Sells new or used automobiles on premises of automobile agency: Explains features and demonstrates operation of car in showroom or on road. Suggests optional equipment for customer to purchase. Computes and quotes sales price, including tax, trade-in allowance, license fee, and discount, and requirements for financing payment of car on credit. (353)

SALESPERSON, BOOKS: Sells books in book or department store: Suggests selection of books, based on knowledge of current literature and familiarity with publishers' catalogs and book reviews. Arranges books on shelves and racks according to type, author, or subject matter. (357)

SALESPERSON: COSMETICS: Sells cosmetics and toiletries, such as skin creams, hair preparations, face powder, lipstick, and perfume, to customers in department store or specialty shop: Demonstrates methods of application of various preparations to customer. Explains beneficial properties of preparations and suggests shades or varieties of makeup to suit customer's complexion. May weigh and mix facial powders, according to established formula, to obtain desired shade, using spatula and scale. (357)

SALESPERSON, MEN'S AND BOYS' CLOTHING: Sells men's and boys' outer garments, such as suits, trousers, and coats: Advises customer about prevailing styles and suitability of garments. Answers questions relative to fabric or design of garment. Selects standard-sized garments nearest to customer's measurements. May mark garment for alterations. (357)

SALES REPRESENTATIVE, RADIO AND TELEVISION TIME: Contacts prospective customers to sell radio and television time for broadcasting station or network: Calls on prospects and presents outlines of various programs or commercial announcements. Discusses current popularity of various types of programs, such as news, dramatic, and variety. Arranges for and accompanies prospect to auditions. Prepares sales contracts. (357)

SALES REPRESENTATIVE, WOMEN'S AND GIRLS' APPAREL: Sells women's and girls' apparel, such as coats, dresses, lingerie, and accessories, utilizing knowledge of fabrics, style, and prices. May specialize according to price range of garment sold. (357)

SECRETARY: Schedules appointments, gives information to callers, takes dictation, and otherwise relieves officials of clerical work and minor administrative and business detail: Reads and routes incoming mail. Locates and attaches appropriate file to correspondence to be answered by employer. Takes dictation in shorthand or by machine [STENOTYPE OPERATOR] and transcribes notes on typewriter, or transcribes from voice recordings [TRANSCRIBING-MACHINE OPERATOR]. Composes and types routine correspondence. Files correspondence and other records. Answers telephone and gives information to callers or routes call to appropriate official and places outgoing calls. Schedules appointments for employer. Greets visitors, ascertains nature of business, and conducts visitors to employer or appropriate person. May not take dictation. May arrange travel schedule and reservations. May compile and type statistical reports. May oversee clerical workers. May keep personnel records. [PERSONNEL CLERK]. May record minutes of staff meetings. May make copies of correspondence or other printed matter, using copying or duplicating machine. May prepare outgoing mail, using postage-metering machine. (362)

SECURITIES TRADER: Trades securities and provides securities investment and counseling services for bank and its customers: Studies financial background and future trends of stocks and bonds, and advises bank officials and customers regarding investments. Transmits buy-and-sell orders to broker as directed, and recommends purchase, retention, or sale of issues. Notifies customer or bank of execution of trading orders. Negotiates stock and bond transactions. Computes extensions, commissions, and other charges for billing cutomers and for making payments for securities. Advises bank officials concerning sale of bond issues and trading of stock. May be designated according to type of securities handled as BOND TRADER; STOCK TRADER; or according to responsibilities assumed as BOND CASHIER. (167)

SECURITY OFFICER: Plans and establishes security procedures for company engaged in manufacturing products or processing data or material for Federal government: Studies Federal security regulations and restrictions relative to company operations. Directs activities of personnel in developing company and security measures which comply with Federal regulations. Consults with local, district, or other Federal representatives for interpretation or application of particular regulations applying to company operations. Prepares security manual outlining and establishing measures and procedures for handling, storing, safekeeping, and destroying classified records and documents, and for granting company personnel or visitors access to classified material or entry into restricted areas. Directs and coordinates activities of personnel in revising or updating security measures due to new or revised regulations. May request deviations from restrictive regulations that interfere with normal operations. (167)

SET DESIGNER: Designs sets for theatrical productions: Confers with play's director regarding interpretation and set requirements. Conducts research to determine appropriate architectural and furnishing styles. Integrates requirements, interpretation, research, design concepts, and practical considerations regarding factors, such as mobility, interchangeability, and budget, to plan sets. Renders drawing or illustration of design concept, estimates costs, and presents drawing for approval. Prepares working drawings of floor plan, front elevation, scenery, and properties to be constructed. Prepares charts to indicate where items, such as curtains and borders are to be hung. Oversees building of sets, furniture, and properties. May build scale models from cardboard, plaster, or sponge. May design stage lighting to achieve dramatic or decorative effects. (061)

SEWER, HAND: Joins and reinforces parts of articles, such as garments, curtains, parachutes, stuffed toys, or sews buttonholes and attaches fasteners to articles, or sews decorative trimmings to articles, using needle and thread: Selects thread, according to specifications or color of parts. Alines parts, fasteners, or trimmings, following seams, edges, or markings on parts. Sews parts with various types of stitches, such as felling tacking, stitch and basting. Trims excess threads, using scissors or knife. May trim edges of parts, using scissors. (684)

SHIPPING AND RECEIVING CLERK: Verifies and keeps records on incoming and outgoing shipments and prepares items for shipment: Compares identifying information and counts, weights, or measures items of incoming and outgoing shipments to verify against bills of lading, invoices, orders, or other records. Determines method of shipment, utilizing knowledge of shipping procedures, routes, and rates. Assembles wooden or cardboard containers or selects preassembled containers. Inserts items into containers, using spacers, fillers, and protective padding. Nails covers on wooden crates and binds containers with metal tape, using strapping machine. Stamps, stencils, or glues identifying information and shipping instructions onto crates or containers. Posts weights, shipping charges and affixes postage. Unpacks and examines incoming shipments, rejects damaged items, records shortages, and corresponds with shipper to rectify damages and shortages. Routes items to departments. May operate tier-lift truck or use handtruck to move, convey, or hoist shipments from shipping-and-receiving platform to storage or work area. May direct others in preparing outgoing and receiving incoming shipments. (387)

SHORTHAND REPORTER: Records examination, testimony, judicial opinions, judge's charge to jury, judgment or sentence of court, or other proceedings in court of law by machine shorthand, takes shorthand notes, or reports proceedings into *steno-mask*: Reads portions of transcript during trial on judge's request, and asks speakers to clarify inaudible statements. Operates typewriter to transcribe recorded material, or dictates material into recording machine. May record proceedings of quasi-judicial hearings, formal and informal meetings, and be designated HEARINGS REPORTER. May be self-employed, performing duties in court of law or at hearings and meetings, and be designated FREELANCE REPORTER. (362)

SILK-SCREEN PRINTER: Tends silk-screen machine that prints designs or lettering on glassware, pottery, and metal and plastic items, such as appliances, instrument dials, and toys: Bolts framed silk-screen onto machine, and installs and adjusts workpiece holding fixture, stops, and guides, using handtools, ruler, and workpiece pattern. Attaches squeegee to pneumatic drive mechanism, using wrench, and couples air line to mechanism. Regulates air pressure and manipulates squeegee to adjust squeegee pressure and angle of sweep. Applies printing compound to screen, using spatula or brush. Places workpiece in or on holding fixture, presses button to lower screen, and depresses pedal or pushes button to activate squeegee. Observes silk-screen and workpiece to detect printing defects caused by rip in screen and applies glue to rip to repair screen. Cleans silk-screen, using brush and solvent. May thin printing compound, using specified thinner. May tend firing oven to dry printed workpiece. (665)

SOCIAL WORKER, DELINQUENCY PREVENTION: Works through community action programs to ameliorate social conditions tending to cause juvenile delinquency and provides counseling and guidance to juveniles: Aids civil authorities to plan urban, suburban, and rural development to insure provisions for meeting social needs of youth. Works with individuals and groups in danger of becoming delinquent, through individual and group guidance and through use of community resources. Refers juveniles to community agencies, such as settlement houses, child guidance clinics, and health clinics, for mental, physical, and social rehabilitation. Works closely with law enforcement agencies, schools, employers, health, welfare, and recreation agencies. Usually attached to public agency. (107)

SOCIAL WORKER, PSYCHIATRIC: Provides psychiatric social work assistance to mentally or emotionally disturbed patients of hospitals, clinics, and other medical centers, and to their families, collaborating with psychiatric and allied team in diagnosis and treatment plan: Investigates case situations and presents information to PSYCHIATRIST, PSYCHOLOGIST, CLINICAL and other members of health team, on patient's family and social background pertinent to diagnosis and treatment. In consultation with PSYCHIATRIST may work directly in treatment relationship with patients, individually or in groups. Helps patients to respond constructively to treatment and assist in adjustment leading to and following discharge. Interprets psychiatric treatment to patient's family and helps to reduce fear and other attitudes obstructing acceptance of psychiatric care and continuation of treatment. Serves as link between patient, psychiatric agency, and community. May refer patient or patient's family to other community resources. Usually required to have knowledge and skill in casework methods acquired through degree program at school of social work. (107)

SOIL SCIENTIST: Studies soil characteristics and maps soil types, and investigates responses of soils to known management practices to determine use capabilities of soils and effects of alternative practices on soil productivity: Classifies soils according to standard types. Conducts experiments on farms or experimental stations to determine best soil types for different plants. Performs chemical analysis on micro-organism content of soil to determine microbial reactions and chemical and mineralogical relationship to plant growth. Investigates responses of specific soil types to tillage, fertilization, nutrient transformation, crop rotation, environmental consequences, water, gas or heat flow, industrial waste control and other soil management practices. Advises interested persons on rural or urban land use. May specialize in one or more types of activities relative to soil management and productivity and be designated as SOIL FERTILITY EXPERT. (061)

SPECIFICATION WRITER: Interprets architectural or engineering plans and prepares material lists and specifications to be used as standards by plant employees or contracting personnel in material processing or in manufacturing or construction activities: Analyzes plans and diagrams, or observes and makes notes on material processing, to determine material and material processing specifications, or specifications for manufacturing or construction activities. Writes technical descriptions specifying material qualities and properties, utilizing knowledge of material standards, industrial processes, and manufacturing procedures. May draw rough sketches or arrange for finished drawings or photographs to illustrate specified materials or assembly sequence. Workers usually specialize and are designated according to engineering specialization, product, or process. (267)

SPEECH PATHOLOGIST: Specializes in diagnosis and treatment of speech and language problems, and engages in scientific study of human communication: Diagnoses and evaluates speech and language competencies of individuals, including assessment of speech and language skills as related to educational, medical, social, and psychological factors. Plans, directs, or conducts habilitative and rehabilitative treatment programs to restore communicative efficiency of individuals with communication problems of organic and nonorganic etiology. Provides counseling and guidance to speech and language handicapped individuals. May act as consultant to educational, medical, and other professional groups. May teach scientific principles of human communication. May direct scientific projects investigating biophysical and biosocial phenomena associated with voice, speech, and language. May conduct research to develop diagnostic and remedial techniques or design apparatus. See AUDIOLOGIST for one who specializes in diagnosis of, and provision of rehabilitative services for, auditory problems. (107)

SPECTROSCOPIST: Conducts spectrographic examinations of metal and mineral samples under established procedures, using spectrograph, spectrometer, densimeter, and other measuring instruments: Analyzes densimeter or spectrometer readings to measure density ratio of specific elements in sample. Computes percentage composition of sample by comparing intensity ratio with standard charts. Investigates deviations from standard, performing further examinations by other spectrographic procedures and methods to establish degree of conformance to standard. Records quantitative determination, procedure, and standard applied for each sample examined. (281)

STATIONARY ENGINEER: Operates and maintains stationary engines and mechanical equipment, such as steam engines, air compressors, generators, motors, turbines, and steam boilers to provide utilities, such as light, heat, or power for buildings and industrial processes: Reads meters and gages or automatic recording devices at specified intervals to verify operating conditions. Records data, such as temperature of equipment, hours of operation, fuel consumed, temperature or pressure, water levels, analysis of flue gases, voltage load and generator balance. Adjusts manual controls or overrides automatic controls to bring equipment into recommended or prescribed operating ranges, switch to back-up equipment or systems, or to shut down equipment. Visually inspects equipment at periodic intervals to detect malfunctions or need for repair, adjustment or lubrication. Maintains equipment by tightening fittings, repacking bearings, replacing packing glands, gaskets, valves, recorders, and gages, and cleaning or replacing burners or other components, using hand and power tools. May be required to hold license issued by state or municipality, restricting equipment operated to specified types and sizes. May oil and lubricate equipment. (382)

STATISTICIAN: Conducts research into mathematical theories and proofs that form basis of science of statistics and develops statistical methodology: Examines theories, such as those of probability and inference, to discover mathematical bases for new or improved methods of obtaining and evaluating numerical data. Develops and tests experimental designs, sampling techniques, and analytical methods, and prepares recommendations concerning their utilization in statistical surveys, experiments, and tests. Investigates, evaluates, and prepares reports on applicability, efficiency, and accuracy of statistical methods used by physical and social scientists, including STATISTICIANS, APPLIED, in obtaining and evaluating data. (067)

STOCK CLERK: Receives, stores, and issues equipment, material, supplies, merchandise, foodstuffs, or tools, and compiles stock records in stockroom, warehouse, or storage yard: Counts, sorts, or weighs incoming articles to verify receipt of items on requisition or invoices. Examines stock to verify conformance to specifications. Stores articles in bins, on floor, or on shelves, according to identifying information, such as style, size, or type of material. Fills orders or issues supplies from stock. Prepares periodic, special, or perpetual inventory of stock. Requisitions articles to fill incoming orders. Compiles reports on use of stock handling equipment, adjustments of inventory counts and stock records, spoilage of or damage to stock, location changes, and refusal of shipments. May mark identifying codes, figures, or letters on articles. May distribute stock among production workers, keeping records of material issued. May make adjustments or repairs to articles carried in stock. May determine methods of storage, identification, and stock location, considering temperature, humidity, height and weight limits, turnover, floor loading capacities, and required space. May cut stock to size to fill order. May move or transport material or supplies to other departments, using hand or industrial truck. (387)

SUPERINTENDENT, BUILDING: Directs activities of workers engaged in operating and maintaining facilities and equipment in buildings such as apartment houses or office buildings: Inspects facilities and equipment to determine need and extent of service, equipment required, and type and number of operation and maintenance personnel needed. Hires, trains, and supervises building service personnel. Assigns workers to duties such as maintenance, repair, or renovation and obtains bids for additional work from outside contractors. Directs contracted projects to verify adherence to specifications. Purchases building and maintenance supplies, machinery, equipment, and furniture. Plans and administers building department budget. Compiles records of labor and material cost for operating building and issues cost reports to owner or managing agents. May prepare construction specifications or plans, obtaining advice from engineering consultants, assemble and analyze contract bids, and submit bids and recommendations to superiors for action. (167)

SUPERINTENDENT, SALES: Plans and promotes sale of new and custom-built homes for building contractor: Plans and organizes sales promotion programs and techniques in cooperation with suppliers of household appliances, furnishings, and equipment. Locates and appraises undeveloped areas for building sites, based on evaluation of area market conditions. Interviews prospective clients and shows homes under construction to display construction features and quality of work. Reviews plans and specifications for custom-built homes with client and ARCHITECT to clarify costs and construction details in preliminary negotiations for contract. Recommends construction features and available decorating options, such as cabinet installations, to aid client in formulating plans. Answers questions regarding work under construction. May assess client's financial status to determine eligibility for financing home through contractor. (157)

SUPERVISOR, WORD PROCESSING: Supervises and coordinates activities of workers engaged in preparing correspondence, records, reports, insurance policies, and similar clerical matter and in operating specialized typing machines, such as magnetic-tape typewriting and composing machines: Advises other departmental personnel in techniques and style of dictation and letter writing. Recommends changes in procedures to effect savings in time, labor, costs, and to improve operating efficiency. Assigns new workers to experienced workers for training. Assists subordinates in resolving problems in nonstandard situations. Evaluates job performance of subordinates and recommends appropriate personnel action. Performs duties as described under SUPERVISOR. (137)

SYSTEMS ENGINEER, ELECTRONIC DATA PROCESSING: Analyzes data-processing requirements to determine electronic data-processing system that will provide system capabilities required for projects or workloads, and plans layout of new system installation or modification of existing system, utilizing knowledge of electronics and data-processing principles and equipment: Confers with data-processing and project managerial personnel to obtain data on limitations and capabilities of existing system and capabilities required for data processing projects and workload proposed. Analyzes data to determine, recommend, and plan layout for type of computer and peripheral equipment, or modifications to existing equipment and system, that will provide capability for proposed project or workload, efficient operation, and effective use of alloted space. May specify power supply requirements and configuration. May recommend purchase of equipment to control dust, temperature, and humidity in area of system installation. May specialize in one area of system application or in one type or make of equipment. May represent consulting firm or equipment manufacturer. (167)

TAXI DRIVER: Drives taxicab to transport passengers for fee: Picks up passengers in response to radio or telephone relayed request for service. Collects fee recorded on taximeter based on mileage or time factor and records transaction on log. Reports by radio or telephone to TAXICAB STARTER on completion of trip. May drive limousine or custom-built sedan to pick up and discharge airport passengers arriving or leaving on scheduled flights. (463)

TEACHER AIDE: Assists teaching staff of public or private elementary or secondary school by performing any combination of following duties in classroom: Calls roll and prepares attendance records. Grades homework and objective examinations, using answer sheets, and records results. Distributes teaching materials to students, such as textbooks, workbooks, or writing paper and pencils. Keeps order in classroom, library, and halls, and on school grounds. Sets up and operates equipment, such as film and slide projectors and tape recorders. Prepares requisitions for library materials and stockroom supplies. May type and operate duplicating equipment to reproduce instructional materials. (367)

TEACHER, ELEMENTARY SCHOOL: Teaches elementary school pupils academic, social, and manipulative skills in public or private educational system: Prepares teaching outline for course of study. Lectures, demonstrates, and used audio-visual teaching aids to present subject matter to class. Prepares, administers, and corrects tests, and records results. Assigns lessons, corrects papers, and hears oral presentations. Maintains order in classroom and on playground. Counsels pupils when adjustment and academic problems arise. Discusses pupils' academic and behavior problems with parents and suggests remedial action. Keeps attendance and grade records as required by school board. May teach combined grade classes in rural schools. (227)

TEACHER, KINDERGARTEN: Teaches elemental natural and social sciences, personal hygiene, music, art, and literature to children from 4 to 6 years old, to promote their physical, mental, and social development: Supervises activities, such as field visits, group discussions, and dramatic play-acting, to stimulate students' interest in and broaden understanding of their physical and social environment. Fosters cooperative social behavior through games and group projects to assist children in forming satisfying relationships with other children and adults. Encourages students in singing, dancing, rhythmic activities, and in use of art materials, to promote self-expression and appreciation of esthetic experience. Instructs children in practices of personal cleanliness and self care. Alternates periods of strenuous activity with periods of rest or light activity to avoid overstimulation and fatigue. Observes children to detect signs of ill health or emotional disturbance, and to evaluate progress. Discusses students' problems and progress with parents. (227)

TEACHER, SECONDARY SCHOOL: Teaches one or more subjects, such as English, mathematics, or social studies, to students in public or private secondary schools: Instructs students in subject matter, utilizing various teaching methods, such as lecture and demonstration, and uses audio-visual aids and other materials to supplement presentations. Prepares teaching outline for course of study, assigns lessons, and corrects homework papers. Administers tests to evaluate pupils' progress, records results, and issues reports to inform parents of progress. Keeps attendance records. Maintains discipline in classroom and school yard. Participates in faculty and professional meetings, educational conferences, and teacher training workshops. Performs related duties, such as sponsoring one or more special activities or student organizations, assisting pupils in selecting course of study, and counseling them in adjustment and academic problems. May be identified according to subject matter taught. (227)

TELEPHONE OPERATOR: Operates cord or cordless switchboard to relay incoming, outgoing, and interoffice calls: On cordless switchboard, pushes switch keys to make connections and relay calls. On cord type equipment, plugs cord into switchboard jacks. May supply information to callers and record messages. May keep record of calls placed and toll charges. May perform clerical duties, such as typing, proofreading, and sorting mail. May operate system of bells or buzzers to call individuals in establishment to phone. May receive visitors, obtain name and nature of business, and schedule appointments. (662)

TELEPHONE SOLICITOR: Solicits orders for merchandise or services over telephone: Calls prospective customers to explain type of service or merchandise offered. Quotes prices and tries to persuade customer to buy, using prepared sales talk. Records names, addresses, purchases, and reactions of prospects solicited. Refers orders to other workers for filling. May develop lists of prospects from city and telephone directories. May transcribe data from order card to keypunch card, using vari-punch machine. May type report periodically on sales activities, using typewriter. (357)

TELEVISION-CABLE INSTALLER: Installs CATV (community antenna television distribution cables) on customers' premises: Measures television signal strength at utility pole, using electronic test equipment. Computes impedance of wire from pole to house to determine additional resistance needed for reducing signal to desired level. Installs terminal boxes and strings lead-in wires, using electrician's tools. Connects television set to antenna system and evaluates incoming signal. Adjusts and repairs antenna system to insure optimum reception. (281)

TELEVISION AND RADIO REPAIRER: Repairs and adjusts radios and television receivers, using handtools and electronic testing instruments: Tunes receiver on all channels and observes audio and video characteristics to locate source of trouble. Adjusts controls to obtain desired density, linearity, focus, and size of picture. Examines chassis for defects. Tests voltages and resistances of circuits to isolate defect, following schematic diagram and using voltmeter, oscilloscope, signal generator, and other electronic testing instruments. Tests and changes tubes. Solders loose connections and repairs or replaces defective parts, using handtools and soldering iron. (281)

TELLER: Receives and pays out money, and keeps records of money and negotiable instruments involved in various banking and other financial transactions, performing any combination of following tasks: Receives checks and cash for deposit, verifies amounts, and examines checks for endorsements. Enters deposits in depositors' passbooks or issues receipts. Cashes checks and pays out money upon verification of signatures and customer balances. Places holds on accounts for uncollected funds. Orders supply of cash to meet daily needs, counts incoming cash, and prepares cash for shipment. May compute service charges, file checks, and accept utility bill payments. May photograph records, using microfilming device. May operate various office machines. May sell domestic exchange, travelers' checks, and savings accounts. May open new accounts and compute interest and discounts. (362)

TRAINING REPRESENTATIVE: Prepares and conducts training programs for employees of industrial, commercial, service, or governmental establishment: Confers with management to gain knowledge of identified work situation requiring preventive or remedial training for employees. Formulates teaching outline in conformance with selected instructional methods, utilizing knowledge of specified training needs and effectiveness of such training methods as individual coaching, group instruction, lectures, demonstrations, conferences, meetings, and workshops. Selects or develops teaching aids, such as training handbooks, demonstration models, multimedia visual aids, and reference works. Conducts general or specialized training sessions covering specified areas, such as those concerned with new employees' orientation, specific on-the-job training, apprenticeship programs, sales techniques, health and safety practices, public relations, refresher training, promotional development, upgrading, retraining displaced workers, leadership development, and other such adaptations to changes in policies, procedures, regulations, and technologies. Tests trainees to measure their learning progress and to evaluate effectiveness of training presentations. (227)

TRAVEL AGENT: Plans itineraries, and arranges accommodations and other travel services for customers of travel agency: Converses with customer to determine destination, mode of transportation, travel dates, financial considerations, and accommodations required. Plans or describes and sells itinerary package tour. Gives customer brochures and publications concerning travel and containing information, such as local customs, points of interest, and special events occurring in various locations, or foreign country regulations, such as consular requirements, rates of monetary exchange, and currency limitations. Computes cost of travel and accommodations, using calculating machine, carrier tariff books, and hotel rate books, or quotes costs of package tours. Books customer on transportation carrier and makes hotel reservations, using telephone or teletypewriter. Writes or obtains travel tickets for transportation or tour and collects payment. May specialize in foreign or domestic service, individual or group travel, specific geographical area, airplane charters, or package tours by bus. May act as wholesaler and assemble tour packages. (157)

TREE TRIMMER: Trims trees to clear right-of-way for communications lines and electric powerlines to minimize storm and short-circuit hazards: Climbs trees to reach branches interfering with wires and transmission towers, using climbing equipment. Prunes treetops, using saws or pruning shears. Repairs trees damaged by storm or lightning by trimming jagged stumps and painting them to prevent bleeding of sap. Removes broken limbs from wires, using hooked extension pole. Fells trees interfering with power service, using chainsaw (portable powersaw). May work from bucket of extended truck boom to reach limbs. (664)

TRUCK DRIVER: Drives truck with capacity under 3 tons to transport materials in liquid or packaged form and personnel to and from specified destinations, such as railroad stations, plants, residences, offices, or within industrial yards: Verifies load against shipping papers. Drives truck to destination, applying knowledge of commercial driving regulations and roads in area. Prepares receipts for load picked up. Collects payment for goods delivered and for delivery charges. May maintain truck log according to state and federal regulations. May maintain telephone or radio contact with supervisor to receive delivery instructions. May drive truck equipped with public address system through city streets to broadcast announcements over system for advertising or publicity purposes. May load and unload truck. May inspect truck equipment and supplies, such as tires, lights, brakes, gas, oil, and water. May perform emergency roadside repairs, such as changing tires, installing light bulbs, fuses, tire chains, and spark plugs. (683)

TYPIST: Types letters, reports, stencils, forms, addresses, or other straight-copy material from rough draft or corrected copy. May verify totals on report forms, requisitions, or bills. May operate duplicating machines to reproduce copy. (682)

URBAN PLANNER: Develops comprehensive plans and programs for utilization of land and physical facilities of cities, counties, and metropolitan areas: Compiles and analyzes data on economic, social, and physical factors affecting land use, and prepares or requisitions graphic and narrative reports on data. Confers with local authorities, civic leaders, social scientists, and land planning and development specialists to devise and recommend arrangements of land and physical facilities for residential, commercial, industrial, and community uses. Recommends governmental measures affecting land use, public utilities, community facilities, and housing and transportation to control and guide community development and renewal. May review and evaluate environmental impact reports applying to specified private and public planning projects and programs. Usually employed by local government jurisdictions, but may work for any level of government, or private consulting firms. (167)

VETERINARIAN: Diagnoses and treats diseases and disorders of animals: Determines nature of disease or injury and treats animal surgically or medically. Tests dairy herds for tuberculosis and brucellosis, and inoculates animals against diseases, such as hog cholera and rabies. Performs autopsies to determine causes of death. Inspects animals intended for human consumption, before and after slaughtering. Advises on care and breeding of animals. Engages in general practice, treating various animal species, or specializes, restricting practice to dogs, cats, and other pets, or to single species, such as cattle, horses, or poultry. May engage in particular function, such as research and development, consultation, administration, teaching, technical writing, sale or production of commercial products, or rendition of technical services for commercial firms. May specialize in investigation, prevention, and control of animal diseases communicable to man through direct contact, insects, food, or contamination of environment. (101)

VICE PRESIDENT: Directs and coordinates activities of one or more departments, such as engineering, operations, or sales, or major division of business organization, and aids chief administrative officer in formulating and administering organization policies: Participates in formulating and administering company policies and developing long range goals and objectives. Directs and coordinates activities of department or division, for which responsibility is delegated to further attainment of goals and objectives. Reviews analyses of activities, costs, operations, and forecast data to determine department or division progress toward stated goals and objectives. Confers with chief administrative officer and other administrative personnel to review achievements and discuss required changes in goals or objectives resulting from current status and conditions. May perform duties of PRESIDENT during absence. May serve as member of management committees on special studies. (117)

WAITER/WAITRESS, INFORMAL: Serves food to patrons at counters and tables of coffeeshops, lunchrooms, and other dining establishments where food service is informal: Presents menu, answers questions, and makes suggestions regarding food and service. Writes order on check or memorizes it. Relays order to kitchen and serves courses from kitchen and service bars. Observes guests to fulfill any additional request and to perceive when meal has been completed. Totals bill and accepts payment or refers patron to CASHIER. May ladle soup, toss salads, portion pies and desserts, brew coffee, and perform other services as determined by establishment's size and practices. May clear and reset counters or tables at conclusion of each course. (477)

WIRER, CABLE: Installs cables and solders wires to connect electrical instruments mounted on control apparatus, such as panelboards and telephone crossbar frames, according to diagrams and blueprints: Pulls assembled crossbar frame or unit to work area, using monorail chain hoist or handtruck. Ties preformed wiring cable to brackets. Positions arms of cable (groups of wires tied off from trunk of cable) and spreads wires to facilitate wiring. May strip insulation from ends of wires with pliers to prepare for connections. Connects color-coded wires to terminals, using soldering iron or pneumatic wire-wrapping tool. Examines and feels wires to detect loose connections. Writes and ties tickets to wires or terminals in apparatus to identify surplus or missing wires. May secure parts, such as diodes and resistors to specified locations on equipment, using soldering iron or screwdriver. Tapes insulating sleeves over auxiliary lead wires of cable. Pulls or carries wired apparatus to storage area. (381)

WOODWORKING-SHOP HAND: Performs any combination of following duties to facilitate cutting, finishing, storing, cleaning, and shipping wood products, and inspects products prior to shipment: Stacks lumber or wood products on floor or in bins to supply machine operators or assemblers, or in kiln cars, yard, or shed for storage or seasoning. Places sticks between lumber to permit air circulation, and binds stacks together during seasoning. Hammers shaped steel bands into timbers and railroad ties to prevent splitting during seasoning and inserts bolts or metal dowels through split timbers to hold parts together. Dismantles crates and removes nails and other metal from wooden parts to salvage material, using handtools. Applies filler, putty, or other material, using brush, putty knife, and fingers to fill wood pores, holes, cracks, or other indentations. Removes paint, lacquer, and other finishes from wood products, using solvent, steel wool, brush, and cloths, and sands rough spots, using sandpaper or sanding machine, to prepare surfaces for finishing. Traces patterns on lumber stock as guide for machine operator. Attaches articles to wires, cord, or hooks preparatory to dipping. Dips article into vats to coat them with paint, asphalt, or other ingredients. Marks furniture surfaces with crayon or rough-edged object to simulate antique finish. Brushes surfaces with glue preparatory to covering with leather, paper, or other materials. Nails together lumber for cutting, and places lumber on machine table. Examines materials and products for defects, finish, and grade, and accuracy of dimensions and matching panels, using measuring instruments. Stamps grade on product and weighs and records units processed and inspected. Changes cutterheads and blades, adjusts belts, and performs other duties as instructed to facilitate setting up woodworking machines. Loads and unloads materials from railroad cars, trucks, and barges by hand, using handtruck or industrial truck to move material to designated areas. Cleans cars and trucks and lines them with paper preparatory to loading. (687)

WRITER: Writes original prose material for publication: Selects subject matter based on personal interest or receives specific assignment from publisher. Conducts research and makes notes to retain ideas, develop factual information, and obtain authentic detail. Organizes material and plans arrangement or outline. Develops factors, such as theme, plot, order, characterization, and story line. Writes draft of manuscript. Reviews, revises, and corrects it and submits material for publication. Confers with publisher's representative regarding manuscript changes. May specialize in one or more styles or types of writing, such as descriptive or critical interpretations or analyses, essays, magazine articles, short stories, novels, and biographies. (067)

WRITER, TECHNICAL: Develops, writes, and edits material for reports, manuals, briefs, proposals, instruction books, catalogs, and related technical and administrative publications concerned with work methods and procedures, and installation, operation, and maintenance of machinery and other equipment: Receives assignment from supervisor. Observes production, developmental, and experimental activities to determine operating procedure and detail. Interviews production and engineering personnel and reads journals, reports, and other material to become familiar with product technologies and production methods. Reviews manufacturer's and trade catalogs, drawings and other data relative to operation, maintenance, and service of equipment. Studies blueprints, sketches, drawings, parts lists, specifications, mockups, and product samples to integrate and delineate technology, operating procedure, and production sequence and detail. Organizes material and completes writing assignment according to set standards regarding order, clarity, conciseness, style, and terminology. Reviews published materials and recommends revisions or changes in scope, format, content, and methods of reproduction and binding. May maintain records and files of work and revisions. May select photographs, drawings, sketches, diagrams, and charts to illustrate material. May assist in laying out material for publication. May arrange for typing, duplication, and distribution of material. May write speeches, articles, and public or employee relations releases. May edit, standardize, or make changes to material prepared by other writers or plant personnel. (267)

YARD WORKER: Performs any combination of the following duties, in accordance with instructions of employer, to keep grounds of private residence in neat and orderly condition: Plants, transplants, fertilizes, sprays with pesticides, prunes, cultivates, and waters flowers, shrubbery, and trees. Seeds and mows lawns, rakes leaves, and keeps ground free of other debris. Whitewashes or paints fences. Washes and polishes automobiles. Cleans patio furniture and garage. Shovels snow from walks. May cultivate flowers, shrubbery, and other plants in greenhouse. May wax floors, tend furnace, or groom and exercise pets. May divide time between several homes, working on hourly or daily basis. When duties are confined to upkeep of grounds, may be designated as GARDENER. (687)

ZOOLOGIST: Studies origin, interrelationships, classification, life histories, habits, life processes, diseases, relation to environment, growth and development, genetics, and distribution of animals: Studies animals in natural habitat and collects specimens for laboratory study. Dissects and examines specimens under microscope and uses chemicals and various types of scientific equipment to carry out experimental studies. Prepares collections of preserved specimens or microscopic slides for such purposes as identification of species, study of species development, and study of animal diseases. May raise specimens for experimental purposes. May specialize in one aspect of animal study, such as functioning of animal as an organism, or development of organism from egg to embryo stage. (061)

Chapter 26

For Further Reading

The more you read about ways to get a job, the better. Focus on techniques you can *use*, ideas that give you a new approach. Go to your local business library, and ask the librarian what's available. Browse in the offices of any grass-roots organization or government agency that can help you find work. Look through your neighborhood bookstores.

You'll find lots of anthologies of old résumés. Don't worry about the slight differences in format and terminology. Any one will do. The key question: do you want to list your experience chronologically, or do you want to break out your skills for emphasis?

Whatever book you're looking at, read a chapter before you borrow or buy. See if you could really *act* on what you read there. Does it seem to apply to your situation? Does the advice make sense?

Here are some of the books I've found most helpful. They discuss the whole job search, from self-analysis through résumés to interviews and offers.

BLUE-COLLAR JOBS FOR WOMEN. Muriel Lederer. Dutton. $7.95.
> A thorough and sympathetic guide for women who want to get skills and jobs in traditionally male fields such as construction, heavy industries, machine repair, science, mining, and transportation.

CAREERS TODAY. Gene R. Hawes, Mark Hawes, Christine Fleming. New American Library. $3.95.
> Lists good jobs with salaries, chances for promotion, number of openings every year, and likely growth rate.

CAREERS TOMORROW. Gene R. Hawes. New American Library. $4.95.
> A survey of the highest-paying professions in the coming decade, with tips on how to "break in."

GO HIRE YOURSELF AN EMPLOYER. Richard K. Irish. Anchor/Doubleday. $4.95.
> Lively, opinionated, full of inside dope. Especially helpful if you're interested in what he calls "judgement jobs"—management slots in private industry and government.

GUERILLA TACTICS IN THE JOB MARKET. Tom Jackson. Bantam. $2.95.

> Seventy-nine actions you can take to get a job without relying on employment agencies. Interesting case histories and dialogues.

HOW TO GET A BETTER JOB QUICKER. Richard A. Payne. New American Library. $2.50.

> Excellent advice for anyone aiming at a management job. Stresses discovering your own "worth points."

THE COMPLETE JOB-SEARCH HANDBOOK. Howard Figler. Holt, Rinehart, and Winston. $5.95.

> Amusing outline for a course in job hunting. Particularly good on communications skills.

WHAT COLOR IS YOUR PARACHUTE? Richard Nelson Bolles. Ten Speed Press. $6.95.

> A rambunctious strategy for people changing careers or reentering the job market. Not so useful if you know what you want, but crammed with good ideas, and pertinent facts for any job-seeker.

WHAT EVERY WOMAN NEEDS TO KNOW TO FIND A JOB IN TODAY'S TOUGH MARKET. Jean Summers. Fawcett. $4.95.

> Friendly, fast, and accurate. Most helpful for reentry women.

Index

Teacher, 94–5, 258–9
Teacher aide, 113, 258
Teaser letters, 105
Technical writer, 264
Telephoning for jobs, 115–119
Telephone operator, 259
Telephone solicitor, 11, 12, 260
TV-cable installer, 260
Television and radio
  appearances, 72
Television and radio repair, 260
Teller, 9, 85, 260
Temporary agency work, 11
Tending, 18
Things, 14–21
Trade associations, 111
Trade schools, 48–50
Training, 40
Training representative, 260
Transferable skills, 59–66, 68
Transportation industry, 38
Travel agent, 113, 261
Tree trimmer, 261
Truck driver, 261
TV repair, 260
Turndowns, 53–56
Types of jobs, 7–13
Typing, 139
Typist, 11, 113, 262

Unemployment, 5, 35–37, 38,
  152
United States Air Force, 40, 52
United States Army, 40, 52
United States Civil Service, 9
United States Coast Guard, 40,
  52
United States Department of
  Agriculture, 40
United States Department of
  Defense, 40

United States Department of
  Labor, 39, 45, 112, 169
United States Marine Corps, **40, 52**
United States Navy, 40, 52
United States Post Office, **10**
Urban League, 43, 46, 47
Urban planner, 262
Utilities industry, 38

Values, 5, 13, 14–21
Veteran status, 39, 49, 134, **141**
Veterinarian, 262
Vetter, Betty, 38
Vice president, 262
Vietnam veteran, 134, 141
Volunteer work, 35, 40, 68, **93**

Waiter/waitress, 11, 263
Wall Street Journal, 110, **112**
Want ads, 100–110, 113
Weight, 44
What Color is Your Parachute?,
  267
*What Every Woman Needs to
  Know to Find a Job in Today's
  Tough Market,* 267
Where the jobs are, 110–114
White-collar jobs, 8–9
Wirer, cable, 263
Women's Equity Action League, **44**
Women's Switchboard, 46
Woodworking, 263
Word processor, 113
Writer, 12, 264
Writer, technical, 264

Yard worker, 265
YWCA, 42

Zeta Phi Beta, 44
Zoologist, 265

About the Author

Jonathan Price has worked as a hash-slinger, bookstore clerk, window-washer, telephone sales rep, secretary, bubble-gum tester, TV journalist, college professor, video artist, training developer, word processing consultant, job counselor, and technical writer. Now 41, he lives in a lime-green bungalow in Berkeley, California, with his wife, Lisa, son Ben, and dog Applesauce. He occasionally answers his mail.